SOME BOOKS BY

# *Leopold Bellak*

| | |
|---|---|
| *The Best Years of Your Life* | *1975* |
| *Overload: The New Human Condition* | *1975* |
| *Progress in Community Mental Health Volumes I, II, and III* | *1969, 1971, 1975* |
| *A Concise Handbook of Community Psychiatry and Community Mental Health* | *1974* |
| *Ego Functions in Schizophrenics, Neurotics, and Normals* | *1973* |
| *The TAT and CAT in Clinical Use (Revised Edition The TAT and CAT and SAT in Clinical Use)* | *1975* |
| *The Porcupine Dilemma* | *1970* |
| *The Schizophrenic Syndrome* | *1969* |
| *The Broad Scope of Psychoanalysis* | *1967* |
| *Emergency Psychotherapy* | *1965* |
| *The Psychology of Physical Illness* | *1952* |
| *Manic Depressive Psychosis and Allied Disorders* | *1952* |

# *The Best Years of Your Life*

# *The Best Years of Your Life*

## A GUIDE TO THE ART AND SCIENCE OF AGING

*Leopold Bellak, M.D.*

ATHENEUM *New York*
1975

*Library of Congress catalog card number 74-20358*
ISBN *0-689-10611-4*
*Published simultaneously in Canada by McClelland and Stewart Ltd.*
*Manufactured in the United States of America by*
*H. Wolff, New York*
*Designed by Kathleen Carey*
*First Edition*

TO MY FRIEND

*Paul Esserman, M.D.,*

A PHYSICIAN IN THE GREAT TRADITION

L. B.

I would like this book to help the aged

And help the middle-aged to understand their
aging parents (and themselves)

The way Dr. Spock helped them understand
their children (and themselves)

# Acknowledgments

MY wife, Sonya Sorel Bellak, originally conceived the idea of this book. This happened in conjunction with her notion that we should originate a personality test to reflect the psychological features of the aging.

This development is natural enough. Twenty-five years ago, she and I collaborated on the Children's Apperception Test (C.A.T.). Like many of our contemporaries, our thoughts, concerns and interest had switched some time ago to parents, aging elders. The Senior Apperception Technique (S.A.T.) and this book reflect this shift. My wife stopped her own creative work as sculptor just long enough to help me initially sift several hundred computer printouts and other sources of information on the aged, and she tested and interviewed quite a few older people also.

After that, my assistant, Caroline Birenbaum, M.A., brought her high intelligence, her ideas, research, writing and editing ability to contribute a great deal to all of the book, but especially to the chapters on economics and funerals.

Elaine Feiden, M.S.W., of the Westchester Mental Health Association and Joann Lang, M.S.W., provided valuable ideas and information especially in areas of social work, and read the manuscript critically.

Rhoda Katzenstein, M.S.L., lent enthusiastic help in various forms in the early phase of the book.

Paul Esserman, M.D., Professor of Medicine, New York University School of Medicine, and Howard Gorfinkel, M.D., Instructor in Medicine, New York University School of Medicine, were a great help by reading especially the sections dealing with strictly medical aspects.

Another good friend, Fred Dannay, much better known to the world for more than a quarter of a century as Ellery Queen, not only read the manuscript for readability, but served as a constant source of intellectual stimulation and, above all, encouragement. I doubt very much that there is anything about writing—in any form—that Fred does not know.

I am also grateful to Dorothy Tiffany Burlingham, who read the entire manuscript in great detail and offered many valuable observations. She brought to it the understanding that comes from her own eighty-four years of living, including her work as a psychoanalyst, in which she is still active at the Hampstead Clinic that she and her close friend Anna Freud founded decades ago. Speaking of decades ago, I also owe her thanks for having saved my life in 1938.

I am indebted to my friend, W. Ernst Freud, for having spent many hours scrutinizing the manuscript, making a number of very constructive suggestions, and generally being his always warmly supportive self.

I know how difficult it is to work with anyone, and given all I have heard about editors and writers, I set out to collaborate like a porcupine: cautiously. Dorothy Parker, my editor at Atheneum, was a most pleasant person and no difficulties with the manuscript originated with her.

James Oliver Brown, my literary agent, is above all a specimen of a vanishing species, a gentleman. Having published technical professional books for just about three decades, I thought I knew something about publishing. The fact is that Jim not only guided me and looked after me, but also gave me a postgraduate education about the tradebook field.

They all tried their best. I am very grateful to them all. I hope lots of readers will profit from our joint labors.

L. B.

# *Contents*

# *The Best Years of Your Life*

# 1

# *What It's All About*

*The aged should be treated as personalities, not as objects of management.*
I. L. NASCHER

## BETWEEN CHILD AND AGING PARENT

JUDGMENT day is at hand: your aged mother is coming to live with you, not next year but tomorrow! What are you going to do about it? Not only is she allergic to your pet dachshund, but, you suspect, to your spouse as well; and the normal, everyday noises of children at play and other busy-home sounds drive her right up the wall. Well, welcome to the club. This is just one example of the problem that people in their middle years are facing every day. And more of them are facing the problem today than ever before because more people are living to a ripe old age. Life expectancy at the turn of the century in this country was a mere forty-seven years; now it is seventy-two and going up all the time. Scientists project that at the turn of the century more than two-fifths of the population will be over sixty-five years of age—a result of the miracles of modern medicine.

## 1 *What It's All About*

One of Maurice Chevalier's better lines was, "Aging is terrible, but the alternative is worse." Aging may or may not be terrible—and one of the objectives of this book is to help you find ways to reduce its terror for both the aged and the younger person who is concerned with the older—but age is a time of life whose arrival is a constant surprise. The great majority are ill prepared for it.

One of the reasons for this lack of readiness is that aging is a highly variable process. It is not easily predictable. People grow old at different chronological ages—some seem elderly at fifty, and others are youthful at eighty. Occasionally a single event—a fall and the fracturing of a hip bone, for example—is responsible for a sharp change from a well-functioning, self-sustaining individual to a helpless, mentally disturbed old man or woman. The less sturdy stance of the older person results in a fall under conditions more easily negotiated in youth; and the increased porousness of aging bones can lead to a broken hip, which often does not heal well or completely. Flat on your back, as anyone must be after a hip fracture, is certainly no position in which to feel independent; and even when the bone has been set and perhaps riveted as well, the difficulty of getting around and fending for oneself can lead to a feeling of helplessness and dependency.

Allowing for wide variations in mental, physical and psychological endowment, not to mention marked differences in sociological ambience and economic patterns, we can nevertheless make some generalizations. Children are dependent upon their parents. From the time of their early adulthood, they coexist with their parents as competent adults. Then in the next general phase of life, the formerly dependent children must change step and adopt something of a parental attitude toward their aging parents. This is the way it has always gone, and there's little to indicate that it won't go this way for quite some time to come.

No one is saying this is an ideal way for life to progress; no one is making a claim that this way is fair. Many people in middle age have just begun to breathe a long sigh of relief: they have brought up their families, seen their children through to a measure of maturity and independence. Both the financial and emotional drains have eased somewhat. The younger generation's educational—perhaps even marital—future is no longer a pressing worry. This is the moment, maybe even the very first opportunity, to relax a bit, to take a vacation unencumbered by diapers, childish squabbles, measles, colds, or school calendars. But wait, what's this? Suddenly a new crop of "children" has been harvested. The middle-aged adults look around and notice that their parents, while not at present helpless, are approaching the age when they will need looking after. They may already have become physically infirm, or financially or psychologically dependent to a greater degree than they care to admit.

Now, instead of a carefree vacation or a second career, you must launch yourself on a new job: taking care of your mother or father, or both. A good deal of time must be spent on visits to their home, solving their medical problems, perhaps finding them a new place to live. You will be phoning more often than you think you have time for—or less frequently than your conscience dictates. If the first reaction to this discovery is one of exasperation and anger, not surprisingly it will be followed by feelings of guilt. Memories crowd your mind: they were such good parents—or were they? Real or imaginary hurts from childhood may be recalled with some bitterness. Also, it is bewildering to think of parents, formerly the source of support and strength, gradually or suddenly changed to the status of helpless and possibly very demanding children. Now it is they who require "parental" guidance and support.

Another disturbing thought makes the situation worse. You cannot help but realize at this point, if you have avoided it thus far, that you yourself are not a youngster any longer. In another twenty to twenty-five years you yourself will be in your parents' present position. How will you feel? How will your children feel about you? The whole situation pumps a stream of new emotions in you that may run the course from concern to fear to guilt to rage and back to fear again.

The question is, "How to deal with it?"

First of all, remember that you are not alone. This crisis you're facing is very far from a unique phenomenon. There are now twenty million adults in the United States who are over sixty-five years of age: ten percent of the population. Among the other ninety percent you can be sure there are a great many children and grandchildren, as well as aunts, uncles, cousins and people outside the kin family, who share the problems you are now facing.

Second, you are in a better position than any generation before you to get help in solving the problems that your parents present. We are fortunate that increasing numbers of professionals and para-professionals are giving thought to the care of the aged, and to the related problems that involve their offspring, relatives and friends. The increasing numbers of the old have given impetus to more extensive private and governmental programs. Federal projects, state aids, city commissions and neighborhood societies are helping to handle this new factor in our national life. Many ways of helping aging people and their families are being set up all the time.

And third, contrary to popular belief that our society is youth-oriented, growing old is really not as dire a condition as it has been thought to be. Many of the problems of aging are man-made, products of our society, or not infrequently self-created by aging people themselves. It behooves us in the middle years to see that our aging friends and relatives don't defeat themselves. Advanced age does not inevitably bring on physical or mental illness. To the contrary, mental illness in particular is even now limited to a relatively small percentage of older people—and this statistic may decrease in the future.

So don't despair—help is on the way. All manner of assistance is around you, often at no more remove than the distance to your telephone. With so much concern focused on the older half of our population, some difficulties will be handled better than they ever have been before, while others will never occur at all. Understanding and perspective, intelligent planning and good will, and an America only recently awakened to the needs and desires of its senior citizenry will minimize the pitfalls inherent in the situation you now face.

But before going on with the counsel we offer to the young adult or middle-aged person who thinks he may be called upon to help make the years better for some older person, we offer the following words.

## A WORD TO OLDER READERS

Even if you don't require any assistance from others, now that you are over sixty-five, you may find many helpful suggestions in these pages. There is in this book a good deal of information that will be of value to you, your spouse, a relative or a friend. The appendix is a mine of ideas for healthy, active older people; other chapters will give you a good idea how much we now know about the ins and outs of the later years.

If you have recently become incapacitated in any way, it is a shock to your relatives, of course, but above all to you. But if the person who has suddenly lost some faculty or capacity is your husband or wife, *you* are the one who feels the loss the most. You are affected even more than your children because, for practical purposes, there goes half of you. Instead of having a companion and a helpmate, you are suddenly reduced, faced with huge responsibilities, devoid of the support you have counted on all these years.

A good deal depends, of course, on how you felt about yourself—and your spouse—before: before either of you turned that corner into the sunset years, before the specific problem arose. By and large we remain the same kind of people when young, middle-aged and old. So try at least not to blame more than necessary on old age. Maybe that will help you to achieve some perspective and keep all your wits about you. You will need them in making the many urgent decisions now required.

If you have been a rather anxious person all your life, don't be surprised if you are anxious now. Things may not be much worse; it is just that you tend to see them as worse than others might. If you feel let down and bitter about something that has happened to you or to your spouse, chances are that you felt let down and bitter, for better or perhaps for worse reasons, earlier in your life. We all tend to blame on age things that either need not exist or have nothing to do with age. Don't fall into this trap!

In the chapters that follow, a number of problems or disorders are discussed and described. Don't use these pages as a manual for worrying about yourself. *Nobody* could inherit all of the problems mentioned; and only a very small percentage of the aged ever has *any* of them.

One of the messages carried by specialists in geriatrics is that *aging itself is not a disease.* An elderly person is not *ipso facto* a sick person—far from it. Many older people live happy lives with healthy minds, emotions and bodies, able to enjoy work, sexual pleasures, and companionship. And the more we learn how to avoid, treat and cure disease, the more likely we will be to live into our nineties, at the least, with full enjoyment.

Our society is already changing its attitude toward age. It has to! There are simply too many aged people in this country for them to be ignored, socially, politically, or any other way. Americans above the age of sixty-five now number twenty million. And over four thousand reach that age every day. Senior citizens, make your weight felt! And not only in demands for your own betterment. All the rest of this country—and indeed of the world—has use for political thinking that is based on decades of experience and judgment. The brilliance of the whiz kids can only be balanced by the wisdom and maturity of the old gold!

Do what you can for the world—and then let it do what it must for you. Become aware of what society already has to offer you. Some of the myriad services and rewards due you are listed in this book. If they are governmental benefits, take advantage of them. Many of them you have already paid for with your productive years, through your labor or your taxes or your simply having endured. Cash in on what's coming to you—some of it you may not even be aware of. Not all the surprises are over. You may be better off than you thought. Consider, for example, the new freedoms you have.

## THE FREEDOMS OF AGING

As we get older, many of our drives decrease. This fact alone makes for far less conflict, so often the result of the struggle between our drives and our consciences, or our drives and reality. Thus, more peace of mind, an important new "freedom."

Appetite for food usually lessens in age; and this may help you understand the advantages of the decrease in other drives. If you remain healthy, your desire for food will remain strong enough for you to enjoy smaller portions. But your hunger will be less of a driving force than it was, say, in adolescence. You can now taste food more carefully and savor it for the fine nuances. Instead of stuffing yourself, you will derive pleasure from subtlety. The gourmand will become the gourmet. Unlike the youth who constantly raids the refrigerator in search of stimulation of the taste buds, you won't be plagued by hunger, and will be able to pick and choose with more discretion. Regular, modest meals will satisfy you, and missing one or postponing it won't represent much of a problem—unless you are eating out of boredom.

The sexual drive also decreases, not only in terms of frequency, but also in urgency. While the secretions of the sexual glands almost *demand* satisfaction in the adolescent, the young adult and even the middle-aged adult, the demand is less compelling in old age. The male prostate, spongelike, filling with its own secretion, is known to empty itself in a young man's dreams if not given some other kind of outlet; in age this no longer occurs. Having a less peremptory sexual drive gives the older person, man or woman, the choice to enjoy it when feasible, not to be driven by it, as younger people so often are. You have more sexual serenity, and with the relatively lower urgency for fulfillment, more likelihood of leisurely enjoyment and postponement of orgasm.

It is well known that sexual diversity and subtlety is a matter of class. The laboring class has not been famous for complexity in lovemaking, partly because of their relative lack of sufficient time, privacy and energy. Denied contraceptives, they have been afraid of conceiving more children than they can care for. Brief, uncomplicated love-making has been the working-class norm. It has been members of the leisure class, in times past, who have had the time, the energy, the privacy, the occasions to develop the art of love-making. Now that you are older, your position is similar: freed of the urgency of the sexual drive, you can afford to cultivate more sexual subtlety; finished with the fear of conception, you may find many of your inhibitions removed; relieved of many of the demands of everyday life, you have more leisure time. This freedom of choice in lovemaking is certainly one of the boons of advancing age.

Ambition, assertion and the need for status and achievement are strong driving forces in the younger person; this drive has been tempered in the later years by the acceptance of reality, which allows you to see yourself and your attainments more clearly: an important freedom. While a few people remain driven to "succeed" even into age, most who have attained sixty-five can accept their limitations and can watch the world around them with some detachment and perspective. If you have been "successful," you have learned that all success is limited, and limited, too, in the amount of pleasure it can give. If you haven't been signally successful in the eyes of the world, you may have come into the even more gratifying freedom of doing things—your job, or play or other diversions—for their own sake, rather than for the secondary results of money or power or recognition.

Knowing that your years are now limited, you may retain a healthy interest in world events and the life closer around you—but it is less intense, understandably so. The thirty-year-old very reasonably has more of an investment in how the world will look after the next three decades have elapsed than the person of seventy-five. If you are psychologically healthy, you are still very much involved in yourself, your children, your grandchildren, and the rest of mankind in general; but it is likely, and allowably, to be a less urgent interest than when you were still building a career, fending for your livelihood, raising a family. Accept this new freedom.

Embrace the freedom from fear that comes with advancing years. Young people are full of fears. Children, hardly comprehending even the world around them, see themselves as helpless, at the mercy of adults and ill-understood larger things, both real and unreal, of all sorts. Adolescence and early adulthood are full of turmoil and of manifold fears, prime among them being the fear of failing—socially, sexually, as a parent or at your job. Even in full adulthood, you may have feared the future in dozens of ways. Now you are delivered from all these fears.

If you have achieved old age, you can take pride in all that you have survived. There is certainly an exhilarating freedom in realizing the truth of the old saw that "today is the tomorrow you worried about yesterday." Even the fear of death you will find less pronounced than when you were young. Part of that may be *because* it is so much closer, you have built up some defenses. Another part can be attributed to a feeling of depletion or of completion. In many old people a general desire for rest prevails: serenity is the principal desideratum, and that includes the idea of dying.

Freedom from the fear of death is indeed liberating. With this ultimate threat removed, aged people are often especially courageous—feeling that they have little to lose, except perhaps their dignity.

Fear of the loss of loved ones characterizes the life of human beings from earliest infancy on. Now that you're aged, however, you have become inured to such loss. From middle age on, perhaps earlier, you have lost your own parents, a brother or sister, other relatives, many friends. Each such loss has tempered and inured you so that you have greater tolerance for yet another. You have learned to see death as an integral part of life; you have found some religion, some philosophy, or some other emotional adaptation that can deal with it. This is a valuable freedom.

No longer do you have to care about worldly achievement; the crucial, life-sustaining necessities are of prime importance—the luxuries and frivolities you dreamed of earlier no longer are. You are at last free to be yourself, unconcerned about status or the opinions of others, unworried about the future. No more are you at the mercy of the tyranny of glands and hormones—or of despotic parents, teachers, employers. Your age group is the only one that can get away with the beachcomber's attitude. Be a beachcomber—at the edge of eternity.

Robert Browning may have had a point when he claimed that "the best is yet to be." Given reasonably good health, and the satisfaction of the basic needs for food, adequate shelter and companionship, as you grow older you can enjoy a special sense of freedom that borders on adventure. Let's see what you can make of this day that will be constructive or just very pleasant, or both. Let the youngsters worry about the rest. Your age is a time to live scot free.

# 2

# *Don't Panic: Some First-Aid Situations*

*Absence of occupation is not rest,*
*A mind quite vacant is a mind distressed.*
COWPER

SUDDEN or unfamiliar events can cause alarm. Hardships befalling loved ones can cause deep pain, not only to the central character in the drama but to those witnessing. The combination of these two phenomena often creates panic. During the World War II blitz the British found out a lot about panic. During the first bombings people lost their heads and ran in all directions; this behavior was a greater danger to them than the bombs themselves. As soon as clear directions were issued on what to do when the bombers came over, that was the end of the panic and of the panic-induced, home-grown havoc. Even very young children stayed calm—indeed fell asleep during the raids—when their parents knew exactly what they were doing.

Though they are a far cry from the horrors of war, some of the experiences of aging can cause panic, both in the aged person and in his relatives and others close to him. Knowing what to do about any emergency, promptly, will help promote a sense of calm for all concerned so that the situation can be alleviated with efficiency and dispatch.

Now we want to discuss some emergencies that may arise with aged people. If your sense of urgency doesn't unravel into panic, you will be able to meet them with equanimity.

## DEFINE YOUR FEELINGS

Before you can be of any real assistance to your aging parents, you had better clarify some things in your own mind. You and your mother or father are about to enter into a relationship full of more conflict than any since your adolescence. It is up to you to work out a compromise between your love for them, complicated by your sense of obligation, on one side, and the limitations of your patience, conscience and personality—not to mention your time and money—on the other. In some romantic fiction, and perhaps in some dreams, all parents are perfect, and all children are good and loving. In reality, the best criterion of maturity is being able to see one's own parents (or for parents to see their offspring) as just plain ordinary human beings, full of faults as well as virtues, and then still love them. If you have not looked at your parents objectively before, this is the time to try to see them whole, and to stop kidding yourself about their perfection. Whatever shortcomings they have, and whatever mixed feelings you hold, will tend to produce misunderstandings and clashes more than ever now.

As your aged parent becomes more dependent, all the resentments you may ever have harbored against him will be awakened in you, either consciously or unconsciously. At the same time, his own need to be mothered, his own childish tendency toward self-pity, demandingness, even resentment or envy of you, may emerge after decades of repression. Try to recognize these feelings for what they are, in both of you.

The availability of space in either of your homes, the financial state of both households, the health of all individuals involved, and many other factors play a crucial role in this new drama. But, all other things being equal, temperament and personality and the ability to assess them validly in yourself and your parent are the most decisive tools in redefining your relationship with each other.

Let's assume for a moment that you and your parent never got along very well, that the temperature of your mutual affection was, to put it mildly, cool. And that for many years you have been able to be quite uninvolved with your parents. If your conscience now tells you that you should help out, then you had better do so: a conscience is not something you can easily trifle with. If you do something your conscience doesn't approve of, guilty feelings and some form of self-retribution (often manifesting itself physically) are the usual consequences. The wise person learns to live within the boundaries of his conscience, as he learns to live within the limits of his physical stamina or his income. This is very much part of accepting reality. And you must be in touch with emotional reality as well as other, more easily tangible realities before you decide what arrangement is best when aged relatives start needing your help. Think things through clearly.

When you have figured out just where you stand with your own emotions and your conscience, consider the feelings of other people who will be affected by your decision, or who will play a role in making the arrangements. There will probably be unexpected problems in any plan you work out, but things will flow more smoothly if everyone's point of view is aired and responsibility is assumed jointly. Perhaps you and your sisters or brothers can share the load, each performing that function for which he is best equipped. At any rate, force yourselves, even if cooperation has never been your forte, to get together at this time and "reason together."

## THE FAMILY CONFERENCE

If there is a radical change in the needs of aging parents, a family conference is a must. All the people strongly affected by the change—affected psychologically as well as in demands upon their time, money and convenience—should certainly come together for an exchange of views. The least such a conference will do is to put all the problems—or anyway all presently visible—on the table. In the first place, there is a bit of collective mourning to do, even if it is only what we call "partial grief." If your parent suddenly needs a wheelchair, it is a sign that he is growing infirm, and consciously or unconsciously you prepare yourself for his eventual death. It is good to be aware of such concern, not shunt it aside. When you ignore your feelings, they often emerge in some disguised and usually troublesome way.

In open conference, attitudes of all the participants will become apparent and can be discussed—if reason prevails. Who will make what contributions, in time, finances and convenience, must be made clear. Don't underestimate myriad time-and-energy-consuming chores that are involved in caring for a dependent person. Try to establish the financial position (not only how much money but how many other obligations) of each family member to work out a fair contribution to the support of the parent if that is in the cards. Try to discover what degree of sacrifice of present life style each is willing to make, if that is going to be necessary. If the aged relative has ever spoken about the way he would like to live when he is no longer self-sufficient, these feelings should be reported and taken into consideration.

After the rest of the family has met and had a thorough discussion, it is time for them to meet calmly with the aged parent, either in the same group or by delegation of the person or persons most likely to succeed in presenting the case. Some old people staunchly deny the need for any assistance when it is patently clear to others that they must have it. Others become overanxious and panic-stricken. Either sort of person should be given firm assurance that some help is now on its way to permit him to lead as comfortable and independent a life as possible. If he wants to, and seems able to, take part in the making of decisions, he should be encouraged to participate. If on the other hand he seems relieved that the family is taking over major decisions, or he is too incapacitated to take part himself, then you should gently but firmly tell him what has been decided.

## FAMILY COUNSELING

It is quite possible that your family has never been skillful at sitting down to discuss *anything*, and that you particularly dread a conference about such a deeply involving issue as responsibility for your aging parents. Perhaps you are afraid that, face to face, your older sister or richer brother will bully you or manipulate the situation to your disadvantage, but that if things are left alone they will manage to work themselves out. It may be that you don't feel up to the emotional commitment such a conference will require at this trying time. This is not an uncommon state of affairs.

A family conference is much more easily advised than brought about. Some families are simply not accustomed to speaking with each other freely without getting into an argument, hassling over old misgivings, getting lost in irrelevancies. If this is the picture in your family, try again. And again. Make one person the moderator if necessary. Perhaps your doctor or lawyer or another respected friend could conduct the meeting if the family can't agree on one of their own.

And if all these suggestions are invalid, you might arrange to have the conference at some social agency, with the help of a social worker. Fortunately, today many sources of skilled family counseling are available for people in every economic bracket. Not every family takes easily to family counseling. Many people are fiercely independent and don't consider it necessary or "fitting and proper" to seek help for their own "little" problems. They may feel you have to be crazy to consult a psychologist, or they may let crisis after crisis build up until they have a mountain of troubles that look hopeless before they will define themselves as in need of assistance. Sometimes one member of a family holds the others back because they defer to his unreasonableness in these matters.

By inquiring of your doctor, religious advisor, local social-service agency, or even your child's school guidance counselor, you can find the names of various psychologists, social workers, or others whom you may contact about your problem. Then if you feel any of these people can help you, make an appointment to see them, by yourself or with another member of the family circle. Usually the balky member of the family is relieved, after all the hemming and hawing, that you have made the decision. He may benefit a great deal from the visit—even if the discussion is relayed to him secondhand—and join in the next one.

This may be a wonderful opportunity for you yourself to learn how to accept the aid of trained individuals accustomed to dealing with a situation that for you seems overwhelming. Such a person can guide the various members of your family toward a realistic appraisal of responsibilities and options.

Many people, especially of the middle class, think that social-service agencies are only for the poor, or people on welfare. They feel there is a stigma attached to seeking social-service aid. The fact is that social agencies are for all socioeconomic classes. They are highly sophisticated, complex organizations. One division specializes in the treatment of psychiatric problems, another focuses on child-care problems, another on the care of the aged. Some social workers deal only with marital problems or other family matters; some are experts in drug addiction or alcoholism. Social agencies, if not government-sponsored, are supported by philanthropic sources, such as Community Chest or United Fund, or by private endowments or religious organizations. Chances are that you have contributed, either directly or indirectly, to their upkeep, as you do for hospitals, the Visiting Nurse Association and so forth. If governmental, you certainly have contributed to them, through taxes. So their services are there for you; take advantage of them. Social workers are professionals, for the most part, who have graduated from college and then had additional years of training in a school of social work. Then usually they have had field training in a hospital, clinic, social agency or elsewhere. They are a prime resource of which everyone should avail himself when the need arises, without any false preconception that their services are not for him.

## LEGAL ASSISTANCE

Modern life is regulated by many documents. It is wise for *everyone* to let some trusted person know where all his essential documents are kept, and how his personal business should be handled in an emergency. With the aged, this advice becomes imperative. If you are the trusted person, and your aged friend or relative has not yet seen fit to apprise you of the location of his documents, try to correct this situation without frightening the older person.

You may tell him that on some occasion others may have to take over the responsibility for paying bills, filing income tax returns, and the like. Documents will be needed to give proof of eligibility for various services. You should be able to locate such essential documents as a will, an army discharge, insurance policies, Social Security cards, safe-deposit keys, birth certificates, stocks and bonds, a lease, cash, an extra set of house keys. Knowing where these items are ahead of time can save you a lot of headaches when you need to have them at hand.

If there is a chance to anticipate some major problems, make sure that you get power of attorney. Kindly requested, it may be tactfully granted; if not, perhaps some other appropriate legal means of handling financial matters in the event that the older person becomes too severely incapacitated to handle his own finances can be arranged.

If you don't have a lawyer—or if your aging relative does not have one, or share one with you—consult the lawyer referral service of your local bar association (listed under

"Lawyers" in the classified telephone directory). These associations will give you the names of lawyers whose fees you can afford. Or if your income is low enough to qualify you for Legal Aid, then they will provide you with free legal assistance.

## LEARNING TO GIVE CARE

It could well be that both your parents—or an aunt or uncle of whom you are the closest relative—live together, and one shows some of the problems of aging that you have to help deal with. More often your problem occurs when one of an elderly interdependent pair has died, and the other one shows significant signs of aging. If an elderly couple is still intact, your first job may be to help the stronger one cope with the infirm one. Regardless of what ails your aged relative or friend, and what now has to be done for him, *do not make an infant out of him.* It is far better for people to do as much for themselves as they reasonably can. Otherwise, they become psychological invalids. And that may be worse, both for them *and* for you.

If they need physical help, try to find ways in which they can learn to do more and more by themselves—they will usually appreciate it. If there is a spouse or companion, help that stronger person perform as much of the physical aid as possible—he or she will age less quickly if he has this sense of accomplishment. And be sure that *several* of the younger family members learn to perform the necessary physical techniques as required.

At present, the most likely source of this instruction is a doctor or an experienced nurse. In most communities the Visiting Nurse Association can arrange for a nurse to give you a demonstration or can provide care on a regular basis.

Some registered nurses have opened their own offices, in the same way M.D.'s do; they can be consulted by appointment, or will make house calls. Such nurses have more time and more skill for seeing patients through long-range medical care than physicians, and they are less expensive. They can always recommend that the patient should see a physician if necessary.

Hospitals, social-service agencies, adult education programs in schools, senior-citizen centers, and other institutions are beginning to offer courses in the care of the aged; but this trend is still in its infancy. Such courses should become as routinely and ubiquitously provided as lessons in baby care are now. It is imperative that the care of the aged become a widely known skill. If it is not so equipped, *ask your local hospital or other appropriate agency to start such a course*. Demand it.

Acquaint yourself with the products physical-aid equipment—for a person who can't walk well, or is otherwise physically handicapped. Aside from canes or crutches, there are several kinds of "walkers" that support a person and "walk" with him on slides or wheels or rollers. A simple problem is the installation of guard rails for the toilet and bathtub for the infirm person to grasp, and guard rails that will keep him from falling out of bed.

It is easy to master some of the simple physical services that you may need to do for an older person. Anyone can learn to change bedsheets with the patient still in the bed: first roll the patient onto one half the bed; then lift the used sheet off the other half, rolling or folding it toward the center; place the clean sheet on that same half of the bed, tuck it in, and gently roll or move the patient onto it; now, with the other half of the bed free, remove the used sheet, and pull the clean sheet over and tuck it in.

Most things having to do with physical care of the elderly

are that simple once you give them some thought, or have someone show you. It's the *attitude* that matters.

Many older people can handle their physical problems much better than their emotional and mental ones. Your mother may have become absent-minded: her mind wanders or she imagines she hears and sees things, or she complains about people being *after her*. Or your two elderly parents may have started quarreling with a bitterness that exceeds anything you have ever heard before. One may accuse the other of infidelity. Mother may accuse father of trying to poison her; father may say she is always hiding his money. Perhaps they will tell you of the meanness of neighbors who keep them awake by moving furniture around in the middle of the night, or by spying on them. Let me reassure you—complaints like these, bizarre though they may seem to you on first hearing—are rather frequent. They may be the result of the brain's getting less oxygen because of hardening of the arteries. But many such complaints are the result of feelings of insecurity, whether deriving from poorer physical functioning or not.

When the elderly see or hear imaginary things, they are expressing their inability to tell what is real and what is not—sometimes because of impaired hearing or vision, often just from having "lost their grip." If your grasp of reality has slipped, even just a bit, it is easy to imagine—as all of us have when frightened, for instance, in the dark—that horrendous things are going on. Quarrels and accusations are often more intense and bitter as people suffer the changes of old age because they feel more desperate: money, possessions, or someone's love assume more importance because the aged person is more in need of them. If you feel vulnerable, depleted, or unable to look after yourself, a missing cane, a misplaced dollar bill, or a nasty remark have an infinitely more jarring effect than if you are feeling strong, self-sufficient, able to shrug it all off.

Feeling no longer sexually desirable often produces embarrassing *accusations of infidelity* on the part of an eighty-year-old spouse who has cared and loved monogamously for sixty years. Even more upsetting is grandmother's complaint that *someone is making advances* to her, or spying on her while she is undressing. These can usually be construed as pretenses that she is not old and wrinkled, that she can still be the object of sexual curiosity. Take such reports as pathetic attempts to restore to herself a measure of vanity and *amour propre*, and you won't be angry or upset or embarrassed.

The *suspicion of being poisoned* may be a way of trying to make some sense out of a feeling of growing weaker, or may result from the fact that foods really do taste and smell different to the aged because the taste buds and the membrane of the nose have altered. Imagining that *neighbors are making noise* in the night may be the expression of an older person's wish for a companion.

In the face of such behavior, your attitude is most important too. If you can react with understanding and patience instead of alarm and annoyance, you can help the elderly person to comprehend his fears and insecurities and possibly overcome them. Bringing a flower to your old mother, for example, or a new tie to your father may satisfy for a considerable time the emotional hunger such bizarre behavior may be expressing. Explaining the changes that have taken place in your aged parent's taste and smell may be very reassuring. Advising your mother to keep a light on at night may make her feel easier and dispel the fantasy that someone is watching her, or raising a din to keep her awake.

Keep in mind that these problems, which seem to arise

with no rhyme or reason, can just as easily go away by themselves. Arranging for a more active life for your aged relative may help—or for more people to talk with on a more regular basis. If these measures don't suffice, depressions and restlessness may be sufficiently worrisome for you to call on a doctor, who may prescribe some drugs. Psychotherapy or other psychological treatment is often radically and promptly helpful in the aged. Even electric shock treatment, which always sounds to the inexperienced far worse than it is (since the patient feels no shock or other pain) can be given on an outpatient basis; it is often useful to cure depression that drugs and other measures can't reach.

If your aged relative needs in-hospital care for some psychiatric problem, it may be only for a short while, especially if there is somebody who can look after him when he is ready to leave the hospital. For a physical or mental problem that cannot be handled at home, there are of course extended-care facilities, hospitals, homes for the aged, or special living facilities that provide what the ordinary home cannot.

## LIVING ARRANGEMENTS

### IN THEIR OWN HOME

If aged people can remain in their own home, reassured by familiarity, the serious problem of adapting to disruption and residential change is eliminated. Small adjustments in the furnishings of the home will make it easier and safer getting around. Turning a first-floor room into a bedroom will eliminate the need to climb stairs, provided the bathroom is on the same floor. If stair-climbing can't be eliminated, be sure the guard rail is secure. Scatter rugs, loose carpets and highly polished floors should be done away with—they are too slippery and encourage a fall. Lighting should be strong, and a night light should be installed if it isn't already in place. A telephone should be within easy reach of the bed, with emergency numbers posted in an obvious place and clearly visible to eyesight that is not quite what it used to be. See that a neighbor is also equipped with your phone number as well as other emergency phone numbers.

Your aged parent may be able to take care of the most elementary needs, such as washing, dressing, simple cooking and eating well enough to live an independent life; but may need help with marketing and other shopping, heavy housework, laundry or home maintenance, going to the doctor or dentist, and seeking entertainment. Since these requirements recur at regular intervals, it is best to face the fact that they do, and make a regular schedule for them. Then you won't be surprised and annoyed at how often these chores have to be done. The clearer the schedule, the better for both caretaker and the infirm: if a definite arrangement exists, the older person is not put into the demeaning position of constantly having to ask for help, and so is likely to be less demanding.

Your community may offer resources for some of these tasks: transportation to shopping and medical centers, food-buying cooperatives, volunteers (sometimes students) to perform household and home-maintenance chores, the preparation and delivery of meals for housebound individuals, or simply telephoning at regular times to ascertain that all is well or to relieve isolation and loneliness. Find out what services of this kind the community offers and take advantage of them.

## IN YOUR HOME

Fewer people these days have aged relatives living with them than in the past, at least in middle-class America, which is not characterized any more by the homestead family or the extended family. In many ways this is a pity because it deprives the elderly of a family setting as well as denying the younger generations the benefits of more mature advice, wisdom and perspective, of the security of continuity and belonging to a family line. So if it can be accomplished to everybody's satisfaction, taking your elders into your own home may be highly preferable to moving them somewhere else.

It may also be an occasion as welcome as a three-alarm fire. Most people, whether related by blood or not, do not easily live close together. Anyone who has ever had a roommate or a partner in a business, been in the armed services or just plain married knows that. Older people are sometimes even more difficult to share close quarters with because they are more set in their ways, or fussier about their belongings, or frightened about the future. Again, your attitude toward such a living arrangement is all-important: neither you nor the generation on either side of you can expect sainthood on anyone's part. Besides, being a martyr does no one good—not the person you are trying to help, not you yourself, not your mate or your children.

Consider your own life situation, part of which is the psychological reality. Do you have the sort of nature that will make it possible for the older person to live with you without constant friction and unhappiness? Do the other members of your family group as now constituted? Enforced closeness is hard for anyone to bear.

My favorite story to illustrate this theory stars porcupines in the leading role. Meeting on a cold winter's day, two porcupines decided to move together to lend each other some warmth. When they came close, they pricked each other with their quills. Annoyed and hurting, they moved apart again, only to feel the cold creeping back into their bones. Then they jockeyed and backed and filled and moved about until they found just the right space to put between—the ideal distance, at which they could give each other as much warmth as possible without hurting each other.

You and your aged relative are now like the porcupines: you have to find out just what arrangement works best for both sides concerned. There are some combinations of people who rub each other the wrong way—they need a lot of distance. Others like closeness and can bear it well, even thrive on it. Each one of us has a porcupine index that tells us the number (and identity) of people we can tolerate and the degree of closeness we can bear without throwing quills. Being incapable of tolerating too many people too close to you is nothing to be ashamed of—it is part of your metabolism. Some people like very warm air around them and others are uncomfortable unless a room is cool. Similarly, some people like a crowd and others abhor it. People marry for dozens of reasons, but the kind of closeness or distance they need in human relationships is a prime factor in their choice. And since any sharing of a home is a kind of marriage, it is reasonable that you give serious thought to the porcupine tolerance of yourself and your immediate family—and how much variation it allows—before inviting your aging parent into your own home.

If such a move is inevitable, now is the time for the immediate family to have a conference, including the younger children. All sorts of feelings will surface, and it may be a stormy time; but far better now than while grandma is settling in. Talk about your fears and expectations; stress the importance of the sharing of household burdens, which will surely be even more important with an aging relative in the house than it is now.

If your spouse feels resentment over having to put up with your elderly mother—maybe because he never got along with his own?—he will feel everything she does to be a source of trouble. If your children are the kind of people who think only of themselves and their own pleasures, they will certainly have no respect for or patience with a grandparent's needs. Prepare them for the change they will certainly have to make.

Some of the problems can be anticipated. Traditionally it has been the woman of the house who has assumed the major responsibility for the day-to-day care of dependents, whether children, the aged or the infirm. Her husband and children are bound to receive less of her attention, care and affection if she is suddenly made responsible for an additional person with pressing needs for attention. If she also works outside the home, and now has more work to do *in* the home, then arrangements must certainly be made for others to assume some of her regular duties. A good chance for a little shifting around of role playing, and for junior to learn how to make his own bed and clean his own room, for instance.

On the other hand, you may be able to afford some outside help, someone hired to perform some or all of the care of the old person, thus making it unnecessary for any family member to devote a great deal of time or physical effort to the task. If you are in this enviable position, you may feel that personal sacrifice is expected of you nonetheless. Overcome your guilt and rejoice. The martyr role—in which you give up all outside activity and claim that you no longer have any time to yourself—is not permitted. As always, some time away from home for you, unrelated to responsibilities toward others, must still be planned and enjoyed.

Besides, the principal caretaker sometimes tries to do everything herself as a means of attaining power over the situation and all the people involved in it. This is as bad for everyone concerned as her working herself into an illness or a nervous breakdown. So during this pre-moving-in discussion, talk everything out. Take all anticipatory fears and complaints seriously. The difficulty and importance of the job must be recognized by everyone concerned, young or middle-aged. You may decide that it is going to be too much for one person or for two or for three, and here's where a new sharing will come into your home.

If you are having difficulties getting the discussion started, here are some questions that may be useful. Lay this little "test" on the family conference table and see how many yesses you come up with:

1. Will you be able to make grandmother or grandfather feel wanted in your home?
2. Are you ready to be kind even when you are exhausted and annoyed?
3. Are you willing to sacrifice some of your material pleasures to insure your relative's comfort?
4. Is your house arranged so that you can take care of an older person?
5. Will you have adequate help to handle nursing tasks and the additional household chores?

6. Can you insure the privacy of each member of the family under the new circumstances?
7. Do you believe the older person can adjust to living in a household other than the one he heads?
8. Is this the best solution to the problem?

If the answer to all these queries is yes, then go ahead and plan your new living arrangements. Not the least of them will have to do with the rooms of your home. Of course the ideal is that the new member of the family will have his own room, on the first floor (or anyway where he needn't climb stairs), close to the bathroom, a cheerful, sunny room where he can install familiar furnishings—in short, the same criteria apply here as in his own home.

Now all you have to do is to prepare the way by helping establish a receptive mood in all the present members of the family, then encouraging grandmother or grandfather or Aunt Elizabeth to understand the family routine and fit into it. If mother and father and the children have developed a little flexibility in advance, then the old one will probably bend a little too.

When you outline the plan to your aging relative, keep in mind that the decision to move into your home (or that of another relative or friend) is just as hard for him to make as it is for you and your present family. Change of any kind requires careful examination. It's not easy for youngsters to adjust to summer camp, for adolescents to slip easily into boarding school or college, for young adults to join the army or get transferred to another town or city. There is no reason to expect old people to rearrange their lives and move their abode with complete ease. They may have spent many years in their present residence so that it has grown on them like a skin. They may have more specific needs now for their comfort or health. They have their dignity to preserve and may not care to adjust to being just barely tolerated or living in a place where they may feel they have no real function in the life of the home. Try to figure out how to make them feel wanted and needed.

Nearly all *new* situations, for most people of any age, cause states of mind that range from excited anticipation to confusion and disorientation to outright fear. People fear travel because they are afraid of the unaccustomed, the unknown. Many, when they *do* travel, reassure themselves by traveling with a group of compatriots, or very well shepherded by a travel consultant. When a family changes its place of residence, many of its members go through major psychological crises. Psychoanalysts hear about the pain and shock of moving, sometimes not dispelled decades later. All newness looms threateningly.

Imagine then the shock and fear experienced by an aged person, deriving considerable comfort and security from a long-accustomed groove, contemplating a move to a new location, a different house or apartment. The very notion causes him to feel a bit less sure of himself, of being able to make the right decision. And this indecisiveness is bound to spill over into sorting things out for packing and moving. Discarding is physically tiring and emotionally taxing: each decision to get rid of something is a parting with one aspect of life. This painful separation is a tremendous burden for the aged; and they usually welcome a loving relative's help in making this series of decisions. (Some people of course never manage to throw away anything at all!)

Now on top of this trauma, grandmother or grandfather has to adjust to entirely new surroundings, bereft of many of his own long-cherished familiar things, feeling unsure about having made the right decision. He may be nearly paralyzed until he adjusts. Be patient with him.

### IN A HOME FOR THE AGED

There are any number of conditions under which your parent or relative's going to a home for the aged is absolutely the best solution, both for him and for all the other concerned friends and relatives. There is something in us that shies away from this decision if any of the other options can possibly be agreed upon; but on the other hand some articulate older people themselves prefer to go to a home for the elderly when they reach a certain age. If it's *your* decision to make, let's consider some theoretical situations that would seem to indicate it's the right one.

Supposing your mother has lived alone for the past four years, quite independently, cooking for herself, doing her own marketing, socializing with her neighbors, regularly attending the local golden-age club. Then one afternoon, as she was about to cross the street near her home, a street urchin grabbed her pocketbook. She didn't let go quickly enough—and fell, and broke her hip. In the hospital stay her hipbone set promptly, but now she needs a walker and some extended care. She will get this care at the convalescent home she has gone to from the hospital, but what then? The accident has made her feel less sure of herself, and, quite realistically, her old neighborhood is far less safe for a person on the street in the daytime than it used to be. Your own home is bursting at the seams with humanity in other stages of crisis already, and besides, your mother has categorically stated that she doesn't want to come live with you. A home for the aged seems clearly the answer.

Or say that your father has had a stroke. Though he has

recovered most of his functioning, his speech is a little impaired and he isn't steady enough to get around his house with agility. Also, he has hardly any visitors and finds it a lonely life. He would welcome the attention and company he would have at a "home."

Perhaps your aunt has become a little absent-minded. In her confusion she leaves the water in the teapot boiling until the pot burns; she doesn't always remember to lock the door when she goes out; or she sometimes has difficulty finding her way back to the right apartment. Surely an older-persons' home would be reassuring to her.

The decision to go to such an establishment is fraught with many uncertainties for the aged themselves; it does, after all, mark a final chapter. As some older people say, the next home is likely to be a permanent one: in the cemetery. It may also imply the end of individuality, even if that is at present expressed only by puttering around one's own kitchen or garden. But the gain is safety, comfort, care and companionship.

For the younger relative, too, there are emotional difficulties. If there is any doubt whether such a home is really necessary—or whether, with more sacrifice on your part, your aged parent could continue in his own home or in yours—you are bound to feel guilty. Recriminations may be in store; for instance, your parent may contrast the selfless care he bestowed upon you when you were young, or when you were ill, with your seeming callousness now.

You can reduce your load of guilt by being sure that you have found the best facility available; and you can help your relative accept living in a nursing home in various ways. His doctor should be the one to explain the advantages of this new way of life. If possible, the older person himself should be taken to visit two or three homes; he should be encouraged to discuss his feelings about the choices with you, so that together you can select the one he would be most comfortable in. When he does move, he should take along with him some of his most prized familiar possessions so that he will not feel totally strange and isolated from the "things" he's used to. If in addition he is free to come and go in the community and thus maintain his independence of movement, he will be much happier than if confined.

Visiting people in a home or hospital for the aged is sometimes a very upsetting experience for the younger relatives. Be prepared to feel the worst as you are leaving, or just after you have left. While aging itself need not mean illness, there is a concentration of people in homes and hospitals who manifest deformities, derangement or helplessness. This can be a startling scene, especially when you first confront it, not only because you don't wish to associate your slightly enfeebled parent with such tragedy, but because you have to face the possibility that this may be your own fate one day. If the hospital is a good one, you can take comfort in knowing that the care is the best available. And in time, many of the other people there, whose condition at first so startled you, will become familiar, will manifest their individual personalities. It will become apparent that many of them are less ill or incapacitated than you thought.

## CHOOSING A HOME

Just as important as helping your aging parent to accept the idea of living in a home other than yours or his own, and entering into its choice, is your selection of one or more possible places. One of the facts of life is that even with a growing emphasis on the latter years, there is often a limited choice of such homes available to you. Or, if there is a clearly superior one in your area, there is a long waiting list for entrance. You may have to locate a temporary home until the one you really want for your mother or father has a room available.

When it has become urgent for you to find the place, what do you look for? Few things in this life are perfect, and institutional living of any kind is less likely to come near perfection than most situations. But some problems can be averted by a thorough search and inspection plus some questions that you can answer in advance of an actual trip to the facility. Is the home licensed? Is it accredited by social services? Will it accept various assistance plans? Insurance? Medicare? What are the costs involved? Are there extra charges for such services as laundry?

Go there yourself before you take your parent along to experience the setting. Nonprofit homes often provide better care than profit-making institutions and may offer a standard of comparison, so try to visit one if possible.

Stay at the home for at least an hour. Insist on seeing every floor, including service areas like kitchens.

Entering a home, you can easily get an idea of the prevailing atmosphere, both physical and human. What does it look like? Is it clean, dilapidated, light, airy? Watch the faces of the personnel as they go about their business. Are they reasonably cheerful, or embittered, tense? How do they talk with one another? With the people in their care? If they condescend, or brush people off, beware. If they have too many rules about what a patient may or may not do, if the visiting hours are limited and rigid, it's not good. Old people need visitors, as often and as long as possible. To set up particular visiting hours makes this vital need harder to fulfill. Many excellent homes permit visitors any time—at *your* convenience—and it doesn't interfere with anything. While every institution needs some rules, oftentimes they are arbitrary or tacitly set up for the convenience of the manager and staff, at the cost of the client. Visiting hours in such establishments are designed to make the staff feel undisturbed masters of "their domain." If so, it should not become your aged friend's domain.

It's perfectly true that food in a bedroom may attract vermin and that a radio can be played too loud. But to be denied a box of crackers in one's room hardly makes for minimal comfort; and if the place is being properly looked after, such minor articles of sustenance should not be more of a problem than in any living quarters (a covered container is one solution). Similarly, if there is a reasonable atmosphere and concerned personnel, people tend not to play their radios too loudly.

Does the home have a volunteer service connected with it? Volunteers usually provide uplift: someone who cares but doesn't get paid for caring is often a more reliable source of sympathetic feeling. Also, volunteers represent the world outside, and indeed often access to the outside world as well—if they are the sort of volunteers who offer to take the residents out for shopping and entertainment.

The setting for meals and the quality of the food, naturally, are important: a pleasure in eating knows no age limit. Also, little things connected with the gustatory life of the institution will tell a lot about its spirit. Some homes serve beer with dinner if requested, or wine. That means that the residence is not rigidly concerned only with dire necessity, and that its staff members do not have a puritanical attitude or jailer's mentality. (Beer or wine can be good for the nerves, improve sleeping, accentuate appetite.) Be sure that a puritanical attitude doesn't prevail as well in the matter of "chaperoning." There is no reason for men and women to be kept separated just because they have passed the age of sixty-five. Couples who have met in an old-age home need a place where they can go to keep company, be alone together.

See what facilities the home provides for recreation, physical therapy and medical care. Is there at least a registered nurse on duty at all times? How frequently do doctors see patients and how thorough are their examinations? Are doctors available to speak with relatives of the aged residents? If it is a nursing home, does the head nurse see every patient every day? Check to see that there are wash basins in each room so staff are encouraged to clean their hands after contact with each patient, thus discouraging the spread of infections.

If the home is associated with a reputable hospital or medical school, chances are good for a high medical standard. Check out the rating of the associated medical facility. And, if patients complain that the medical staff uses them as "guinea pigs," look into this report to see whether it's imaginary or real and how you can protect your parent legally from any such occurrence.

So far we have discussed the general problems of institutional living. The fact is that there are different kinds of care-giving institutions for the aged who cannot live independently. The main distinction, not always clearcut, lies between old-age homes (sometimes also known as rehabilitation centers—more as a statement of goal than an indication of substantial difference, since very few older people are able to leave again for another form of living than a home) and nursing homes.

Nursing homes are facilities for people who need active

nursing care. Such individuals are most frequently incontinent, or unable to move well on their own because of a fracture or a stroke; or they may be very feeble, will not eat of their own volition, or suffer from some ailment that requires chronic nursing care. There are facilities also for those who require time-limited nursing care, such as after an operation, which may be called physical rehabilitation centers or extended-care facilities.

In distinction, homes for the aged are institutions which care for aged people who, while unable to live alone and, perhaps, have some disability, can by and large attend to their personal needs most of the time. The fact that greater problems exist with nursing homes than with homes for the aged can easily be deduced: the more care the individual patient needs, the harder it is, unfortunately, to get enough of it. The worst abuses exist in nursing homes because the patients are least likely to protest actively or even be able to tell about the situation adequately. The needs of the patients are most demanding and the personnel attending them are hardly real professionals. Nor are they well paid or rewarded socially for their demanding work. It falls on minimally skilled, insufficiently trained and supervised people to lift patients on and off beds, onto toilets, into bathtubs, or to feed them.

The care of the very incapacitated aged patient is the specter haunting everyone, not the facts of age themselves. Magazine articles and books have been written eloquently describing the appalling conditions in nursing homes. It has also been pointed out that many nursing homes are part of a rather ruthless profit-making industry which has the advantage of being federally subsidized through Medicare and Medicaid payments, without sufficient quality controls being enforced, at least in many instances.

It will take a consumer revolt, constant community pressure, increasing vigilance by local and federal agencies, to raise the level of care provided by nursing homes. This effort has been begun, and it is a worthwhile pursuit for active, healthy members of senior citizens' groups, in particular, to engage in as watchdogs for their less fortunate peers. Lobbying by elderly citizens, for example, recently resulted in passage of more stringent regulations for nursing homes in Rhode Island against the opposition of the nursing-home industry. These included unannounced inspections and total public access to inspection reports.

Above all, it will take further medical advances and prevention of illness to make a real difference.

When your questions have been answered satisfactorily, you have evaluated the available homes and made your selection, and the move has been made, be prepared for some further problems and upsets.

Even after the initial problems of adjustment—and your guilt—have been overcome, there may be some new manifestations of fear and insecurity. When you come for a visit, your mother may tell you that the nurses beat her, that the doctors pay no attention to her, or that other patients steal from her. You may be puzzled as to whether these complaints are those of a confused state of mind or real and justified. The fact is that many such allegations are figments of the imagination and can be ignored, whereas others are actual situations that it is your duty to investigate the best you can. Try to evaluate the mental state of the aged friend, and after you have a pretty clear picture (through the use, possibly, of some "test questions"), take appropriate action, bearing in mind that institutional living is, at best, full of shortcomings, though these must not include cruelty or neglect.

It is important to understand that some problems inevitably occur when people are cared for by others, whether at home by private nurse or in an institutional setting. Sometimes it is possible to work out a means of alleviating the problems; at other times it is necessary to accept the situation as best one can.

For example, I know of a wealthy man who was incapacitated by a stroke which left him with a rare form of incontinence (many forms can be treated rather successfully). He often perceived a need to defecate, which his nurse recognized as a false message sent to the brain by a defective nervous system and who therefore tried to dissuade the patient from frequent toileting. This upset the patient's wife, who was used to her husband being in control not only of himself but of an industrial empire. Now he couldn't even have his wish to go to the toilet met. To make matters worse, he occasionally did lose bowel control without warning, which the nurse, most unreasonably, interpreted as an act of spite. All the wealth and private care did not prevent a very painful situation.

Incontinence and frequent requests to be taken to the toilet present quite a problem in nursing homes, where the staff must respond to many patients, not just one. It has been found that if patients are assured that they will be taken to the bathroom at intervals, determined by observing the usual frequency of their needs, they are able to wait for the scheduled times and are relieved of their excessive anxiety about this matter. Although initially such attention to toileting requirements may be a lot of work for the staff of the home, eventually things run much more smoothly, eliminating situations where patients lie in their feces or urine, possibly contracting bedsores or infection, certainly feeling demoralized. And ultimately, there is much less laundry and disinfecting of the premises required.

After the decision has been made and you have enrolled your aged father, he may cry and insist he doesn't belong there. He could, he believes, live perfectly well by himself. He may even accuse you of simply wanting to abandon him to strangers, or of taking possession of his fortune or belongings. He may feel that things have been misrepresented and that he is the victim of persecution. Again, it is your responsibility to investigate the degree to which his complaints are justified.

The important thing in all these situations is not to panic. It's important for neither you nor your infirm or aged parent, nor your other less afflicted parent, to become alarmed. For if you don't know how to proceed, or can't cope with a whole new set of life problems, there are many experts and a growing number of facilities available for you to call upon for help. Here, for reminders, are some of these aids:

*A social agency* in your community. (See the Appendix.) Call and ask for the geriatric branch, the service for the aged. You can visit them, and if need be, they will come and visit you and/or your elderly relative.

*Homemakers.* The social agency knows about these people, called into service when it is difficult to take care of the home of the aged person. They will come into the home for as many hours as is necessary to tidy up and do some shopping when necessary.

*Physicians.* Either private doctors or those provided by the local hospital or the health mobilization organization will make a house call.

*Visiting Nurses* can call daily or once or twice a week, to give an injection, dress a bedsore, exercise a paralyzed leg, or any number of other treatments.

*Social Workers* can arrange for Medicare-Medicaid or whatever financial assistance is needed. They know about resources, how to fill out the right forms and get what benefits or services are coming to you. So do welfare workers.

The last thing in the world you should be is shy or hesitant about calling upon the aid that you need and deserve and really can't do without in coping with a newly dependent aging friend or relative. To do so is to do a disservice to him *and* to yourself.

# 3

# *The Most Prevalent Special Problems*

*The ruins of himself, now worn away*
*With age, yet still majestic in decay.*
HOMER

ALTHOUGH we can't repeat often enough that to be entering old age is by no means to be sick or deranged or in one's second childhood, there are a number of quirks or problems that are frequently part and parcel of aging. Many of the aspects of aging discussed here succinctly will be handled in more detail in other chapters. In *this* chapter we have listed these frequently encountered phenomena for quick and easy reference.

## ACCIDENTS

The aged suffer accidents more frequently for a number of reasons. One is that their reflexes are slowed so they avoid obstacles or moving objects less readily than younger people. Another is that their coordination is impaired. They may be less steady on their feet because the mechanism in the inner ear that controls balance has deteriorated, or because the hand and the leg do not obey as promptly as they once did the commands given when the eye or ear perceives danger signals.

What might mean just a bump or a bruise or a harmless fall for a younger adult can mean a broken bone for an older person. Bones are made up of two basically different materials intricately interwoven: one is primarily calcium and a few other minerals, the other is gelatinous protein similar to cartilage. In the aged much of the gelatinlike material has disappeared, leaving the bones quite porous. Osteoporosis ("porous bones") is a typical bone disorder of the aged, rendering their bones much more breakable. Since people typically try to avoid falling backward or straight forward, falls to the side predominate. This means landing on one's hipbone. Fractures of the hip, therefore, are among the most frequent afflictions of old age. And while this sort of fracture can often be adequately repaired, even in the aged, the immobilization that follows directly upon such a break may produce physical complications such as painful bedsores or pneumonia.

The fear of accidents in the aged, often so incomprehensible to the vigorous, mobile youngster, is very understandable. They perceive the decrease in their reflex speed, and they are beginning to realize their relative helplessness in dealing with any number of circumstances; and they dread the increased and acute helplessness that accidents can bring about.

Sometimes the aged patient treats the part of the body that has met with an accident as if it were a separate being. Studying such a patient psychologically, I have often found that an older person behaves as if his hurt limb or organ were a child to which he must play mother or father. He babies and speaks of it in the third person, as if it were another independent personality. Because the damaged part involves such a large share of consciousness, it plays an enlarged role, much bigger than life size.

If such an accident befalls your mother or father, be aware of this peculiarity and treat it with a sympathetic and understanding attitude. At the same time, don't show excessive concern or intense sympathy for so long a time that the extra attention becomes a reason for further "investing" in accidents or the fear of accidents. All of us have needs and desires to be dependent and to be fussed over, and everyone is susceptible to temptation and seduction along those lines. If we friends and relatives and professionals show an excess of sympathy, we do the patient a disservice by making him feel more like a dependent child than he needs to. Gentle insistence on the patient's doing as much as possible for himself while invalided and after recovery from an acute injury is necessary. Discussion of some of the causes of his accident may help him too. The accident sufferer may be less aware of the causal connections than are those around him. And pointing out his attitude toward the accident and toward the afflicted part, if it can be done gently and diplomatically, may help too. Childlike regressions to a former state of dependency can only lead to further incapacity and affect the older person's self-esteem.

## ACCUMULATING POSSESSIONS

Some people take great pleasure in throwing things away, in a sort of constant renewal of life through a renewal of objects, of possessions. Others like to accumulate things, to prolong the present or to hang on to the past by hanging on to its appurtenances. An attempt to hold on to continuity, to time that seems to be slipping away, is probably what motivates older people to gather around them a host of possessions, even seemingly useless and valueless ones. A few aged people (remember the pathetic Collier brothers?) collect startling amounts of trash.

This is a harmless characteristic of old age—unless such trash accumulations constitute a health or fire hazard. If the case is so extreme as to be this kind of peril, it may be necessary for you to establish a guardianship of your aging relative, or to place him or her in a caretaking institution. But such stringent measures should be employed only under the most dire circumstances. Otherwise, let him collect—where's the danger in it?

## BEDSORES

Older people who have to spend a good deal of time in bed are more likely than younger patients to develop bedsores. The lower back, the hips and the heels are areas where lesions are most likely to appear; they may be large or small, superficial or several inches deep. If an afflicted older person lies too long in one position, the skin actually dies: the combination of poor circulation and uneven pressure prevents the proper nourishment from reaching the skin in that place. Decreased resistance to infection in the old, together with a lack of cleanliness, can increase the chances of bacterial invasion. Therefore, frequent turning of patients and prevention of breaks in the skin by keeping bed sheets smooth and unwrinkled are important, as is scrupulous cleanliness. Bedsores first appear as reddened skin areas. Should you notice red spots developing, powder them and cover them with soft material. If actual breaks in the skin occur, consult a physician.

## BODILY PREOCCUPATION

It used to be held that a child should be seen and not heard. Something similar might be said of one's body: a body should just be there, fulfilling its functions, not calling undue attention to itself. And with a healthy body this is the case. The moment you have to be intensely aware of your body—because your heart is beating too fast, or your leg hurts, or your stomach has cramps—an alarm goes out. Some people seem to be able to more or less ignore even such dramatic symptoms as these; others react immediately as if to a four-alarm fire, and these people are found in all age groups.

In old age even the healthy body functions less unobtrusively. At the least it works with some minor aches and pains. Digestion and elimination slow down. Even under normal conditions the aging body has to have more attention paid to it than that of the average young person. If your elderly parent had a tendency to keep a steady vigil over his health as a younger person, this tendency will be markedly increased in age; if he took his body for granted in previous years, he may only just now begin to watch it and its functioning with more concentration. If he has a diseased or impaired organ, it may come to play an enlarged role of its own. If there is something wrong with his liver, his mental image of his insides will resemble those funny maps of the United States as seen by a New Yorker: New York seems to cover at least two-thirds of the continental territory, with the Rocky Mountains dividing it from a narrow western slice that is California. To a person preoccupied with one part of his body, that limb or organ looms very large in the mind. This is easy to understand if, for example, you have ever had a bothersome fever blister on your lip. It itches, it burns, it feels swollen; you are sure that everybody sees it and finds it disgusting. The fact is that eight out of ten people you meet won't notice it and that even the two who do don't care. *You* are the person to whom it looms large. The person excessively concerned with his weight feels fat and bloated when the scale shows a two-pound gain; others around him don't notice the difference. This intense relationship with one's own body is often the situation with the aged. It is hard both for them and for those who have to endure their intemperate concern with their bodies and their constant talk about what ails them.

Aside from appropriate medical attention, the cure—or the improvement—of this condition is related to undoing the cause. If undue preoccupation is the result of the lack of other occupation, providing other interests will help. When your attention is focused on the world outside yourself and its human relations and its activity, you pay less attention to your own body and its well-being. If your aging parent is particularly anxious over his physical condition, a careful explanation of the precise implications and prognosis by a patient and kind physician should go a long way to decrease worry. When a real damaging of self-love has occurred, and the complaining is a form of saying "I can't stand the change age has brought to me—I don't feel worthwhile and attractive any more; I am angry about all this," then some brief psychotherapy may be indicated. The results will be in direct proportion to the degree of psychic health or lack of self-centeredness that existed in earlier days.

## DRIVING

Many states now require a periodic eye examination after a certain age for renewal of an automobile operator's license. Where this requirement is not in effect, the decision as to whether an older person should drive a car should be based on his actual mental and physical condition—eyesight, reflexes, muscular coordination, etc.—and his driving record, rather than on his age itself. If his condition, both mental and physical, is not consistent with complete safety on the road, he is a danger to himself and to others and must be forced to give up driving.

So dominant a means of getting around is driving an automobile that if an older person is deprived of his license, it can represent a very serious threat to his life and proper functioning, his sense of himself as a competent person. Aside from the realistic limitations such a loss imposes on his mobility, it must be understood as a real blow to self-esteem and a feeling of independence. Whatever possible should be done to counter both the practical and the emotional problems precipitated. Extra time devoted to providing other means of transportation will help; more attention given to your suddenly wheel-less parent and an improvement in his social life may partially compensate for hurt feelings and insecurity. As much as he or she complains about this deprivation, the older person may feel a secret relief at not having to risk driving any more.

## EATING

Appetite usually decreases in the aged, and the sense of taste alters somewhat. Enough food consumption to maintain a desirable body weight should be encouraged; and the necessary basic supply of vitamins and minerals should be provided. All other things being equal, no special food planning or diet should be necessary if you are feeding an older relative, except that food should not be unduly difficult to chew and digest, especially if the aging person has dentures or poor teeth. Meals for him or her—as for everyone—should be as interesting and appetizing as possible. A small glass of wine, particularly of a relatively dry variety, taken fifteen to twenty minutes before dinner, is likely to have a definite appetite-increasing effect. (An excessive amount of wine, or even a moderate amount of heavier alcoholic drink, has an appetite-suppressing effect.)

## FALLS

Besides the causes mentioned under Accidents, falls in the aged can be the result of other conditions, chief among them dizziness. And dizziness may be caused by a number of different disarrangements, among them anemia, low blood pressure, high blood pressure and arrhythmia (irregularities in the heartbeat). Even such insignificant conditions as a superfluity of wax in the ears or anxious breathing can cause dizziness. Taking aspirin, sleeping pills or some of the drugs prescribed for high blood pressure can produce vertigo in the aged, as can certain normal motions, such as bending the head backward or turning it suddenly to the side. This last movement may produce pressure on the carotid sinus, a small area in the front of the neck close to the muscles that keep the head erect, and cause a fall. Fainting or a convulsion may even result from exaggerated pressure on that spot.

Dizziness and limpness occur in the aged most frequently when getting up from a chair or bed. This is because the abdominal walls have become loosened and much of the whole body's blood has gone to the blood vessels of the abdomen. On arising, an insufficient supply of blood has traveled to the head, causing dizziness and even collapse. You can help prevent this frightening occurrence by encouraging your elderly relative to rise very methodically and slowly, if from a reclining position, assuming a sitting position first, tightening the muscles of the stomach and abdomen. Even tightening a belt before getting up from a chair can help remedy this situation, and prevent a dangerous fall.

A low salt level in the system can cause dizziness and a resulting fall. A greater intake of salt, perhaps in the form of salt tablets, may prove helpful in such cases. So may treatment with drugs like niacin or seasickness pills, which dilate the cerebral blood vessels and thereby decrease dizziness.

A most amazing form of falling in elderly people is called a "drop attack." Standing at a sink or table, a person may fall down without warning—his legs just giving way. Crumpled on the floor with his leg muscles very loose, he may be unable to get up for a few minutes to several hours, but otherwise be perfectly conscious. Though this phenomenon is not well understood medically speaking, it is not a cause for alarm and should not disturb the sufferer unduly.

You can help him by bracing the soles of his feet against the floor or wall so that the muscle tone is soon recovered and he is able to get up again.

Though you can tolerate it easily in your middle years (and may even have sought it on occasion in your youth), the mere sensation of dizziness can cause considerable fear and insecurity in aging people. And the same goes for any loss of muscle control, no matter how transient. Even though she has not experienced a serious fall, recurring vertigo or flaccidness of musculature may engender in your mother a reluctance to walk alone or engage in any independent activity. Try to persuade her to use a cane or walking stick or a "walker," which will make her steadier and less fearful of moving about by herself.

## INCONTINENCE

Incontinence, the weakening of bowel or bladder control, is a terrible cross for the aged to bear because of course it reminds them of a reversion to an infantile state. Fortunately in some forms it is only a temporary condition. Wearing diaper-like undergarments can minimize the dreadful embarrassment of incontinence.

There are medications that can be prescribed for incontinence. And specific training for control of either the bladder or the bowel is possible too: your doctor can arrange a consultation with a nurse especially experienced in this therapy. In some cases surgery of the prostate gland or of the bladder muscles is helpful; and under certain circumstances a rubber tube (a catheter) is inserted to facilitate emptying of the bladder.

Bowel incontinence is sometimes due to an accumulation

in the rectum of hard, puttylike feces, which have to be manually removed. (Drugstores sell disposable plastic gloves, useful for this unpleasant problem: use white petroleum jelly on the fingers of the glove.) Diarrhea that is caused by such impaction will cease once the obstruction is removed. Such impactions, initially due to constipation, may be prevented by the use of suppositories or enemas, or a dose of mineral oil. Mineral oil should be used only occasionally as it may interfere with the absorption of food from the intestine. Elderly people who might cough while swallowing the oil might also breathe some into their lungs. This could be dangerous. Most laxatives taken routinely decrease the bowel's natural tendency to work and may also cause some irritations. Daily exercise, if possible, is a healthy way of avoiding constipation. Some roughage in the diet is another reasonable measure. Many physicians prefer some medication that provides non-irritating bulk or mucillage as a smoothing agent to oil or other laxatives. Many such preparations are available as over-the-counter medicines.

## NAGGING QUESTIONS

Some elderly people become great nags, continually asking questions, a variety or the same one over and over again. Given an answer but continuing to ask the same question, grandmother or grandfather can become a source of great frustration and impatience on the part of the rest of the family.

This annoying behavior, it's important for you to understand, derives not from any desire to be a pest, but from the fact that he feels at a loss. Because of some brain-cell deterioration, he feels insecure, not quite sure of himself. He is a bit confused about the world around him and perceives many changes in his own functioning. Asking the same question again and again is an attempt to check up on his own perception; but since the answer doesn't really relieve his feeling of insecurity, he keeps on asking.

Perseveration, as continual repetition of the same question is called, is a frequent result of brain damage or deterioration, which, incidentally, probably has little if anything to do with the *decrease* of brain cells with age. The most reliable data about brain-cell decrease comes from animal studies, but the evidence about humans is not conclusive, only suggestive. It appears that between young adulthood and sixty-five-plus, as much as one-third of the total brain cells are lost. (Brain cells, unlike muscle, skin and other cells, do not regenerate or grow anew.) Most neurologists, however, believe that a very large percentage of all living brain cells are never used at all, and therefore the loss in aging need not make a critical difference. There is considerable belief that previously unused brain cells can be trained to take over the functions of some that are destroyed in the process of aging. (Karl Lashley, a distinguished neurophysiologist, has named this peculiar ability of brain cells "equipotentiality." Working with animals, he removed various portions of the brain and found that they then lost previously learned capabilities, presumably recorded in the removed part of the brain. When the animal learned again to perform the task as taught to it, Dr. Lashley assumed that other parts of the brain had taken over where the removed cells left off.)

Nagging questions may seem to be concentrated on the whereabouts of people or things: "Where is Joe?" or "Where are my black shoes?" or "Did you take my gold watch?" This sort of query indicates that father is having trouble with orientation, is not always sure he knows exactly where he is. The best way you can help him with this problem is to provide him with a very clearly defined routine in a relatively small area.

Other kinds of questions you can only continue to answer, patiently, truthfully and gently. Besides being inherently annoying, your older relative's becoming such a nag is hard for you to bear because it upsets you more than you may be aware that your parent is reduced to such a regrettable state. Your children may be better able than you to deal with their grandparent's constant questioning: questions-and-answers is a game they may enjoy playing, quite simply. The more concerned you are, the more closely emotionally involved, the more likely you yourself are to react with impatience. If your child or children can't be called upon, it's therefore important, if at all possible, for someone outside the family to care for such an elderly person, at least for relief. Or, failing this spreading out of the daily responsibility, that you find a day-care center.

## OPERATIONS

Surgical procedures are remarkably well borne by most old people. Modern medicine prepares the patient for surgery by building up his blood supply and providing a variety of drugs that strengthen the body's defenses. Anesthesia today is a far cry from what it used to be, and surgery itself and the vital care right after the patient emerges from the operating room are among the greatest advances in the whole field of medicine.

Nevertheless, an aged person whose functioning may not be up to par before surgery may respond with some confusion, including hallucinations or false beliefs, for some time after an operation. Also, surgery and the enforced rest that follows it may change a person from quite robust to really aged. Part of this alteration is due to the desire that we all retain to be taken care of; convalescent care sometimes proves just too much of a lure for someone who feels less than totally vigorous.

It is helpful for someone close to the patient to be with him as he wakes up from anesthesia; this is true for all ages and particularly with the aged. It is reassuring and aids in orientation. (Remember how you have felt when waking up alone from a very deep sleep or, worse still, from a nightmare?) Keep in mind that you should not exhaust the patient, and then just spend some time with him talking about everyday things. This immediate contact with reality will help him regain orientation.

There are special rehabilitation centers for postsurgical aged people where they are tended to physically and mentally. The personnel at such facilities are prepared to deal with the tendency for older patients to slip into a state of helplessness. But this trend is far from universal; the great majority of even very old people today have hardly any side effects from surgery.

## SEXUAL ABERRATIONS

Some elderly people of both sexes may expose themselves sexually; it is usually because they are confused or absent-minded or both. Very infrequently it is done as a prelude to molestation or solicitation; but that is less often the motivation in an older person than in a younger.

Other old people, who don't have a satisfactory sex life

any more because of the loss of a mate, may make definite physical advances to whoever is in close contact with them. Rather than being truly sexual in nature (though we in our culture for some reason seem to resist the idea of strong sexuality persisting into the later years, which it often does, and should), such advances may represent merely a simple need for a social contact. (Literally reaching for a breast, a buttock or a penis may be translated as reaching out for warmth and loving concern.) You may help the aging friend or relative who behaves in this way just by holding his hand while walking or talking with him. And you may forestall any further such demonstrations by showing generally more interest in him or her than you have previously.

## SLEEPING

Two common complaints made by older people are that they don't sleep at night as much as they used to, and that they are restless or frequently awakened during the night with physical complaints. One of the reasons the aged don't sleep as much is that they simply don't *need* as much sleep as the younger adult. Having finished their growing and being less physically active than younger people, their bodies don't have the same requirements for the sound sleep that stems from bodily fatigue. In addition, they may go to bed earlier than they used to, out of boredom or loneliness. This makes the night seem longer and gives the impression of less actual sleep. One simple measure is to increase daytime activity.

A nap during the daytime will give one older person the feeling that he has two days to your every one; in others it may increase the complaints about sleeplessness once he's retired at night. If too much sleeping medication is taken at bedtime, it may not only give him a good night's sleep, but continue to produce drowsiness through the next day, causing frequent cat naps, and thus in part reversing the usual sleeping pattern. In such a case, eliminating all sleeping potions may effect a cure.

Coffee, tea and some carbonated beverages contain an ingredient called caffeine, which is a stimulant. An older person should be persuaded to give up drinking these particular stimulants in any quantity during the day, and especially just before bedtime. Switching to decaffeinated coffee, trying herbal teas, substituting fruit juices or water —or just breaking the pattern of too-frequent coffee breaks —may be helpful.

Various pains (rheumatic, arthritic or otherwise) may interfere with regular sleep; a mild painkiller can sometimes be prescribed against such interruptions. The need to urinate frequently during the night may also play a role in this trouble; many older people therefore refrain from drinking much liquid in the latter parts of the day, and particularly on retiring.

While a clap of thunder in the night may wake you only momentarily, your aging uncle may find it particularly difficult to fall asleep again once awakened because of his feeling of unease about orientation and about impending helplessness. His sleep may actually be improved if there is some light on by which he can quickly establish his whereabouts. Even a radio turned on very low may provide a focus of attention that will prove reassuring and allow him to go back to sleep quickly. Being at the same time not too far away from the rest of the household's sleeping quarters will also be a help.

Whatever physical pain or discomfort or emotional upset

can be alleviated will be an improvement in the sleep of the aged. Sometimes a nightcap of wine or beer will be relaxing and induce sleep. Such a treat is worth a try before consulting a physician about prescribing a mild sedative or sleeping pill to help overcome the pattern of sleeplessness. But under any circumstances you must reassure your parent that a little less sleep than in earlier years is normal and does no harm. Anxiety about insomnia, as all poor sleepers of any age know, only makes it worse.

## SUSPICIOUSNESS

As older people become more unsure of themselves, they start to question everything more carefully and be extra cautious. While this is on the whole a constructive tendency, it may manifest itself in suspiciousness: not believing in their own perceptions and not trusting other people. It may even intensify into persecutory ideas or paranoia. The aged often make a clearcut division that they would have scorned at an earlier age between good and bad people. If you are to be helpful to them, you must align yourself with the "good." Without playing tricks, without directly agreeing, you may have to appear to accept the suspicious person's judgment of some people as "bad." These separations of the sheep from the goats should not become a source of argument between you and your elderly mother: contention will only make things worse as you slowly join in her mind the ranks of the forces of evil.

If one feels helpless, he is especially on guard and fears the worst. Consider the underlying truth of the old joke, "Just because I'm paranoid doesn't mean I have no enemies." Old people often feel helpless—physically, as well as in the sense of being unable to cope mentally as they used to. So they ask more questions, are more wary of being taken advantage of, worry about losing their valuables. Since it is easier (at all ages) not to acknowledge one's shortcomings, an aged person finds it simpler to accuse someone of having taken her pocketbook than face the fact that she has become so forgetful that she doesn't know where she left it.

Some persecutory ideas can trouble both the aged and his family equally. For instance, some sense of not being a sexually desirable companion any more can translate itself into the wish that people would take a definite sexual interest in one. As the conscience doesn't easily admit such thoughts to the surface level of consciousness, they sometimes get twisted around inside and emerge as accusations that people are making advances or spying on intimate situations.

The family can help by overcoming any reaction of huffiness or ridicule. Don't get upset by such expressions of suspiciousness; instead say something like, "In some ways getting older sure hurts your vanity, doesn't it? You could almost wish that people would flirt with you!" A direct interpretation like this can profitably be followed by attempts to help your aged relative stay well groomed and attractively dressed. Keep a simple formula in mind: the less reason your older friend has for feeling undesirable, the less he has to feel guilty over wanting to be attractive, and the less guilt he feels, the less likely he is to harbor imaginary ideas about being spied upon or sexually molested. And another one: the more a person can be helped not to feel helpless, the less likely he is to feel persecuted.

# 4

# What Do We Mean By Aging

*Many grow old before they arrive at that age.*

SIR THOMAS BROWNE

WHAT is your real age? What your calendar says, or how you feel, or what the Social Security Act tells you? There are many concepts of human aging, and many ways in which the human being can grow older. We'll try to deal with a few of them in this chapter.

## YOUR M.Q. (MATURITY QUOTIENT)

An outstanding characteristic of our era is rapid change. Drastic changes in a familiar city or landscape confuse us; sudden alteration in any aspect of our daily lives also leaves us at a loss. The meaning of aging has undergone a transformation too. Life expectancy has changed greatly in the last century, and with it so have styles of living. In the early 1900's many women of forty-five were old and behaved that way. If you remember your parents when they were the age you are today, chances are you think of them as having been much "older" than you are now. That is not all self-deception: you not only have some twenty years more of life ahead of you than they did (statistically speaking), but you are also in much better physical shape. Superior nutrition, better life- and energy-saving drugs, more affluence and all its concomitants make you really much younger at fifty or fifty-five than your parents were. And hence you behave quite differently.

But you often wonder about this change in life style. How *should* you live? Are you behaving badly, "too young for your age"? What is your real age? Well, that depends. . . .

Chronological age is easy enough to define: you know your birth date and can perform simple arithmetic. But beyond that a definition of age becomes more difficult, even in the case of children. If, for instance, a youngster is shorter than his parents think he should be at any particular chronological age, they may take him to an orthopedist. This doctor will X-ray the bones of the child's legs. The long bones of arms and legs start out as soft as cartilage. A hard bony core develops in the middle of the shank and at both ends of the bone (i.e. where the calf bone connects with the knee joint at one end and the foot joint at the other). These hard cores grow toward each other, narrowing the strip of cartilage between them until they join into one big hard bone. If they have not yet grown together, he will make a guess as to how much longer it will take for them to meet. Though the boy may be sixteen, the doctor may say that his bone age is only fourteen, that he will continue to grow for another two years, and he will guess the number of inches. This bone age is a kind of biological age, controlled by an individual biological clock, that is not quite in phase with the chronological or calendar age. In some children the parts of the long bones join very early—the bone "age" may be greater than the birth date would suggest, going by the norm.

Something similar may happen at the other end of the life cycle: some people who are chronologically eighty are biologically only sixty. Their bones, eyes, ears, skin—even their reflexes and blood pressure—may be those one expects, according to the norm, to find in a sixty-year-old.

The age you *feel* is your subjective age. Some people feel far older than they are according to the calendar, others much younger. This subjective feeling does not necessarily coincide with the biological age: some quite ill people remain spirited and mentally young though biologically old—and vice versa. Some misanthropes and hypochondriacs outlive people who feel hale and hearty and well.

Social age is a more complicated matter. Society has diverse mores to confuse the picture. For instance, according to Social Security regulations and current custom, one attains retirement age at sixty-five. Also, in our society young people are expected to be lively and very interested in sex; but society tends to look with some reservation at people in their sixties, seventies or eighties who insist on being both lively and still interested in an active sex life. You are supposed to be mature when you enter a profession or take a steady job; and if you don't like earning a wage, you are considered "immature." You are expected to act your age at many different points in your life—but *what* age, which kind of age? What kind of maturity?

This sort of social regulation varies, of course, from culture to culture. Dr. Bernice Neugarten, an American researcher in aging, speaks of the "social clock" regulating people's expectations: being "early" for going to college, "late" to get married, "just right" for entering a profession. She has invented the term "personal-life time" (in contrast to social or historical time). Part of this conception is the fact that people around fifty to fifty-five tend to look at life as "time left to live" whereas before that age they think of "time since birth." (This may be a good basis for a new two-party system!)

All of this can be confusing: we are too many ages, and it's hard to keep them aligned or synchronized. Remember the trouble children used to have as a result of "rapid advancement" (sometimes called "skipping grades") in school? A smart boy or girl could be jumped a grade or two if his intelligence surpassed that of his classmates. Many children so advanced were not physically and emotionally matched with their scholastic achievement and felt out of place and out of phase in physical growth and sexual development. Girls particularly are always highly conscious of the onset of puberty, and if their own lags behind that of their classmates, it can be a source of emotional maladjustment.

The I.Q., or intelligence quotient, worked out by Alfred Binet may help us to work out the M.Q., or Maturity Quotient. Briefly, your I.Q. is 100 if you can perform the tests that fifty percent of all children of your calendar age can; if your intelligence-test age is higher than your calendar age, your I.Q. is over 100, if lower, then your I.Q. is under 100. For an M.Q., the testing should include headings such as *psychological factors*—ability to learn new material, memory, flexibility, motivation, attention span; and organic factors—skin elasticity, perceptual acuity, circulatory functioning, brain-wave patterns, reflex speed.

In working out actual tests to determine maturity quotient, one might discover that skin elasticity is not a differentiating factor but that blood-vessel elasticity is. Or the speed of reflexes might be found to be useless but the ability to persist at a task significant. If and when reliable and valid criteria are found, they, like the raw data of intelligence tests, can be evaluated for their contribution to the accurate biological age. Then, if chronological age is divided by biological age, a person sixty years old by the calendar and sixty years old biologically would have a maturity quotient of 100, following the norm. The ratio for someone who is sixty chronologically but only fifty biologically would be 60 to 50, a maturity quotient of 120. This would indicate that he is considerably younger than average, just as someone with an I.Q. of 120 has above-average intelligence.

Such an M.Q. would help us avoid a good deal of confusion in the welter of kinds of aging that surrounds us today. It could eventually be as useful in helping us to plan retirement rationally, on an individual basis, as an I.Q. is for planning vocational or professional training. Neither quotient is infallible of course, but both could be useful. I can only hope that researchers in gerontology will agree with my suggestion, will continue to investigate the measurable criteria of biological age, and will come up with some nearly foolproof means of testing for maturity quotient.

## BIOLOGICAL CONCEPTS OF AGING

The mere passage of time need not bring what we usually associate with age—the inevitable slow running down of the body machinery toward eventual halting in death. We know of at least two types of cells that are immortal: the ameba (which simply goes on multiplying *ad infinitum*) and cancer cells (which multiply continually and at various rates of growth). All other animal cells seem to live a programmed length of time, even though they undergo changes. How this growth happens has yet to be agreed upon by science. What causes the cells of living things to age? Is it possible to slow down, or even completely stop, this process? Could it be reversed? Fascinating questions under constant study. Recent discoveries have brought forth a rash of predictions that control over cellular aging is possible within the foreseeable future, perhaps within our lifetimes. Here, again briefly and simply, are some of the concepts of aging currently being explored.

## THE GENETIC THEORY

The genetic theory relies heavily on the supposition that every human cell is something like a miniature computer, programmed to perform in a specific way. Each cell receives its own programmed message for maturation and eventual aging from the biological molecular computers, in this case DNA, the basic life material. The schedule of cell growth that culminates in bodily maturity seems to indicate that there is a genetic program for aging. Experiments have shown that when individual cells are put into a culture in the laboratory, their artificial life outside a human body is related to the age of the donor (the person from whom the cells were taken). In one experiment, cells were taken from the arms of a hundred human subjects ranging in age from prenatal to ninety. The cells from younger people multiplied more often; that is, they lived longer than the cells from older people. It appears therefore that the key to aging may well be hidden in each individual cell.

There is much popular belief, some of it scientifically based, that longevity runs in certain families. There is also evidence that aging is controlled by a certain part of a person's genetic inheritance, that the rapidity with which he grows old is "in his genes." In a human disorder called progeria, blessedly very rare, aging is so rapid that very young children develop wrinkled skin and degenerative heart disease and die of "old age" by eleven or twelve years of age. When cultured, their body cells rarely double more than a few times—they are believed to have a genetic programming that speeds up the aging process tremendously. The biological clock of these poor unfortunates has run amok.

The implications of the genetic programming of human cells is that it may be possible to increase the ordinary human life span by altering the genetic cell machinery. Exercising at least limited control over the aging process is believed by the genetic theorists to be attainable in the near future.

## FREE RADICAL THEORY

A widely held theory holds that substances known as "free radicals" are what cause aging within the cells. The free radical is a type of molecule with a strong tendency to react with anything with which it comes in contact. Radiation can produce free radicals; and they are known to be responsible for turning butter rancid. Antioxidants (such as vinegar or lemon juice) are used as food preservatives because of their property of neutralizing the effects of free radicals. Those who believe that free radicals cause aging are strong advocates of antioxidants as a means of prolonging life. Both the vitamin E and the vitamin C controversies stem, in part, from the ability of these vitamins to counteract the free radicals.

If indeed free radical molecules cause damage to the time clock theoretically built into every human cell, then it is possible that the life span can be increased by finding a means of interfering with their activity.

## CROSS-LINKING

Another more difficult theory being explored for its relationship to the aging process is known as cross-linking. It is based on the fact that the blood vessels, bones and skin become more brittle as we get older. Their flexibility is maintained by long fibers of collagen, an elastic, rubbery substance that is the basic constituent of all cartilage and connective tissue. The grotesque gargoyles on the cathedral of Notre Dame were patterned upon children who had a certain type of collagen disease. Leprosy, a baffling and dramatic illness of the human body, is due to disturbance of the collagen.

As we grow older, certain chemical substances form between the long fibers of collagen, creating "cross links." These links decrease the flexibility of the organs, especially the blood vessels. If the substance that causes this cross-linking could be discovered, certain troublesome symptoms of aging could be modified. The skin would retain its youthful texture, the bones would become less brittle. And most important of all, the blood vessels, instead of looking like rigid pipes, would resemble garden hoses, thus permitting freer flow of blood and reducing high blood pressure, strokes and heart disease.

Some years ago, large numbers of sheep in the West were dying mysteriously—their bodies almost literally falling apart. It was found that the animals had eaten a variety of wild tea that had the chemical effect of breaking the cross links between the collagen fibers until the blood vessels and other organs simply disintegrated. This was flexibility carried to a fatal degree. If a substance with a controlled and ideal amount of cross-linking could be found, the youthful properties of the body could be prolonged, resulting in an extension of the normal life span.

### LOW ANIMAL PROTEIN

One theory holds that the human being lives longer on a diet with a lower intake of animal protein. Experimentation with mice has produced greater longevity when the protein content of their diet is low. This theory may be borne out by the Australian aborigine and by the fascinating Hunza tribe. In Hunza, a part of West Pakistan, people live (200 times as often as Americans do) for more than one hundred years in perfect mental and physical health. Hunza men not infrequently father children at the age of ninety. In the 1920's Dr. Robert McCarrison, an English surgeon, spent seven years among the Hunza. He reported: "During the period of my association with these people I never saw a case of asthenic dyspepsia, of gastric or duodenal ulcer, or appendicitis, of mucous colitis, or cancer. . . ." The Hunza eat mainly bread made of whole, unrefined grain, leafy green vegetables, potatoes and other root vegetables, peas and beans, fresh milk and buttermilk, clarified butter, cheese and fruit. They eat meat only on rare occasions. Thus you can see that their diet, although it contains much protein, is almost totally free of *animal* protein.

Regrettably, a crash low-animal-protein diet won't do the trick in our culture. It takes a lifetime of such a diet to produce the desired effect (and probably a good many other changes in our life styles as well). But some adaptation of the diet of long-lived peoples into our culture could conceivably prolong life.

## AUTOIMMUNITY

Certain diseases associated with aging are thought to occur when natural immunities within the body attack the human cellular structure itself. When we are vaccinated against smallpox, for example, a minuscule amount of the weakened smallpox virus is introduced into our bodies. The body then manufactures defenses against the real disease, the deadly pox. In other words, we acquire immunity. Under certain circumstances, the body develops excessive immunity reactions: it reacts to its own tissues as if they were foreign intruders or disease viruses. Arthritis, among other disorders, is thought to be the result of the attack of one's own immunity bodies against oneself.

The spleen may well be the number one villain in this regard. Experiment has shown that when the spleen was removed from mice who were expected to die of cancer within two years, their life expectancy doubled. Removal of the spleen, as the producer of immunity bodies, seemed to protect them from the harmful immune reactions to themselves. If we can figure out how to train some other organs to do the useful work of the spleen in the aged, then perhaps we will be able to lick this self-destructive tendency of the aging body.

An outstanding researcher in the field of aging, Dr. Alex Comfort of the University of London, suggests that even if we should not succeed in prolonging the life span radically in the immediate future, it is entirely within our reach to delay changes in skin, bones, heart and lungs—perhaps through diet—without knowing much more about the causes of aging than we do right now. If any such biological miracles should come to pass soon, tremendous new problems will arise. Whether such innovations bring an actual increase in life span or "merely" a significant expansion of the years of maximum health and vigor, we can expect major social, economic and sexual changes in their wake. Technological advances and the population explosion have led to ecological problems; we are justifiably concerned now about pollution, food supply, living space. Geriatric advances will add to these problems and cause a revolution in the policies and practices of insurance, birth control, and retirement, to name just a few. The whole concept of marriage and family life will once more need to be completely overhauled. Nevertheless, says Dr. Comfort, viewing the whole prospect of increased health and longer life within our lifetimes, we should get used to the idea. When the age-old quest for the fountain of youth has ended, we must rejoice and begin a new search: for the answers to the new problems created.

## SOCIAL CONCEPTS OF AGING

Tithonus, of Greek mythology, was a young and handsome man when Aurora, the goddess of dawn, fell in love with him. As many a mortal daughter still does, she sought help from her father, Jupiter, whom she beseeched to make Tithonus immortal. Jupiter acceded, and Tithonus lived on and on; but while Aurora remained eternally young, he became grizzled and feeble. Aurora eventually locked him away and when his pitiful cries continued to annoy her, she turned him into a grasshopper—proving that to be desired by a goddess is not always a blessing.

Many Americans can look forward to a Tithonus-like career. While it's doubtful they will share his ultimate fate, their increased longevity may bring them many more years of hoary old age than their forebears expected. The added years may not bring more years of contentment. But one thing that we ought to make it our business to change as quickly as possible is our misconception in this land that the younger years are the only ones worth living. In reality, many of our attitudes toward people past middle age are holdovers from a past that has already fled. A book called *Life Begins at Forty* by Walter Pitkin was a sensation, an eye-opener, when it was published in the 1940's. Today a similarly revolutionary book would have to be called *Life Begins at Sixty*.

In societies where nutrition and hygiene are poor and where living conditions are catastrophic, as they are in so many parts of Asia, Africa and South America, for example, thirty-year-old men and women often look as old as North Americans who are in their sixties. And Americans who today are seventy years of age do not resemble at all the average person of that chronological age in 1900, or after World War II, or even ten years ago. And of course, except in calendar years, they are *not* as old.

In this age of rapid transition, it is not always easy to determine which of the characteristics commonly associated with old age really are due to aging. Are some of the phenomena we notice in the aged actually evoked by the role imposed by our contemporary society on them? Let's look at some of our concepts of aging through a comparative examination of the ideas of mental illness we hold now and those held by society as recently as twenty years ago.

Until the era of Enlightenment, the mentally ill were patently mistreated, confined willy-nilly to jails and dungeons. Even into the mid-1950's, mental patients in America were frequently declared insane by a judicial process that offered little consideration or protection. They were disposed of in huge state hospitals often housing as many as 10,000 patients. One physician frequently had total responsibility for 500 men, women and children. Nutrition was poor, treatment was minimal, and little if any interest was shown in any patient as an individual. Hospitals often were forty or fifty miles from the patients' homes, and even relatives who might have shown interest found them difficult to visit. As a result, patients often developed more bizarre symptoms, and few recovered and were released.

Although it has taken too many years, our attitudes toward and treatment of the mentally ill have undergone profound changes. With the advent of psychotropic drugs and other new approaches, the situation has improved rapidly in recent years. We now know that much of what had been considered mental illness was in reality the result of "treatment" based on a concept of every mentally ill person as a hopeless case. Today such patients are treated in general hospitals near their homes, in unlocked wards, or in their homes. Adequate psychiatric treatment and other therapy make it possible for them to return to productive life within a short time. Effort is made to see that mental patients maintain contact with the natural environment, with their homes, with the realities of life. Research has shown that many of the severe symptoms of mental disturbance resulted from the inactive role patients were forced to play in the unnatural, uncaring setting of the large, impersonal institution.

In a sense, our current social concepts of aging frequently

force the aged into a state of mental and physical uselessness. And as has proved to be the case with the mentally ill, it is likely that many of the problems we associate with old age are the *result* of outmoded society-produced attitudes. Forced retirement from work they are still able to perform, segregation of the elderly from the mainstream of life, ignoring of or impatience with their needs and desires, all have fostered a deterioration of our older generation. This has been a disservice, not to mention a waste of valuable resources, perhaps even more deplorable than our treatment of the mentally ill.

If the muscles of the body are not used, they waste away; doctors call it atrophy. When the mind is not used, it too atrophies with disuse. When today is just like yesterday and the day before, and there has been no call upon your knowledge or skills or capabilities, there is no reason why confusion about time and place should not develop. With little or no contact with the active world, it is easy to develop delusions and hallucinations: not only isolated mental patients, but shipwrecked castaways and prisoners in solitary confinement develop such symptoms. Experiments with subjects locked in soundproof, lightless rooms, suspended in such a way as to remove the sensation of gravity, have generated in otherwise normal young people psychotic phenomena similar to those found in psychosis that shuts out all sensation and perception. Little wonder that people forced into isolation by nothing more than old age should show similar disturbances or disuse atrophies. Every mechanic knows that an unused tool or engine tends to develop defects. Anyone who has ever had an arm or leg in a cast knows what happens to the immobilized muscles. It may well be that certain so-called degenerative diseases of the muscles or the bones are simply the result of their insufficient use in older people.

Although many problems of the aged manifest themselves as psychological and medical, both their causes and their cures may well be social. Or sociological. To the extent that the care-giving professions, the population at large and the aged themselves become aware of this possibility, social change will occur. One of the most powerful factors working toward this change is the increased voting power of the elderly. As of 1971, ten percent of the U.S. population was over sixty-five years of age. The Census Bureau estimates that by the year 2000 this figure will increase to forty percent, or well over eighty million people!

The state of Florida, with nearly a million people already who are over sixty-five, deserves special mention here because it highlights an important aspect of the old-age picture that is becoming vitally important to the entire country. About fifteen percent of Florida's voting population are older citizens, sixty-five and up. Any politician interested in Florida votes finds that he has to address himself to issues that are vital to this group. The implications are obvious: not only on crucial bread-and-butter issues, but in the shaping of national attitudes toward war and peace, for example, this mature and seasoned collective voice must be listened to. This group of voters has a strong influence on the shape and tempo of future change and progress. The younger citizen now concerned that our technology may have outrun its usefulness may find hope in this development: the mature citizen is likely to have less interest in space travel, extended automation or the paving over of all that is still green in America; and he will express this conservatism in votes. The older citizen may indeed return to a once-cherished role as a moderating influence in the polling booth, simply through dominance by numbers.

The increased economic power of the older generation also carries with it the potentiality for enforcing much change. As a very simplified example, consider the spectacle in many resort hotels in the fair-weather-all-year-round sections of our nation. Many of these establishments were originally built to cater to the needs of vacationing businessmen and convention visitors. Most of the lobbies formerly serving as showcases for the requisite expensive call-girls are now decorated with ramps for wheelchairs. From prostitution to facilities for the infirm or retired in one easy generation!

Society's attitudes toward children have changed drastically since the turn of the century. Child labor, rigid upbringing characterized by severe punishment for minor infractions of family rules, punitive and unimaginative education—all these have given way to better understanding and more responsive handling of children. Improvement in nutrition, the information revolution, more enlightened upbringing and a generally higher standard of living and education have resulted in a better deal for the younger generation, who have succeeded in applying enough pressure to achieve lowering of the voting age and the general recognition of youth as a responsible and contributing segment of the population. There is reason, therefore, to hope and expect that Western society's attitude toward people beyond the middle years—and the role assigned them—will change just as drastically and constructively. And for similar reasons.

# 5

# *The Fear of Aging*

*Grow old along with me!*
*The best is yet to be,*
*The last of life, for which the first was made:*
*Our times are in His hand*
*Who saith "A whole I planned,*
*Youth shows but half; trust God: see all nor be afraid!"*

"Rabbi Ben Ezra" *by* ROBERT BROWNING

THE prospect of aging is sometimes a frightening one. It frightens your elderly parents and relatives, and it frightens *you*—for their sakes and for your own. In our contemporary society even children are afraid of aging. This is not surprising; youngsters sense their parents' fear of growing old in our youth-centered culture. There are other factors too: a child of five can see that his grandmother doesn't get around as well as his mother does, and that his grandfather's skin doesn't feel quite like his father's. When a death occurs within the child's environment, chances are that it will be an old person who dies, and he can associate age and dying. It is of course part of a parent's job to try to allay fears in his son or daughter; and when you have helped him not to fear growing up, he will partly have conquered his fear of growing old.

But as years go by, it will crop up again. The fountain of youth is a very old story. Greek and Roman legends and mythology often dealt with magical means for avoiding age and for recapturing lost youth. Forty years before Christ was born, Cicero wrote on aging (and much of what he said makes inspiring reading still today). Throughout the Middle Ages the search for a grand elixir of life was a major theme. Alchemy flourished. Medieval texts were written on the subject, and some circulated for centuries, going through dozens of editions. Among the many secrets of eternal youth were exercise and diet programs, moderateness and temperance, magic potions made from specific plant or animal matter, and partaking of the waters of particular spas.

The concept of the fountain of youth probably originated as a Hindu fable, but it was well known in Europe during the Middle Ages. Ponce de Leon hoped to find the fountain in the New World. European artists and cartoonists often dealt with it in satiric form: Cranach the Elder, for example, showed streams of doddering humanity arriving at just such a fountain on stretchers, in carts and wheelbarrows, even by piggyback—and leaving on foot, transformed into vigorous and beautiful youthfulness. In a seventeenth-century print, another means of rejuvenation was pictured as a windmill: old hags entered one of the windmill's doors and emerged from the other side as luscious young maidens swooning into their lovers' arms.

# 5 *The Fear of Aging*

In the first few decades of the twentieth century, the names most popularly associated with attempts at rejuvenation were Steinach and Voronoff. Steinach, an Austrian surgeon, proposed that tying or cutting the duct that carries secretion from the testicles would restore or improve male sexual performance, and that this might possibly bring general rejuvenation with it. Painting the lymph nodes where thigh and abdomen join with iodine was also thought to have a stimulating effect. Voronoff, a Russian surgeon, was best known as the "monkey gland man," since his cure for aging was the implantation in men of parts of monkey testicles. Voronoff assumed that this would prolong youth by providing extra testicular hormones.

The most celebrated of all the searchers after eternal youth in later decades of this century is probably the late Paul Niehans, a Swiss doctor who attempted rejuvenation—or the prevention of further aging—by the injection of the cells from fetal lambs, matching the organ of the lamb to the organ in the human being that he considered needed treatment. Among his thousands of patients were reputed to be such illustrious names as Bernard Baruch, Pope Pius XII, Winston Churchill, Charles Chaplin, and the Duke and Duchess of Windsor. A considerable number of European doctors currently follow more or less closely the techniques pioneered in Dr. Niehans' clinic, variously claiming a general revitalizing of the body and with it a cure for many of the more frequent ailments of old age. Regrettably, there is no convincing proof that the injection into the human body of cells from unborn sheep or any other animal does produce beneficial effects.

A Rumanian physician, Dr. Ana Aslan of Bucharest, has for twenty years been using a drug called Gerovital to relieve the general debilities of old age, as well as some of the specific ones, including arthritis and arteriosclerosis. Gerovital consists primarily, though not entirely, of procaine, which is best known in America by its trade name, Novocaine—the anesthetic your dentist often injects into your gums before painful work in your mouth. Dr. Aslan is said to have treated Marlene Dietrich, Nikita Khrushchev and Ho Chi Minh; and though these notables are reported to have been enthusiastic about her results, investigation in the United States into the properties of Gerovital has so far produced no evidence of its curative properties.

At present, vitamin E as a rejuvenator has some enthusiastic supporters. It is an antioxidizing agent; and one of the theories of aging holds that excessive oxidation of some cellular processes is responsible for aging. At the time of this writing, however, there is no solid, generally agreed-upon experimental evidence that vitamin E has an anti-aging effect, or for that matter any other effect on the human body. Still, it is hard to suppress a feeling of hope that in all the experimentation and research that is being carried on, a revolutionary miracle drug or technique will soon be developed.

At any rate, the search for the elixir of youth goes on. Diets of various kinds, special exercise regimes and even quirkier new "discoveries" make interesting reading, for both young and old. I can only recommend caution with regard to new ideas and fads dedicated to the proposition that the process of aging can be halted. There is little doubt that the medical profession is always slow to accept proof positive of any claim, an attitude that is on the whole a good and protective thing. But this conservatism may encourage people to feel that they can be one step ahead of official sanction in their desire to regain youth and perfect health. Beware: some "panaceas" are perfectly benign and useless; other can do you actual harm.

## 5 *The Fear of Aging*

Recent history—the atomic bomb, capricious warfare, an increase in crime and violence—has contributed to our awareness at an early age of the finiteness of life, and of its tenuous nature. This recognition is reflected in an eagerness to cram as much as possible into the youthful period. Nor is death the only thing that youth is newly aware of: it is now more conscious than ever of old age, and it doesn't like what it sees of aging in our culture.

In many societies, unlike our present-day one, aging is not viewed as a threatening condition. Even in most parts of Western Europe, hardly to us a foreign culture any more, there is far less concern about aging. Older men and women are more readily seen as sexually desirable there than in the United States, where youthfulness is usually equated with sexual desirability. European women often prefer men considerably older than themselves; European men frequently prefer a mature woman to a young girl. In our culture, far too many men fear the day when pretty young women will no longer see them as sexually attractive; too many women think of themselves as no longer desirable when they pass the age of forty-five. In the American setting, aging is feared as a loss of femininity or of masculinity almost akin to castration. It is a tragicomical fact that the more pride a person takes in his or her sex appeal, the more terrifying looms the prospect of growing older. On the other hand, a man or woman who has never been particularly concerned with physical endowments is less likely to feel fearful of the process of aging; the person to whom physical prowess has never been a point of pride is less threatened by the onset of infirmity.

## 5 *The Fear of Aging*

# THE VITAL DELUSIONS

Those false beliefs that provide us with a sense of security when we are young and well I have called "the vital delusions." Part of the process of aging is the giving way of some of these misconceptions. There are four basic delusions: the delusion of immortality ("I'll never die"); the delusion of unlimited possibilities ("The world is my oyster"); the delusion of freedom of will and action ("I can do anything I make up my mind to do"); and the delusion of an attainable state of bliss ("I shall find perfect happiness"). All four are interlocking—and all four are related to aging.

The delusion of immortality, separated from any philosophy or religion of which it may be a part, is simply the unspoken belief that we will continue to live. It seems impossible to exist without some planning for tomorrow, the day after, and the day after that, indefinitely. The *possibility* that we may die at any moment exists, but we don't conduct our lives in recognition of it; most of the time we behave as if there will never be an end, as if our lives had no limits. The person who dwells constantly on whether he will indeed be alive tomorrow can't act freely or realistically—his actions are too inhibited. The value of the delusion of immortality can best be appreciated in times of great danger. The soldier who believes that death is something that will happen only to the other fellow reaps great value: "Why worry? Only the bullet with my number on it will get me." This delusion produces a certain sense of comfort, may even be what's behind the report of incredible combat bravery.

There are other useful applications. A hunter lost in the

wilderness who hallucinates food and water is denying his predicament in a way that may sustain him until he is rescued. Someone with stomach cancer may reject the meaning of radiation treatment, insisting that he will recover from his "ulcer." To a certain extent, we all hold the notion that "it can't happen to us." The protective armor of denial, however, can disintegrate shatteringly with the death of someone near to us, or on the occasion of a near-fatal accident. The vital delusion of immortality then becomes a little more difficult to sustain, especially as we get on in years. When the joints ache with arthritis, endless tomorrows are harder to contemplate.

The delusion of unlimited possibilities is closely interwoven with the sense of immortal life. Almost every youth (in our culture) feels superior to almost every older person, in opportunities, in potentialities, in luck, regardless of any other factors affecting their respective status in life. Youth derives this feeling of unlimited possibility from its sense of unlimited time ahead. The young man can say to himself, "That old man has had it. There he is, but how far is that? A world without end lies before me. I've got plenty of time. Everything is possible." Of course we know that time itself is one of the most perplexing and elusive of all personal experiences; eventually it deals a serious blow to the belief in possibilities without limit. In fact the termination of youth can be defined as that point in life when the time before one no longer appears unlimited.

The delusion of complete freedom of will and action, a very subjective feeling, becomes progressively more difficult with age. The child just beginning to try his wings, the supple youth brimming over with boundless energy, feels free to move in any direction with a sense of physical power that gradually disappears with age. As it becomes harder to move around, as lifting the body—or even a limb—begins to present a bit of a problem, one is all too aware of a lack of freedom of action. The youth plans his life with a strong confidence in his free will. He can make all manner of choices with regard to friendship, love, marriage, work, education, vocation, where and how he will live. He is to a large degree unaware of the many, many factors that determine his selections and courses of action: his own personality, his genetic heritage, social mores, economic variables, and so on. He fully believes he is master of his ship, that he has only to decide and it will sail in any direction he ordains. Only when he is older will he realize that he may not have had all the choices that he imagined.

The likelihood of attainable bliss accompanies the youth's feeling of freedom of will and action. Isn't the "pursuit of happiness" guaranteed him by the Constitution? Conjugal bliss is typically expected by young newlyweds: the reality of possible strife or disappointment and separation, infidelity, divorce do not enter the picture before the wedding. Happiness through success at one's work is the only thing envisioned as careers are embarked upon; competition, interoffice politics and just plain ineptitude and failure do not rear their ugly heads. Significantly, the age at which the majority of middle-class people enter private psychotherapy is the middle thirties. By all conventional standards these patients are successful. They are usually married, have children, live in comfortable homes, have finished a good education; they are enjoying financial and vocational success. What brings them into treatment, whether the presenting symptoms are depression, anxiety or some other disturbance, is the fact that they have begun to feel the limitations of their lives. They no longer possess the feeling of free will and action; they despair of attaining a state of bliss. The realization dawns that they perhaps have gone as far as they are likely to go. It is at this point that many of today's early middle-aged Americans worry about life being over soon. They consider an alternative life style. They want to assert their freedom of will and action once more. In opting for a different way of life they hope to find happiness again—in the country, going "back to the land," in a commune with a novel concept of family, in distant lands where both custom and terrain are new, entering a radically different occupation. Not so many people in their mid-sixties feel the need for this overhauling of their lives.

Some delusions of course are vital to all of us: a certain amount of denial of hard truths and "selective inattention" are essential in daily life. There can be no normal functioning without ignoring at least some of the disturbing external and internal stimuli. Life itself, for some, is bearable only if some of the delusions are held in the face of contradictory evidence. Much of the misery of aging is caused by the impossibility of hanging onto vital delusions. As time chips away at them, fear often takes their place.

But not all aging people are fearful to the same degree; a factor other than chronological age plays a role. That vital difference is how one feels about oneself, how one is involved with people and things outside himself. The person with strong interests, deep emotional attachments and an interest in ideas; the individual with a commitment, not merely to attaining a goal but to life itself, has a better chance for happiness and stability, at any stage of life. Simple acts—expending energy, investing interest, giving affection or love to others and having it returned—prevent feelings of stagnation, of isolation, of uselessness. And hence fearfulness: the person busy with living life usually has little time for fear. Simply having arrived at a certain age is no reason for no longer being busy with life, of which age is but one phase.

There is no sense in denying that old age brings with it many disadvantages, but there are distinct advantages to be capitalized on. By virtue of greater experience, older people have more perspective. They are natural teachers, having so much trial and error behind them. Perspective can help the aged to achieve serenity although it does not automatically come with age. Growing up is a struggle. When parents complain about their difficulties, responsibilities and problems, the adolescent often responds, "Do you think it's easy being a kid?" (Both are right of course.) Grandparents, on the other hand, are often happy just to be past the turmoil of becoming. They are what they are and have in a sense earned the right to be themselves. The days of fighting for a career and a family—and of fearing its problems—are over.

With a little perspective, the aging person can look at his life with some satisfaction. In every life there has been some success: in work, in certain other personal achievements, as a parent or spouse, as a friend, or as a thoughtful and productive citizen of the nation or community. It has not all been disaster. Moreover, experimental studies suggest that many of the mental functions do not decline with age. If speed of physical response *does* decline, well, a storehouse of experience in life situations compensates, in all but emergency situations. Biologists agree that in the absence of severe physical illness, aging need not be what it is too often feared to be.

For neither the young nor the old can an assured state of unmitigated bliss be an end in itself. Work and love must serve for their own sake rather than the attainment of an end. The best chance for a reasonably happy life lies in the very act of living, not crudely and hedonistically, but as a participating social being. It is a curious fact that the absorption in other people and *their* lives can lift away the oppression that withdrawn self-involvement produces.

In old age there can be no hunting for greener fields; but working the fields one already possesses can continue to bring gratification. Drives and emotions must be stabilized to the point where the means have become the end. In youth there is a certain pleasure in being a gourmand, eating heartily and hugely; after maturity, it is far better to be a gourmet, choosing carefully, tasting and savoring every morsel. And what holds true for food holds true for dealing with practically every other aspect of life. Goethe treated this theme in *Faust*. Symbolizing the restless human spirit, Faust has studied medicine, philosophy, theology, jurisprudence; he has tried love and mysticism, all in a fruitless search for happiness; he is even willing to offer his soul to the devil for a single moment of happiness. At long last Faust finds redemption by accepting life as an end in itself. Goethe spent many decades writing *Faust*, and he was a very old man before his protagonist finally found peace. Could it be that the ebbing energies of old age make it more palatable to accept life as an end in itself? And not anything to be feared?

## ALL IN THE MIND

Myth often plays a role in our baseless fears of age. Foremost among them is the myth that sixty-five absolutely and irreconcilably marks the beginning of old age. This anachronism reflects the social needs and life expectancies of forty years ago, not of today. In the 1930's sixty-five was selected as the bench mark for purposes of Social Security legislation.

This choice of retirement age had no relation whatsoever to the process of aging, but it became fixed in the minds of a number of people as the turning point. At present, seventy-five would be a better choice, more realistic. People age at different times and at different rates, depending on a wide variety of factors, some of which we have already discussed. To feel that one is "over the hill" simply because he has lived for sixty-five years can be a most destructive notion. Some people at that point actually force themselves to live up to the arbitrary declaration that they are old, instead of living the vigorous, enjoyable lives of which they are capable. We can only hope that the fallacy of compulsory retirement at sixty-five in corporate and public life will be exploded before long.

Another of the more unfortunate myths is that deterioration of the brain is a part of normal aging and therefore one must expect all sorts of difficulties—certainly a fear-inspiring prejudice. The plain fact is that most people of sixty-five and older suffer absolutely no brain damage. They should neither expect occasional malfunctioning of their gray matter nor ascribe any such symptoms to aging.

"I am getting old" is indeed a mental state; it is a frame of mind that by its very existence can produce something like self-hypnosis, affecting bodily and mental functioning, mood, and general outlook on life, all of which can interact and influence one another negatively. It bears repetition here that to a great extent patterns of personality that existed in earlier life continue into older life. Attitudes that have been dormant for many years can be brought out by circumstance, even the circumstance of aging, or thinking that you're aging. A person who was very active and manifestly independent in his middle years may, under the impact of the mental set of aging, permit previous latent needs for dependency to surface. It is as if he or she has been waiting for a signal to return to a childlike state. Such an individual now clings to sympathetic friends and to everyone in the family. Feelings of helplessness, the fear of injury and a self-concept of fragility tend to interfere with nearly all the pleasures of life. Sexual activity and enjoyment are among the most frequent casualties in one with aging as a state of mind.

It is often difficult of course to feel "the right age." As with so many others, the concept of age has undergone radical change in the last decade or two. When we present-day adults think of our parents at the age of fifty or sixty, we tend to think of them as old people because in many ways they were. Set in their ways, they felt they had to "act their age" by being composed, sedentary, serious. And surely this held true for people at seventy and beyond. With advances in nutrition, medicine, the dissemination of information, means of travel, even in moral attitudes, all this has changed. Today more and more older people are doing things formerly reserved for the very young: they ski, bicycle, skate, water ski, play tennis, and travel to remote and difficult parts of the world. A friend of mine in her late sixties recently returned from a camera safari in Africa, which she undertook, she explained, "before it was too late." When I chided her for thinking she was getting on toward the time when she couldn't make such an ambitious trip, she answered, "Oh, I don't mean too late for me, silly, I mean that some day soon all those magnificent animals may be extinct!"

Yet many people today at fifty, sixty, seventy, even eighty, keep the traditional concept of aging too much in mind, tending to think of themselves, and thus to act, in terms that were true for previous generations. They insist on acting their age even when their age by the calendar doesn't relate at all to their biological or social age.

It is foolish to play games and kid oneself (or someone else) into make-believe youth. On the other hand, researchers in gerontology agree that there is a distinct difference between chronological and biological age. Most of them feel that what are usually considered the effects of aging are more likely the unnecessary results of disease. If an aging person can be kept free of debilitating illnesses, there is little reason why he should show many of the characteristics that we generally associate with old age.

Most futurists believe that within a decade major changes in patterns of aging will occur: how people look, feel, behave as the years roll on will be radically different. If our society will also change its *idées fixes* and permit chronologically older people to live, work and love up to their full potentials, rather than forcing them to conform to out-of-date legislation and passé myths, it will indeed be another world. Reeducation is necessary. Then much of the fear of aging will disappear, centering as it does on the uneasiness that can come with sickness, helplessness and the loss of dignity. To that extent it can be said that aging is often only in the mind—of the beholder as much as the person beheld.

## THE SCAPEGOAT MECHANISM

Some of us blame our misfortunes on our parents, our ethnic identities, our names, even our physical size or makeup. And of course many of us blame all of our ills on our age. While each of these factors, and others, can play a role at various times, the need for a scapegoat is all too prevalent; and age makes as useful a scapegoat as any. I know people who suffered terrible aches in their joints in early youth, due to injury, rheumatism or perhaps muscular strain. But when similar pains develop in the sixties, they claim, "My age is catching up with me." People who were hypochondriacs in their twenties tend to be hypochondriacs in their old age; the only difference is that they once were young hypochondriacs and now they are old ones. When someone you know is unduly preoccupied with the idea of aging and tends to complain about it, blaming just about every trial large and small on his aging, there are a number of practical approaches.

Keep in mind that most of us do not have as much perspective on ourselves as we have on other people. To help someone else to objectivity about how he sounds may go a long way to a more positive attitude. After all, in a sense he is only uttering a *cri de coeur:* "Look at me, I'm aging. Everything is terrible for me and wonderful for everybody else." If he is at all capable of a bit of perspective on himself, if in other words he retains a touch of a sense of humor, tell him as tactfully as possible exactly what he is doing. If you can, play a tape of himself back to him and force him to listen. He may stop the complaints out of sheer embarrassment.

If we can convey, kindly and diplomatically, that unfounded feelings and complaints about aging are a form of self-pity, envy, excessive self-love and self-preoccupation, we may help the older relative or friend change his outlook, and be happier, less fearful. Such behavior, basically, is related to that of the child who brings every little bump and scratch to his mother, saying, "Look at me, what a poor child I am." Only in the case of the aging person, it is playing parent with himself. It is like splitting one person in two: one is the suffering child and the other the fussing mother or father who comforts by declaring, "What a poor child. How terrible that you now move more slowly and forget things on occasion."

Another effective approach is a tougher, more realistic one. There are undeniably certain undesirable aspects to growing old—but the alternative is worse. Point out that there are few if any situations in any of our lives that do not involve some difficulties, even hardship and pain, no matter what stage we are in. Age and its attendant problems is simply one of them. The infant cries with the pain of teething; the schoolchild is often bewildered and hurt by the adult world; adolescents have their crises, often severe enough that few of us would care to go through that particular period of life again. Illness, loss of friends and relatives, unemployment perhaps, the trials and tribulations of education, marriage, a career—all occur during life. Remind your mother, father or friend of past conflicts: the anxieties of dating, the quandaries of becoming engaged, decisions about work and places of residence, uncertainties in bringing up children. Aging has its inconveniences and difficulties, and they require us to adjust, to adapt to a new situation, just as any change in life did.

Some older people feel tremendous sympathy and compassion for younger ones who still have to struggle an uphill road. If in addition to a measure of disengagement and detachment, your aging aunt or uncle finds compassion, he can be very pleasant to be with. It is a permissible pleasure for those who have "ripened" to feel that the world's problems for the next two or three decades are now for his juniors to wrestle with. As one man put it to me, "I have paid my dues; it's time now for me to enjoy the privileges." But it is not necessarily a part of aging for one to lose all sense of identification with those who are now left to do the wrestling.

If, on the other hand, your recently retired uncle is one of those who spends a lot of time lamenting that he has only a few years left to live, you can tell him that he is statistically wrong. A man of sixty-five can expect to live thirteen more years, on the average, while a woman of sixty-five can look forward to about sixteen more years. Even at seventy-five (because life expectancy goes up the longer you live) a man may expect to live an additional eight years, while the woman has ten more years.

And if "nothing can be done about my problems" is a keynote of your aging parent's litany of complaints, you also have the wherewithal for gentle contradiction. Physicians experienced in ministering to the elderly consider it an unfortunate myth that older patients are untreatable. In their experience, elderly men and women respond remarkably well to all kinds of medical programs. The recurrence of illness in old age is an occasion, just as at any age, for proper treatment—not for unreasoning fear or for resignation to a general decline.

# 6

# *Personality and Character Changes in the Elderly*

*You are as young as your faith, as old as your doubt; as young as your self-confidence, as old as your fear; as young as your hope, as old as your despair.*

S. ULLMAN

MOST of us tend to think of people in terms of stereotypes and to pigeonhole them in groups. And one of the easiest ways to group people is by age. In fact age group has become part of the language. We refer to "youth," to "middle age" and to "old age" and expect certain kinds of behavior from each category, regardless of individual personality and character. Our tendency to stereotype is partly a reaction to fear, particularly fear of our own aging. This lack of understanding creates an atmosphere between the generations, in which many of the benefits of intergenerational contact are lost.

Mere chronological age is a poor basis for identifying a person: people come in endless variety, and of course venerable people are as individuated as those of any other age, perhaps more so. Generalizations about specific traits of character of the aged do not hold true for the vast majority within that "category." As they move into their sixties and seventies, many people retain the same personality traits they had in their youth or middle age; others experience an identity crisis in much the same way that adolescents do. Some older folks become more self-seeking and self-centered, realizing that there is not so much time left for enjoyment. Some use age as an excuse for bitterness and a return to dependency. Still others choose to deny their age.

Economic and social status unquestionably play a role in age, as again they do at every stage of life. Financial resources can greatly facilitate one's adaptation to the "sunset years." The freedom to travel, to escape climate that you have just begun to notice is harsh, the availability of physical comforts, a choice of activities, and, above all, adequate medical care are all very important aids in making the transition.

Since the study of geriatrics is of a somewhat recent vintage, there are more hunches and notions than hard facts about how personality develops with age. There have been no longitudinal studies: that is, following of a group of people over a period extending from no more than thirty-five years of age to seventy-five and later. (It would be even better to have started at a person's birth and studied his personality development throughout life.) Psychologists have come to realize that the present behavior of an individual can best be understood in terms of his past life and personality; they are beginning to devote time to developmental studies of the psychology of adulthood, charting changes in personality as they occur over extended periods of time.

Patterns are emerging. Life histories already available suggest that patterns of behavior in the aged reflect long-standing life styles. There is a clear, consistent follow-through in any individual's ability to cope with life's challenges and problems—and the methods remain the same—as he moves from middle to old age. In the absence of major catastrophe or physical disaster, the personality traits of an aging person can be predicted from those that are evident in middle age. There is no one psychological pattern by which all people grow old. There is no inevitable winding down, withdrawal or inability to deal with life situations.

But a *few* generalizations can be made. If a person has been optimistic most of his life, it is likely that he will retain a positive view of life with advancing years. On the other hand, those who did not do well psychologically in middle age may very well require counseling, psychotherapy or some other aid in adapting to aging. There is *some* agreement that individuals suspicious and uninvolved with others in their middle years are more likely to become paranoid as they grow older. The "mellowing" in old age is the exception rather than the rule.

Personality development through life's various stages is affected by more than biology. Every aspect of life has been changing, today more rapidly than ever: environment, the family, work and social situations, all undergo constant change, which must be taken into account when studying adult personality. Some changes are developmental, others situational.

Life satisfaction—or how the aging person views himself and his past and current role—*has* been studied very widely. Some of the conclusions suggest that the aged regard growing old more negatively than young people, others that just as many older people take a positive view of themselves. Morale in the elderly seems less affected by the years themselves than by poor health and the inability to remain active. It is a known fact that decrease in intelligence or awareness in the aged can be reversed by changing the environment around them, as well as altering others' expectations of them. There is no irreversible biological process, chemical process or heredity pattern that affects the vital mental functions.

## KANSAS CITY STUDIES OF ADULT LIFE

Much of what we do know about the personality and its changes in old age comes from systematic studies by a group of investigators on the Committee on Human Development at the University of Chicago. They are known as the Kansas City Studies of Adult Life because the field work was carried out in Kansas City. The first series of studies included data from more than seven hundred men and women of all social levels, aged forty to seventy. A second set of studies covered a group of nearly three hundred persons aged fifty to ninety, who were interviewed over a six-year period. To date, participants total more than 2000 persons.

Certain vital questions were pursued, among them, "What are the changes in personality associated with chronological age in the second half of life?" "Are retired persons who remain actively engaged in their family and community happier than those who are relatively inactive?" "How do long-standing personality differences affect human relationships?" From these studies Bernice Neugarten, a professor at the University of Chicago and an outstanding researcher on gerontology, has suggested that as people age they tend to become more egocentric and to invest more interest in themselves than in other people or concerns outside of themselves. Yet the ability to cope with particular problems, whether hypothetical or real, does not decrease with increasing age. Unless illness or some other specific misfortune interferes, the aging person does not become less capable or adaptable.

In Dr. Neugarten's exploration of life satisfaction, five aspects were measured:

1. The extent to which an individual takes pleasure in the activities that constitute his everyday life.
2. Whether he believes his life is meaningful and accepts it, past and present.
3. Whether he feels he has succeeded in his major goals.
4. Whether his self-image is positive, rather than negative and derogatory.
5. If he maintains happy and optimistic attitudes and moods.

It appeared that there was *no decrease in satisfactions as people grew older*. If they enjoyed a good deal of life satisfaction in the later years, it was more usual than not that they had experienced it earlier. Where it didn't appear late in life, it was generally found that they had never experienced it.

Social interaction was another aspect of human life thoroughly researched by the Chicago team, and one that is subject to the most controversial conclusions. Investigators

E. Cummings and W. E. Henry originally posited two theories: (1) that both society and the aging person withdraw from each other, and (2) that the individual's withdrawal is accompanied by a decreased emotional involvement in relationships in which he had been engaged earlier in life.

The latter hypothesis, which came to be known as the "disengagement theory," proposed that the elderly person who disengaged successfully was likely to retain a sense of psychological well-being and a high degree of life satisfaction. One way in which the theory has been interpreted is the assumption that the aged person has found his place in the order of things; as it used to be said of certain social classes, "He knows his place and he stays in it." He accepts his station in life and has adapted to it.

Nevertheless, some members of the Chicago team had doubts about the theory, and Dr. Neugarten reinvestigated the entire area of disengagement. She found that high life satisfaction was more apparent in socially active and involved persons than in those who were inactive and uninvolved, although that relationship was not consistent. The pivotal factor in predicting personality development among the aging is the personality type that was established at an earlier age. Long-standing life styles, consistency rather than inconsistency, dominated the way in which individuals move from one age to another.

It is the immense variety of personalities among any age group, including the oldest, that is most striking. Age is not a leveler of individual differences. It is the type of personality that you have in the middle years that is most important to success or failure in adapting to aging. People who have always adapted well, who have a flexible psyche and character, are those most likely to adapt well to old age.

## INTELLIGENCE GROWTH AND MEASUREMENT

Although behavioral studies take a larger share of the limelight, inquiries into the intellectual processes in the aged are beginning to break new frontiers. As in so many other areas, the research has not yet been pursued long enough to produce completely reliable data. Certain clear indications nonetheless are beginning to emerge. One of the most significant findings is that intelligence does not tend to decrease in a simple relationship to age. In other words, there is no evidence that the older one grows the less intelligent one becomes. The one major study with contrary findings involved a group of people who had suffered considerable disease of the heart and blood vessels; it may be that intelligence decreases in those who are seriously ill but not in those who are by and large healthy. Another study concluded that people with markedly high blood pressure showed a marked decline in intelligence as age increased; but those with only mildly elevated blood pressure showed no change. In fact those with only slightly higher than normal pressure sometimes functioned better (possibly because this condition supplied more blood to the brain).

Almost fifty years ago it was declared that different facets of intelligence may decline at different rates, and this conclusion seems to be borne out in certain more recent studies. The most widely used means for measuring intelligence is the Wechsler Adult Intelligence Scale, which tests ability to think abstractly, figure memory, vocabulary, practical judgment, and so on. One study of aged people, using the Wechsler Scale, reported that there was a greater decline in performance aspects than in verbal skills. Other studies revealed that the earliest and greatest losses appeared to occur in memory, spatial relations and reasoning ability. But it appears likely that even these results may be socially and culturally induced, rather than genuinely the effects of age.

During the past decade, evidence has been emerging that makes a strong case for the continued development of intellectual efforts throughout late adulthood and old age. There is definite evidence that the aging of the intellect is brought about not by the advent of years but society's expectations and the environment in which the aged so often are placed. Deficiencies in the cultural milieu of much of our senior population correspond to the deprivations of minority groups and disadvantaged children. Amidst the cultural and informational changes so characteristic of our society, the oldest generation should have opportunities for continued education and intellectual growth. Society as a whole must take the responsibility for educational programs that will keep the aged in touch with the world around them, since it is often their isolation from this world that is responsible for the deficits in their intellectual functioning. Efforts must be made to stimulate the life of the mind in the elderly, since chronological age should truly have no bearing on our expectations of them.

One fascinating and iconoclastic deduction of some studies of the aged is that there is no hard evidence that old people are more rigid in their views than young people. There goes *that* old saw out the window!

## MEMORY

The popular opinion is that old people can't recall what they had for breakfast but remember exactly what happened at

Christmastime twenty years ago when little Mary broke her doll. This sort of failure of recall of immediate events may be a fact, but scientists are far from sure about its nature. Nor is the whole mechanism of memory a simple thing. Memory, say psychologists, has at least three components: (1) you have to "register"—take in what is happening; (2) you have to "store" experiences; and (3) you have to be able to "retrieve" data, that is, to get experiences "out of storage," to recall events or information.

We know that all of us "register" far more than we are aware of. If hypnotized, for instance, subjects can remember much more of what they saw when they entered a room than they *think* they saw, or can recall under ordinary circumstances. Our "storage" system is more capacious than we imagine; when a brain surgeon touches part of the brain with a point, the patient can often recall whole scenes out of his early childhood that he had no idea he had experienced. (Brain surgery is done under local anesthesia with the patient retaining consciousness, because the brain itself has no pain sensation at all.) What one can recall is often subject to emotional interference, as anyone who ever had examination anxiety or stage fright knows very well.

Whether old people really remember long-past events better than recent ones is also a complex question. It may be that they do so only because Mary's crying when she broke the doll she got for Christmas is probably an oft-told tale. If grandmother had been asked, and had told, twenty-nine times between breakfast and lunch what she ate that morning, then we could compare the actual ability for recall. Psychologists try to study memory for events that are neither very recent nor very old. They use lists of words and digits of different length. As in all experimental studies, a lot of factors enter that further put the results in doubt. For instance, how much motivation can a subject have for remembering such words or digits, as compared to what happened to a beloved granddaughter? So even the meager results have to be taken with a large grain of salt.

As far as they do go, experiments comparing the performance of people over sixty-five with those of middle age and younger suggest that the ability to receive and retain information does not really decline with age. What does become more difficult is to perform certain tasks: retain longer lists intact, for instance. Memory traces may fade faster for older people if their memory span is overtaxed. Or maybe they just lose interest in foolish experiments sooner. The only useful information gathered from these ingenious but time-consuming experiments is that, whatever the reason, old people find it easier to remember things if they are presented with a small amount of material at a time, have ample time to "digest" it, and the material is presented in such a lively manner (spacing instructions, presenting written material in contrasting colors) that it is easy for them to "code" the information for storage in the computer we call the brain. (I suspect that these conclusions hold true for the memory of the young as well as the old.)

Some very recent research offers convincing evidence that a loss of memory in elderly people is the result of depression rather than dysfunctioning. Researchers from the Psychology Department of the City College of New York and from the Psychiatry Department of the University of Chicago examined some elderly patients complaining of memory loss for organic impairment of brain functioning and for depression at the same time. The depressed older people who complained about memory loss had actually a better memory, by objective standards, than the nondepressed people. Again, when they tested people who had organic brain damage, they found that only those who were also depressed complained of bad memories. All this research is subject to confirmation or rejection, but so far it sounds impressively like a blow at the fallacy of memory loss in the aged.

## SEXUAL INTEREST AND FUNCTIONING

As in so many other areas, myth far outruns available knowledge about sexuality and aging. Whatever solid information we do have contradicts the legendary as well as most of society's ingrained attitudes. There is little or no evidence that either interest in sex or the ability to function sexually decreases with age (again, unless affected by a specific illness). Somewhat more is known about sexuality in the aging male than the female, but what studies there have been of women confirm the data given by men; by and large they are in agreement.

Dr. Alex L. Finkle, a distinguished urologist, writes: "Hormonal insufficiency appears to have little if any effect on sexual potency in advancing age. Reasons for impaired or terminated sexual activity are primarily psychogenic or sociopsychologic." Studying a group of males ranging in age from sixty-five to eighty-six years, Dr. Finkel found no evidence that patients convalescing from "minor cardiac infarctions" (a mild heart attack) are badly affected by engaging in sex, or any reason why this particular heart disease should affect sexual functioning. He also quotes a cardiologist who suggests that persons with angina pectoris may take nitroglycerine either preventively before sexual relations or during intercourse. This heart specialist does not think that any particular position for coitus matters for a person who has suffered a heart attack or a stroke. His advice is simply not to exceed one's own comfortable tolerance with regard to effort.

Dr. Finkle states that most patients retain potency even after an operation for a benign or malignant tumor of the prostate, even if female hormones are being given to prevent a recurrence. As with so many other functions in the aged, if sexual performance was good before the prostatectomy, it is likely to be good afterward.

The organic factors that cause impotence are few: diabetes (sometimes), certain spinal cord injuries, alcoholism. But certainly simple aging is not one. Those who were active and potent in earlier life are quite likely to continue to be so in advanced age. The widespread notion that if one has been sexually active during youth (whether by masturbation or actual intercourse) he will have "shot his bolt" is simply a myth. The facts are to the contrary: the more one was and remains active, the greater the likelihood that he will continue to function sexually well into the eighties.

Masters and Johnson noted that heart rate and blood pressure increase during various phases of intercourse, but found no reliable evidence that the increase was of any special danger to people who have had heart attacks or strokes. In fact, another pair of "sex" doctors, Drs. Hellerstein and Friedman, found that the increase in heart rate and blood pressure during intercourse came to less than the simple act of walking up two steps. In their study, no patients reported impotence after a coronary.

Throughout my own experience with heart patients, their cardiologists not only did not forbid intercourse, but indeed suggested that it was desirable not only for its own sake but for the relief and release of tensions that themselves are more likely to do harm than intercourse. My observations of these same patients seem to confirm that advice.

Very often it is a disapproving attitude by their children,

peer groups or others that makes older people feel guilty enough to completely disengage from any sexual activity. Males are made to feel like "dirty old men"; women "silly." Another area in which society and its attitudes must change. While sexual ability does not disappear with age, unfortunately inappropriate guilt too easily appears.

The availability of an attractive and willing partner seems to be the single most important factor in maintaining a satisfactory sex life into advanced age. And this is true for both men and women. All the available evidence indicates that neither hysterectomies nor other organic problems affect the sexual drive of women who previously enjoyed sexual interest and activity. Estrogen replacement in postmenopausal women may possibly increase sexual interest, though the data are not clear. The only definite usefulness of estrogen is during menopause, when the symptoms of estrogen deficiency such as flushes, headaches and excessive sweating may be relieved.

It should be remembered, too, that sexual activity does not mean only genital penetration. There is no reason why old people should not continue to enjoy the privileges of early youth (and later adulthood) and indulge in masturbation (auto or cooperative) as well as kissing, fondling, touching and fellatio—or anything else that is done between consenting adults in privacy. It would be a great pity if our age of sexual enlightenment that gives freedom to youngsters were to insist on rigid taboos for their grandparents.

And let's face it: there *is* a social taboo against sexuality in the aged. If a man past early middle age shows manifest sexual interest, especially in someone very much his junior, he is scorned. An older woman showing sexual interest, especially in someone younger, is ridiculed or pitied. When you come right down to it, sexual interest between contemporaries if they are aged is not viewed with equanimity or tolerance either. The origin of this particular taboo is probably an offshoot of the general taboo against sex in force in our society until very recently. Sex was, and often still is, considered sinful and something to be ashamed of. This attitude toward sex as an object of guilt and embarrassment starts in childhood, when too many parents are less than candid with their children. How many adults today were told as little ones that they should not "touch themselves" lest their hands or genitals fall off, or they become ill! Naturally they grew up feeling that sex is dirty—how could they help it? As a result, young children are almost inevitably embarrassed by any evidence of sexual affection on the part of their parents, even if these parents are only in their thirties. Adolescents are, or were until recently, characteristically embarrassed by any evidence of their parents' sexuality. There are many who feel that their mother and father at the ripe old age of forty are assuredly too old still to engage in sexual relations! This prohibitive attitude toward sex in the aged is then but a carryover of a feeling about sex in general, and sex in parental figures in particular. Somehow, the young (college-age) population has won some sexual freedom; the elderly have yet to win their fight for sexual liberation.

According to the U.S. Census Bureau, 18,000 couples over sixty-five years last year listed themselves as living together though not married. (The number not so listing themselves is likely many times greater.) They live "in shame," and their shame is often very intense. The plain facts are economic: many a widow would lose her Social Security income (and possibly some other forms of inheritance) were she to remarry. Therefore, many elderly couples live together without benefit of clergy or city hall clerk.

There are of course many who don't have the choice of

whether to live out of wedlock or not: many elderly people live in homes for the aged and other institutions segregated by sex, where there is no occasion or provision made for privacy for sex or even expressing affection. Typically men and women are assigned either different floors or separate parts of one floor. Bedrooms are usually shared with roommates, and privacy is otherwise nil. Even doctors and nurses and administrators of centers for the aged are still quite oblivious to the fact that their charges have need for love and sex. They actively abhor the idea, or discourage it, or at the very least make no provision for it. Only very slowly is the notion getting around that this is not an appropriate state of affairs.

It has been reported that the American Association of Homes for the Aged is considering drawing up a bill of rights of the aged: I hope so, and I hope such a document will take into account the right of privacy, and the right to a sex life. What is needed is not only the recognition that there is a great deal of sexual vigor after sixty-five, or that the possibility for sexual satisfaction be built into homes for the aged. It is not even enough that the attitudes of administrators and medical staff change, or that the general public assume a more flexible stance in this regard. Above all, the aged themselves need encouragement and guidance with regard to their sexual life.

To start with, they need reassurance that to have sexual desires is not unusual or abnormal or immoral. In the second place, they need to understand some of the physiological changes that take place after a certain age. By and large it takes older men somewhat longer to attain erection, and their ejaculations may be minimal or rare—but this is not the end of pleasure. Older men must be counseled that the changes they observe do not mean that their sexuality is over—it just changes somewhat. And the same holds true for women: their mucous membranes may be drier than they used to be, or thinner and more easily chafed. But proper lubrication with a variety of simple jellies (or sometimes prescribed ones) can remedy any unpleasantness resulting from those physiological facts.

In our child-oriented society, a tremendous effort has gone into sex education for the young, the adolescent, the young adult. What we need now is some concerted try at sex education for the aged! There are only about twenty million aged in the United States at present (if we go with the arbitrary age of sixty-five as the beginning of "age"). But 4000 more people reach this turning point every day. And our older population is increasingly healthier. Society *has* to plan for them the way it planned for the baby boom after World War II. Among the plans should be the sexual life of the older population—and this phenomenon should be taken into account educationally, culturally, socially and economically. Sex is too important a part of life to be scanted or ignored simply because the portion of life it takes place in is the last third!

# 7

# *Problems of the Psyche*

*Our nature is not unlike our wine:*
*Some sorts when old continue brisk and fine.*

SIR JOHN DENHAM

THERE is a widespread misconception that most older people suffer from disabling mental disease—that mental disease in old age is inevitable and irreversible. This is an idea that should be wiped out of public consciousness.

The *fact* is that fewer than one percent of the patients in mental hospitals in the United States are over sixty-five years of age. There is another two percent who have enough of a psychiatric disturbance to reside in institutions other than a mental hospital. And an extensive survey of eight communities reported that from four to eight percent of the aged outside of any institution show some evidence of psychosis.

In other words, all studies agree that less than ten percent of the over-sixty-five population suffer from any kind of *severe* mental illness. Measuring the milder forms of mental illness not only becomes arbitrary, but it must be seen in light of the large-scale studies that report that up to eighty percent of the general adult population tend to suffer from some kind of emotional disorder.

There is almost general agreement among experts that mental illness occurring among the aged is caused, at least in part, by stress; and that it could be decreased or improved by changes in the situation of the aged in this country. Among the stresses are economic, social and psychological ones: loss of income; loss of role and status; loss of spouse, friends and relatives; enforced isolation and inactivity because of disability; and for some, loss of certain mental functionings such as memory and speed of response.

In addition, certain organic bodily ills are strong factors. It is not easy—sometimes impossible—to say just what role organic processes, such as hardening of the arteries, may play. But it is likely that up to half of those ill enough to be institutionalized suffer from some organic impairment.

It remains to be seen whether early attention to diseases of the heart and blood vessels, better diet, systematic activity, and other approaches will make some of these disorders reversible, or even prevent them in the future. There is almost universal agreement that much of what is considered the effects of aging is not, medically speaking, aging at all, but rather the result of unprevented, unrecognized or untreated *physical* illness.

Not all old people experience personality changes. Many of the changes that *do* occur are relatively common to older people. For example, because illness and death among persons close to them are frequent experiences for most aged people, they manage to maintain a rather detached attitude toward these events, as if they might thereby protect themselves from sickness or dying happening to *them*. This is a necessary defense mechanism, but it can easily give an erroneous impression of callousness. Following are some of the more common personality changes that take place in the aged. They are not properly speaking mental illnesses, but can sometimes be mistaken for them.

## COMPARTMENTALIZATION

There are many ways in which aged people adapt to their situation. They may do only one thing at a time because they are physically incapable of juggling several tasks at once—or because their memories are impaired and they easily lose track of what they are doing. The ability to learn new things *presumably* decreases with age (there are few experimental data on this, and what exist are certainly not unanimous), so often old people attend to only one relatively new task at a time. It is as if they put each chore into a compartment of its own and manage each compartment separately, because that is easier.

Also, so that they can manage to handle what needs to be handled, the aged tend to see and hear what they wish to in a somewhat self-protective way. They notice things selectively, as it were. Then they can handle emotionally and intellectually only those matters they feel they can manage.

## BODILY PREOCCUPATION

One of the more frequent peculiarities of older people is great concern with their bodies and their bodily functions (although just as frequently this is a personality characteristic that is developed earlier in life and simply carried into old age). The matter of bowel movements, sleep and appetite begin to play a marked role in the lives of some older people. This again is a defense against anxiety: the older person is aware of the many changes going on in his body, and one way of trying to deal with that situation is by taking particularly good care of the physical plant and watching just about everything that goes on with it. Regrettably, this tendency is especially upsetting to other people around the older ones—it arouses everybody's anxiety about their own well-being. In the face of this undue concern with the body, even a young person can't help wondering whether he will be in as good shape as the old relative when he reaches that age. Anxiety tends to make us not the nicest people we're capable of being, and when feeling such nervousness we may brush off brusquely topics of bodily function when they're brought up by mother or father.

## BIZARRE ACCUSATIONS

What usually distresses families of older people the most is to find them "talking nonsense." Painful episodes may build up around a grandparent's accusations that are absurd but sometimes close enough to reality to hurt. Confusion about time, place and identity can add to the pain. It is very embarrassing when sexual behavior or sexual delusions are included: a friend or relative may be mistaken for a wife or girlfriend; a very elderly woman may report that she is pregnant and in fact accuse someone of having raped her. It takes great understanding and control of one's own emotional reactions for the younger friend or relative to bear up in such circumstances.

A great deal of emotional difficulty can be engendered when aged people enter institutions. They may accuse the family of putting them into a home to get rid of them; if anyone cared, they complain, they could be taken out (although at times this may be truly impossible). They may accuse their children of putting them away to get hold of money or possessions. They may even accuse someone in the family of trying to poison them. Accusations of being harmed or plotted against may shift rapidly from family member to family member, from friend to friend.

Many institutionalized people insist that a nurse, another patient, or even a doctor has mistreated them physically, or abused them in some way. Unfortunately, relatively helpless people in institutions sometimes are taken advantage of; on the other hand, some of the accusations may be delusional. *Most* such reactions are mechanisms of defense; and in the aged, they are often quite transparent. It is possible that a decreased blood supply and poor nutrition are sometimes related to the occurrence of delusions. More often, however, a withdrawal from active contact with people, whether by happenstance or choice, leads to an emergence of inner images, memories and beliefs to the degree that reality is overshadowed.

## LOQUACIOUSNESS AND CLINGING BEHAVIOR

Because of a great need for evidence of love and affection, some older people become very "sticky"—they do everything possible to maintain the interest and attention of the people around them. The excessive loquaciousness that is often observed is just a desperate attempt to spin out the yarn as long as possible as a bridge to the other person. (This tendency is hardly limited to the old but can be observed in younger people if they feel lonely.) When the people around them become impatient with this talkativeness, they make the older person feel more insecure again, and a vicious cycle is established.

Sometimes old people offer all sorts of new and previously carefully guarded information. Old family scandals are likely to be disinterred, and skeletons pop out of the family closet. One rapidly deteriorating woman informed her middle-aged son that he had a half-brother he had never heard about, born to his father out of wedlock. A young woman who put great stock in her Scots heritage was told by her father on his hospital bed that she was half Jewish. Sometimes these stories come out because the aged person doesn't want to take the information to the grave with him; sometimes they are an expression of spite and revenge, before the door closes. Often such tales are confabulated—that is, invented or partially distorted. This may be a bid for attention by a person who feels increasingly like a fifth wheel.

The vicious cycle of constant talking can be interrupted by a few reassuring words that you will come back again soon, that now it's time for a glass of juice or a mid-afternoon cup of tea. And the vicious-sounding gossip of fabrication need not cause you such consternation if you understand the reason why it is coming out now. The more ways you can think of for reassuring your institutionalized relative, the more likely you are to ameliorate or do away with bizarre forms of behavior.

## REALITY DENIAL

The simplest way to deal with unpleasant facts at any time of life is simply to deny them. The aged in particular engage in this defense mechanism a great deal. It is much simpler for your mother to deny that she is no longer capable of caring for herself in her own home than to acknowledge the painful reality. The result may be that her children will be accused of locking her up and not permitting her to live among familiar and comforting surroundings. And surely this kind of accusation will cause guilt feelings in those responsible for her well-being.

A little bit more complicated a mechanism than simple denial of unpalatable realities is what psychiatrists call projecting: one's own ideas and feelings are put onto other people, or onto the outside world, instead of recognizing that the feeling, thought or desire comes from within oneself. Sometimes the projected feeling or desire behaves as if it were put through the lens of a camera—and comes out upside down. For instance, a frequent hallucination of older people involves annoyance with people who don't let them sleep; the aged person will insist that the neighbors upstairs purposely jump around at odd hours of the night to wake him up. Sometimes he will just complain of this disturbance; occasionally he will knock on the ceiling with a broom. Actually, the aged person may feel lonely at night and *wish* someone would take an interest in him; *he* may be the one who is stamping around in the dead of night, unable to sleep like a log the way he used to. Neither the failure to sleep soundly and long nor the wish for somebody to want to be in touch with him is acknowledged, but both are projected onto a somebody-who-makes-noise-to-wake-him in the night.

## REGRESSION

In interpersonal relations, the aged often revert to behaving like children, because of their helplessness, and making parental figures out of the adults around them, particularly those who are concerned with their care. This may involve the doctor, nurse or volunteer worker—and also the adult son or daughter who is caring for them. The one good and useful aspect of this development is that sometimes the elderly who see the caretaker as an authority figure react the way a child might. Then reassurance or guidance from this person is not rejected but can go a long way toward alleviating many of the daily problems the aged person may present. If your father or uncle feels like a child again, very small tokens of affection can improve his mood radically. At the same time, if for instance a phone call doesn't come when it is expected, he can become very depressed. He will react to loss of love, real or imagined, almost as sharply as in early childhood or infancy.

## SELFISHNESS

Often disturbing to members of the family is the fact that the older person seems to have lost some of his consideration for others, which has given way to a concentration on getting something he wants for himself. The fact is that many an aged person is so dependent on some physical comfort—for example, the chair that he feels best in—that he will be quite rude about getting it. He is much more selfish than he might have been once upon a time. Sometimes stealing is an expression of a desperate fear of not having enough food or money. The older person feels threatened by his inability to be as competent as he used to be. This desperation leads to what otherwise is considered asocial behavior. Again, reassurance can go a long way to ameliorate this upsetting behavior. If unchecked, especially in old-age homes and hospitals, it can lead to complications.

## REPETITIOUSNESS

The repetitiousness for which the aged are famous (or infamous) is a form of clinging to reality by holding onto what they know to be the truth. Repeating the same statement over and over again is like sticking to a well-known path when one is scared of getting lost in a wilderness. This habit, though, can be extremely burdensome to those living with someone aged. Understanding the purpose of the repetitiousness may help you to cope. The more reassuring you are, and the easier you make it for older people not to have to learn or do too many things at the same time, the less need there will be for them to repeat and repeat the same bit of information. It is simply a form of self-reassurance that they still know where they are, who they are and what it is all about.

## DELUSIONS AND HALLUCINATIONS

When someone holds a false belief and clings to it despite good evidence against it, it is called a delusion. Hearing and seeing things which are not seen and heard by others is called hallucinating. Delusions can be better understood if we keep in mind that they serve to bridge the gap between fact and desire. Their main purpose is to cope with unacceptable reality and inadmissible feelings. Delusions in old people—such as feeling that they are young, wealthy, sexually desirable, when they no longer are—are often simply compensatory; they hide reality and make up for the fact that the opposite is true. Both delusions and hallucinations *can* be successful in protecting people from painful awareness. More often they are only partially effective. When they fail, the fears and misgivings they were supposed to mask will break through. Then, instead of serving as pacifying tools, they are merely a heavy burden. Such imaginings can center around a person who played a threatening role in the old person's childhood, they can be concerned with a dangerous fire, they sometimes presage immediate and painful death, against all of which the hallucinator is helpless.

There are times when delusions and hallucinations in the aged become mixed up, overlap, fluctuate rapidly in content. At one moment they may be working successfully, lulling the aged person into happiness, only to give way suddenly to frightful visions and suspicions. Occasionally both kinds of delusional matter can exist side by side; almost in the same breath a person can be proud, demanding and boisterous—and terrified, cringing and dependent.

Some delusions, often caused by guilt, are very painful. A man in his eighties developed overnight the delusion that he suffered from syphilis of the brain. He was extremely disturbed and cried because he was both shamed and worried about what this disease was doing to his brain. Apparently he had had a sexual dream and felt that this was "dirty." His early adolescent fears emerged. The old fear, combined with guilt, plus the awareness that he was not functioning mentally as well as he once did, merged into the alarming delusion that his malfunctioning was due to a venereal disease.

Let's take another example. An aging uncle experiences

some sexual impulses and desires. They may take the form of childhood impulses, such as the desire to peek through a keyhole, or expose his body, much as children do. If he is disturbed, he will act on these desires. More often, however, the wish will hit the mirror of the conscience, which will respond with, "Who, me? Absolutely not!" The image will then deflect onto anyone who is conveniently nearby. It then becomes, "She wants to spy on me by looking through my keyhole when I am undressed," or "He is exposing himself," or "She has designs on me." The next step is for your relative to devise elaborate measures to avoid being seen, to escape being spied upon. He will direct angry accusations toward his friend or companion, who is but a reflection of his own image. Because, no matter what one's age, it is always easier to blame someone else for one's own problems or guilt-raising impulses.

Sexual feelings are not the only ones to be distorted in this way. Out of a feeling of deprivation, childish greeds are reawakened in some elderly people. If conscious recognition of the impulse is unbearable, anything can be used by the mind, whether it makes any sense or not. When the delusions take the form of accusations against the family, members of the family often feel strongly enough to argue for the truth—in vain, of course. If the accuser were able to listen to reason and to perceive reality, he would not have had the delusion in the first place! Relatives very often react by feeling aggrieved and showing anger, only making things worse for themselves and for their elderly charge.

Delusions can be very embarrassing when they involve sexual preoccupations. A middle-aged man I know went to visit his eighty-year-old mother. He was horrified when she told him she had just had an abortion, and further insisted that he was her husband (not her son) and that she had aborted their child. This man was somewhat reassured when told that such delusions are not at all unusual. We know that ideas normally buried deep in the unconscious—or only partly experienced—can emerge without inhibition in psychoses and in drugged or other intoxicated conditions. His mother's thought, "My son is so handsome, I would want to marry him if I were his age," can be translated, loaded with taboo as it is, into a disturbing delusion. Some old guilt feelings about an abortion also happened to rise upsettingly to the surface at the same time.

Loss of the ability to concentrate and control events and memory often plays a major role in the delusion that everyone is taking things away. The delusion of being stolen from is simply an expression of "I don't know just what is going on any more. I can't keep track of things. I feel powerless."

All of us have had experiences in dreams that are similar to hallucinations and delusions. There is no general agreement why these manifestations of psychoses occur in old age. There is no clearcut evidence that hardening of the arteries—arteriosclerosis—has any definite relationship to psychoses; but then, no one knows precisely what is responsible for aging either. Curiously enough, delusions may come and go spontaneously in old age. Nobody quite knows why these fluctuations in reality-testing, memory, and other functions occur. A delusionary attack can last from minutes to months.

Psychiatrists in training have to learn to recognize these phenomena in themselves so that they will not be upset or intolerant of patients with these symptoms. To a certain extent, all specialists dealing with people with emotional problems should learn how the process works in themselves in order not to be unduly troubled, annoyed or shaken. As a lay person who may encounter delusions or hallucinations in an elderly charge, you will find them easier to live with when you understand these frightening things for what they are. Delusions and hallucinations are attempts on the part of the human consciousness to deal with fears, anxieties, hopelessness and helplessness, sometimes successfully and sometimes not. Because all of us must deal with a certain amount of irrationality beneath the surface, we should realize, too, that seeing it in others in a pronounced form is producing an echo of fear that we might act in a similar fashion.

Some drugs help make delusions disappear. Thorazine, for example, and other psychotropic drugs belonging to a chemical family called phenothiazines can be effective. Elderly people need, and should have, much smaller doses of such drugs than more robust younger adults. This must be left to the discretion of a competent physician. Specialists in geriatrics generally prefer a minimum of medication because drugs often have undesirable side effects.

Psychiatrists specializing in the elderly can sometimes help them conquer delusions by psychotherapy, as they can with younger people. But the effects are less often lasting unless other positive circumstances also enter the picture—such as changes in some of the unpalatable aspects of life like isolation or physical illness.

Delusional behavior in old age can be stopped or prevented from happening at all by making sure that the aged person has sufficient social contact and interesting occupations. It is not unusual to find that an elderly person who was delusional when you arrived has become completely oriented as to time, place, your identity and his own by the end of the visit. He may have become entirely rational as a result of an hour's conversation about common-sense things and other subjects of interest to him. Unfortunately, however, the effect of active personal contact is transitory.

The aged person may relapse into irrationality an hour after his visitor has gone if simply left to sit alone in a chair or bed—or even in a day room where nobody talks to anyone else.

## DEPRESSION

Depression is a widely occurring emotional problem that observes no age qualification. There are, in fact, competent psychiatrists who have described depressive reactions in infants. Babies who don't have sufficient contact with their mothers or some substitute figure show a loss of appetite and a lack of interest in anything around them. Even their faces acquire a depressed expression. If depression can be said to be more a part of old age than any other time of life, adolescence is certainly the runner-up. Suicide rates are highest, in this country, for people over sixty-five years of age, and next highest for adolescents.

Why should depression be such a widespread disorder? Experts have suggested many specific reasons, such as feelings of low self-esteem, intense criticism of self, or helplessness. Even a sense of failure in meeting high intellectual, economic or moral standards can cause depression. A loss of any kind is likely to lead to a depressive reaction: loss of a job or a friend, or loss of a limb by amputation. Then consider the loss of stamina, beauty or strength that occurs to those over sixty-five: the human condition alone can produce a state of depression in old age.

Since depression is so prevalent, it is important that we recognize its symptoms. Among the things you should be alert to (and which are serious enough to merit extra attention, professional or otherwise) are a general feeling of fatigue, loss of appetite, sleeplessness and weight loss that is unaccounted for by physical disease. Constipation is very frequent in depression. Studies have shown that less saliva is produced by a depressed person, that the intestines move less, and that the amount of gastric juices produced decreases. This is understandable when we remember that a reverse reaction occurs during an appetizing experience: when you're hungry, think of something that you particularly like to eat—cake and ice cream, a frankfurter dripping with mustard and relish, a plate of caviar—and you can feel your salivary glands (up under your ears) activate; the gastric juices start pouring out, and your stomach and intestines react with rhythmical contractions.

When anxiety is intermingled with depression in such a way as to make it hard to say whether the sufferer is primarily depressed or anxious, we use the term "agitated depression." Tendencies of restlessness, anxiety and depression are commingled. The person so afflicted tends to talk about the same things repeatedly, frequently accompanied by body scratching and wringing of the hands, which is a substitute demand for physical attention. "Depressive equivalents" are certain complaints which do not appear as depression but serve as a cover-up for the condition. These equivalents can be headaches, backaches, stomach pains, constipation, a feeling of bloatedness. Itching skin is often a depressive equivalent.

Knowing the cause of the depression can help you to devise a specific treatment. If you know, for instance, that your aged mother is depressed by the recent death of her husband or sister, then it is useful, as soon as the period of mourning is over, to try to improve your mother's social life in as many ways as possible. You can encourage her to increase contact with old friends, or suggest seeking new ones. You can structure her daily life, scheduling specific things to do at given times. This is important, even if it involves making up a timetable.

There are few things more depressing and generally harder to bear than empty time. The depressed person suffers from a lack of energy, and as a result, his self-starting mechanism is particularly frustrated. Doubt, ambivalent feelings and the inability to come to a decision play outstanding roles in depression. Therefore, helping to make out a schedule and insisting that it be followed, even if you encounter resistance, is especially helpful. You don't need to restrict the schedule to major events: it may include even a clear listing of everyday activities—mealtimes, when to go shopping, at what time to take a walk and where, when to arrange with a few peers to meet informally for tea or to watch a particular television program. Social clubs, golden-age clubs and discussion groups can be extremely valuable for airing problems connected with the causes of depression.

If the depression becomes more serious than seems feasible for you to handle alone or within the family circle, then a psychiatrist, social worker or psychologist experienced in dealing with the problems of the elderly may provide effective help. Aside from individual therapy, group therapy involving peers can produce good results.

There are a number of drugs available which have an antidepressant effect. And for very severe depressions electroshock treatments can be used with no more danger than at any other age.

## MANIC STATE

Manic and excited states also occur in the aged, although much less frequently than depression, and almost exclusively in people who have had manic-depressive psychoses or manic phases earlier in life. These manic phases sometimes continue into the sufferer's seventies and later. The manic feels normal and often feels elated and highly optimistic; he cannot understand why others think there is anything wrong. Manics usually need little sleep, are extremely active, talk rapidly; they may be briefly irritable to the extent of feeling persecuted, only to have the good mood return suddenly. Since sexual interest and drive also increase during these episodes, inappropriate sexual behavior occasionally occurs in aged manic individuals.

Several drugs may be useful in the control of manic behavior: lithium carbonate is currently the most favored. It is a highly toxic drug, however, that needs close supervision by a physician experienced in administering it, who has access to a laboratory that can check the blood level of his patient.

Because elderly people in manic phases behave in many ways that are considered inappropriate, they can cause great embarrassment and anger in their families. Try to remember that gross or indiscreet sexual interest, excessive anger, drinking and gambling while in a manic state is an expression of illness, and no more of a strike against patient or family than the measles. When the manic excitement subsides, with or without a drug, the patient is usually regretfully shy or even depressed. It seems that society will accept much more readily unhappiness and depression—especially in the old—than it will an excess of activity and zest and joy. A sad commentary.

## SUICIDE

The most recent year for which complete statistics are available on suicide is 1960. In that year 21,281 people committed suicide in the United States. Of those, twenty-eight percent were over the age of sixty. For aged white males, the rate was four to six times greater than for the average person. The suicide rate of white women also climbs with age up to age fifty and then declines. Until recent years, blacks had lower suicide rates than whites, but figures for black males are beginning to parallel those for white males. The highest suicide rates are seen among divorced people, followed by the widowed, followed by those who have never married. The lowest are among those with intact marriages.

These data lend themselves to different interpretations, of course. It may be that having an intact marital relationship prevents the feeling of loneliness that plays a role in suicide, or it may be that the people who have managed to maintain a marital relationship (instead of staying single or having been divorced) are more stable to start with. One explanation why suicides in older men should be that much higher than for older women (in view of the fact that old age is as common among women as men, or more common) may be that the loss of status and of functioning is more acutely felt by men in our culture, which expects more from men. Such statistical data are, however, not only difficult to explain reliably but also meaningless when you are dealing not with masses but with individuals. Many diseases—peptic ulcers, for example—will show a great predominance in the male part of the population for decades, only to change and be found just as commonly in women, or show different sex preferences in different cultures.

The most important fact to keep in mind about suicide is that aged people, at least in our culture at the present time, *are* markedly suicide-prone. Being old apparently doesn't mean being resigned to life as it is, with all its burdens and disappointments. One of the stimuli for people to make attempts on their own lives is their feelings of inadequacy or guilt. When people accuse themselves of all sorts of wrongdoing in an irrational manner, they can easily become suicidal, at age nineteen or ninety. Again, tolerance of older people's shortcomings, together with reassuring understanding of their plight and loving concern for them are what the doctor has ordered from you.

# 8

# *Treatment of Some Common Mental Ailments*

*In sickness, the mind reflects upon itself.*
PLINY THE ELDER

IN approaching the treatment of some emotional and mental problems of the aged—whether caused by organic or psychological factors or that combination which even the experts can't quite separate into its parts—it is important to keep a few general principles in mind. In the first place, once again, not every person of chronologically advanced age has such problems. In the second place, those who do may have them more as a manifestation of social and psychological situations imposed on them (such as uselessness, loneliness) than because of poor nutrition, illness or other physical conditions. In the third place, conditions affecting the aged are not necessarily hopeless. Our own frame of mind—and also that of many physicians—is too often overly pessimistic. None of us likes seeing infirmity because it brings our own vulnerability too easily to mind. When we are young, it's easy to believe that time will take care of almost everything; this is harder when we are old. Physicians, even the good ones, often have an unconscious desire to perform magic and make everyone good and whole and sound again; this is more difficult to achieve with older people.

Responding to the needs of the aged for dignity, attention, security and reassurance will very often take care of most of their problems. When none of these measures suffices, and ordinary attempts at understanding care cannot deal with the problem, professional help may be able to make a considerable contribution. To diagnose the nature of emotional or mental difficulties, psychiatrists, psychologists and neurologists have a variety of techniques, tests and machines available. These aids range from methods for diagnosing brain damage to those identifying specific fears and conflicts.

The tests used for diagnosing impairment of brain functions are less well known to the general public than some of the others, like the Rorschach test, for example. For studying brain disturbance, the patient may be asked to copy geometric designs, draw various figures, or arrange cubes in geometric patterns. Some of these tests have been used ever since World War I and usually are even more sensitive indicators than the electroencephalogram. There are also specific tests for the exploration of disorders of thinking; they include such tasks as finding answers to problems, sorting out various objects and grouping them as to kind, such as fabrics of different colors.

## THE SENIOR APPERCEPTION TECHNIQUE AS A GUIDE

For very specific study of the content or nature of anxiety, unhappiness and conflict in the aged, the Senior Apperception Technique (S.A.T.) was designed. It consists of a series of sixteen pictures showing elderly (and other) people in various daily life situations. The illustration on page 134 is an example. The senior citizen is asked to look at the picture and tell a story about it. What he says and how he says it invariably give the listener accurate clues to what is on his mind. In relatively simple ways the skilled psychologist, social worker or psychiatrist can learn more about the nature of the patient's anxieties from such a projective technique than he can from just an interview.

To illustrate how the S.A.T. can be employed, we shall reproduce two responses to the picture on page 134, together with the interpretation that the tester made of the material, restricted to the most obvious implications. It should be stressed that this test is not a plaything for social occasions; it should be employed only by people properly trained in its use.

Here is Mrs. J. F.'s narrative:

> This is an afternoon at the Senior Citizen Center. Four people are playing cards. They have known each other for some time. The man on the left looks like he had been a teacher and he is reading a magazine. One woman is looking out the window, rocking back and forth. She is here for the first time. She wonders if the two women on the right are whispering about her. They look well dressed and their hair is stylish. Maybe they feel superior to that woman at

> the window with a simple bun. While she is rocking back and forth she is thinking of how she used to play cards with her husband and some neighbors. In a little while bingo will start and they will all have a good time.

This story was told by a seventy-five-year-old woman being interviewed for the possibility of entering a home for the aged. The account makes quite clear what her concerns about the home are: Identifying with the woman alone, she is afraid of being the outsider. She seems concerned with social acceptance, feeling inferior to the others. The single man is made into a teacher, that is, an intellectual; the two women might look down on her socially. There is some tendency to feel sorry for herself, but she can rally her psychological resources. The end of the story sees her participating in the social life, but only in a ready-made situation—a bingo game. She does not, for instance, tell a story of the man coming over to her, or of herself joining the two women. This suggests that providing structured social activities for her on entering the home will be especially necessary to break the ice. If she turns out to be standoffish, it will be because she herself is afraid of not being accepted. The rocking and the memory of playing cards with husband and friends suggest some depressive tendencies, but they appear rather superficial.

In contrast, sixty-nine-year-old Mrs. P. L. tells the following story on viewing the same picture (the one reproduced on page 134:

> That woman on the left looks quite mad. She pretends that she is angry at the cards she holds but she is really quite angry at the woman sitting on her right because that one has flirted with the man all the time. She is so interested in flirting that she messes up the game. After a while the woman on the left says she has a headache and wants to

lie down. The nurse gives her an aspirin and she falls asleep.

Mrs. P. L. was given the test in a psychiatric outpatient clinic to which she had been referred by the medical department because she frequently appeared with a variety of complaints for which no physical cause could be found. Her narrative—one among several with a similar theme—suggests that she has considerable sexual interest that she does not acknowledge. In the story she tells, the flirtatious behavior is ascribed to the "other woman." It might be the sexual stimulation that causes Mrs. P. L.'s headaches, or the effort of not acknowledging her interest in a man to herself, or the anger aroused by her attempt to see in others what goes on in herself. She apparently chooses physical complaints as a way out of her conflict between sexual feelings and what her conscience—or maybe reality—lets her do about it. She is likely to demand care (the nurse who gives aspirin) and has a tendency to withdraw socially as a further defense. Discussing her problems by using the story as a springboard may bring her tensions into the open. And some ways of permitting and expressing her needs may keep her from imaginary ailments and unhappiness.

It is in such ways that this apperceptive technique (S.A.T.), and others, can be of help in identifying psychological problems of various natures. The professional "listener" can then decide what the appropriate treatment should be. After hearing an older person respond in like manner to a number of different pictures, the psychologically trained expert can often identify the sources of conflict and promptly treat the existing disturbances.

The possibility of successful professional treatment of emotional problems in later life is generally considered much more likely by experts in the field of geriatrics than by the lay public, or even by those in the health profession not specifically acquainted with the problems of the aged. It's important that we all keep this fact in mind, for only if we do will we avoid unnecessary feelings of hopelessness and resignation on the part of both the elderly and their relatives and concerned friends. Troubling problems—even those that are repressed—may very well lend themselves to treatment.

## PSYCHOTHERAPY

In the absence of serious brain damage, even "deep psychotherapy," which is based on insight, can be highly successful with older people, especially with acute problems. Dr. Alvin Goldfarb of New York City's Mount Sinai Hospital has suggested that some elderly people do better with a fifteen-minute session, instead of the customary fifty minutes. This apparently is the case when the role of the psychiatrist or other professional is one, primarily, of an ally and protective friend of the aged patient.

It is a popularly held opinion that the duration of a neurotic problem (how long the patient has been afflicted with that particular neurosis) is more relevant than the patient's calendar age when it comes to relieving the problem through psychotherapy. From my own experience, several people in their late sixties, and some in their seventies, have lost some phobias that they had, at least off and on, during most of their earlier lives. Agoraphobia (fear of open places) seems to be one that is accessible to therapy in the late years. Five years after counseling with me, several patients still seem free of this fear—they are able to walk in the street alone or drive a car a considerable distance away from home and shelter. One man of seventy-two whom I treated for insomnia had nightmares that stemmed from problems that went back to his childhood. He responded well to psychotherapy. On the other hand, in my experience, certain problems, such as marked hypochondria, are unlikely to respond to psychotherapy in old age if they have been of lifelong standing. Problems that have to do with extreme forms of self-centeredness are not among the good prospects for successful treatment.

Often the problems of the elderly are directly related to tensions within the family; those can be worked out by having members of the family present at therapeutic sessions and airing the situation. Group therapy, where several people with complaints discuss their problems jointly, is another effective treatment: there tends to be considerable similarity in the problems of the aged. Talking things out and having a number of problems of several people aired simultaneously gives perspective and a feeling of not being alone in your misery. Some community centers provide opportunity for group psychotherapy for people living in their own homes rather than institutions.

## OTHER FORMS OF THERAPY

When someone is hospitalized, the professional has a chance to provide various subtle therapeutic measures to which only brief reference need be made. Many of them are grouped under the heading of *milieu therapy:* creating a total environment that has a curative effect. For instance, an older patient can play a definite role in governing the institution as a community. A thing like resident government can play a very constructive role in fostering feelings of adequacy and useful activity.

*Occupational therapy* plays a definite role: the making of things with the hands. This should not be simply "busy work," but should permit the patient to take some pride in his production. Patients often like to give the products of their handiwork to members of their families, and it thus serves as an important emotional connection.

*Rehabilitation* for all sorts of problems from joint diseases to learning how to socialize are part of the program of many of the more enlightened institutions.

## DRUG TREATMENT

Many drugs in general use, including antibiotics, are of course of great help with the aged. There are a large variety of drugs for help with specific ailments such as high blood pressure. There are drugs believed by some to improve brain functioning but considered worthless by others. Some physicians believe that high doses of vitamins, especially niacin, promote dilation of the blood vessels of the brain and thus ameliorate dizziness, confusion and forgetfulness. Dr. Ana Aslan, a Rumanian physician, believes that injections of a drug similar to Novocaine can improve brain functioning.

There are many experiments under way to determine whether hyperbaric treatment (exposing the elderly person to oxygen under greater pressure than normal barometric pressure) can improve brain functioning. The theory is that the higher oxygen pressure leads to more oxygen absorption by the blood (almost double), which in turn increases the oxygen supply in the brain cells (which is uncertain), thus bettering mental functioning (also uncertain at this writing).

A large number of psychotropic drugs are available. This group of drugs can have an antipsychotic or antidepressant effect, can quiet excitement and manic behavior, and can allay anxiety. All experts in the field of geriatric medicine caution against overenthusiastic use of these excellent drugs, since the elderly are more sensitive to most drugs than younger adults are. It should be kept in mind that the smallest amount that does the job should be used in all instances. Possible toxic side effects may include a recurrence of the confusion for which the drug was administered in the first place.

Chlordiazepoxide (Librium), diazepam (Valium), clorezepate dipotassium (Tranxene) and other anti-anxiety drugs may be very useful. Besides allaying anxiety, meprobamate (Miltown or Equanil) and diazepam tend to have a muscle-relaxing effect, which makes them ideal for the relaxation necessary to permit the onset of sleep without being, strictly speaking, hypnotics or "sleeping pills."

For the treatment of depression, most of the relatively safe drugs are not likely to have any immediate effect. Among them are drugs with chemical names like imipramine, amitriptyline, nortriptyline, and trade names such as Elavil, Tofranil, Norpramine. Amitriptyline tends to have both an antidepressant and a relaxing effect, and, given in daytime, it can improve sleeping patterns.

Unfortunately, practically all these drugs can have unpleasant side effects—dryness of the mouth, unwanted sleepiness, some blurring of vision. Used in excess, they can produce irritability, tenseness, even delusions of a paranoid nature, followed by depression. Even if properly administered and used to advantage, they may have to be decreased slowly in dosage so as not to cause withdrawal problems.

Among the most important tranquilizers are the phenothiazines and their relatives, the drugs most frequently used to quiet people, or even to counteract delusions and hallucinations. The most widely used is called chlorpromazine (trade name Thorazine), though there are many others, such as haloperidol, which can have a major quieting or even antipsychotic effect if properly prescribed and supervised. These, too, can cause a variety of side effects, including rashes, depression and drowsiness; but by and large they are very useful drugs whose advantages outweigh the side effects by a wide margin.

A combination of tranquilizers and antidepressants may at times be especially useful; they can enhance each other's effect without canceling each other out. For instance, an antidepressant can counteract the depressing effect of a tranquilizer, while the tranquilizer can counteract the effect of irritability and tension of the antidepressant. Sometimes physicians prescribe their own mixtures of these two classes of drugs. Commercial preparations, too—those that can be bought on prescription—come in various mixtures of these drugs; for instance, a mixture of amitriptyline and perphenazine is marketed as either Triavil or Etrafone. These are flexible medications that are produced in various ratios of tranquilizer to antidepressant.

For the care of the manic person, with extremely agitated episodes of restlessness and boisterousness, the drug of choice is usually lithium carbonate. Produced under at least two different names by different manufacturers, it is a drug that requires particular caution because it easily reaches toxic levels. It is customary for a physician to take a blood sample to determine the current lithium blood level in the patient, then, having established the normal level, to prescribe the lithium. The blood level should then be checked often, even in the absence of any obvious undesirable side effects, to make sure that the therapeutic level has been reached but not exceeded. The toxic effects of this drug include vomiting, nausea, diarrhea, stomach pains, sleepiness, muscular weakness and frequent urination; if any of these occur the drug should be stopped and the situation reevaluated.

All of these drugs, of course, must be prescribed and supervised by a physician, among other reasons, to make sure that there are no contraindications to their use. It is useful, however, for both patient and relatives (or other caretakers) to understand their action. It is also imperative for you to know that most of these drugs should not be discontinued completely and suddenly, even when no longer necessary, since this in itself may cause unpleasant effects.

If you are the person with prime responsibility for the care of an elderly friend or relative, it is of great importance for you to understand what the medication is about and what it is supposed to do. Intelligent observation can often guide the physician to changes that may be necessary. Also, after using most of these drugs for any length of time, a blood count should be done (especially of the white blood cells) to determine that an undesirable and dangerous alteration of the blood has not occurred. This is another way in which friends and relatives can be helpful in keeping track of what's going on with the elderly patient.

Also, simple remedies should not be ignored just because we have access to more sophisticated ones. There is many an experienced physician who believes that a glass of wine, especially just before lunch or dinner to stimulate appetite, or to relax and even improve the vascular system, is a good thing. There is some evidence that wine may also be effective as a mild tranquilizer, not only because of its alcohol content but also because of some other chemical substance quite normally part of natural wines.

For many aches and pains, and for occasional insomnia and other discomforts, small amounts of aspirin may not only suffice but may be the best drug of all to use. Long known and widely used as it is, we still don't understand all the beneficial effects of aspirin. It is likely that it has anti-inflammatory as well as painkilling and possibly anti-infective effects. On the other hand, it should be kept in mind that, unless buffered either by combination with an antacid or taken with food, aspirin may irritate the stomach enough to cause bleeding of the stomach in an occasional person. Also, an overdose, like an overdose of many a "harmless" medicine, can kill.

## ELECTRIC SHOCK TREATMENT

There are many other forms of treatment for the emotional and mental problems of the aged. Even though it has come in for controversial publicity in recent years, electric shock treatment is not the ogre you may suppose. It is still often used and should be, particularly for deep depressions that don't respond to drug treatment, and for the amelioration of delusions and hallucinations if drugs have not cured them.

Otherwise known as electric convulsive therapy (ECT), it was invented in the 1940's and has been refined a great deal since then. Usually the patient is required to refrain from eating for four hours before the treatment. He is given an injection to reduce mucous secretions, and also a muscle relaxant, which represents one of the improvements over the original electric shock treatment: preventing muscular contractions has cut down on the possibility of a bone fracture occurring during the treatment—a matter particularly important in the elderly. Some therapists also give the patient a quick-acting barbiturate to put him to sleep and allay any pretreatment fears.

Most experts consider electric shock treatment of patients in their seventies or even their eighties no hazard, if there is no serious illness contraindicating it. The patient does *not* feel any pain during the treatment, even without any intravenous barbiturate administered first, since he is immediately unconscious and remains so for a few seconds. Treatment schedules vary: some therapists prefer to give one treatment for three consecutive days and then a few more on alternate days. Seven to eight treatments are the usual number for elderly people. A certain amount of confusion is likely to be present in the patient directly after treatment, and some memory defects may be in evidence for as much as six weeks after electroshock—the more so, the more treatments are given. Sometimes a follow-up shock treatment once a week for some weeks is indicated, and this seems to cause few further effects on the memory. The primary thing to remember about ECT is that it is *not* painful, it is *not* "savage," and it is often a very effective cure for some kinds of mental disorders in the elderly.

# 9

# *The Aging Brain and Mind*

*Orandum est ut sit mens sana in corpore sano.*
JUVENAL

NOT all older people become "senile." Some very old people, including many famous in history, function extremely well. Even at very advanced ages, some display brain functioning vastly superior to many younger people, or even to themselves at an earlier date. Nonetheless, symptoms of senility, disorientation and impairment of judgment, learning, perceptions and the ability to reason may be found in people from forty years on.

Medical science is not entirely clear about what goes on in the brain in old age, or which of the changes observed in the microscope really cause trouble. Much of what is blamed on organic change may be psychological; whereas many psychological changes may have an organic basis. A few problems are relatively clearcut; they are discussed below.

## ORGANIC PSYCHOSES

Ordinarily, mental disorders are very roughly classified into two categories: those for which there is some somatic organic physical reason, primarily brain damage; and those which are called variously psychogenic, psychological or functional. Organic disorders can occur, of course, at other times than old age and may be transitory in nature. If someone drinks too many cocktails and becomes confused or violent, or feels he is being mistreated, and if the behavior is extreme enough, he may be considered to be suffering from an acute organic psychosis of an alcoholic nature. If all goes well, the disorder clears up promptly. Similarly, some serious kidney infections produce toxic substances which affect the functioning of the brain, causing hallucinations and delusions. When the kidney condition improves and the harmful substances are no longer being discharged into the bloodstream, the symptoms disappear.

The organic psychoses of old age are sometimes difficult to differentiate from psychoses caused by psychological or even social factors. Though organic disorders result from afflictions of the brain, they often interact with existing psychological conditions, and it is often the latter that determine the specific manifestations of the underlying brain dysfunction.

Let me offer you a sort of parable to illustrate this. An acquaintance of mine has a heart disorder that ordinarily causes him no problems. One summer he decided to do some mountain climbing and set off with a heavy knapsack on his back. It wasn't long before he found that the weight in addition to the rigorous activity made his heart beat rapidly and his legs swell. The burden on his heart made it perform badly. Just so can a psychological burden make the brain perform poorly.

To make things more complicated, the brain, like the rest of the body, is exposed to many kinds of damage throughout the normal course of life—the effects of an infection, an occasional concussion. In this respect the brain is not very different from a joint which may have been dislocated or sprained at some time and, in the process of repair, developed arthritis. The brain too, as we advance in age, will show signs of some impairment without demonstrating any apparent mental disorder.

When, however, an elderly person shows evidence of some psychiatric problems—and neurophysiological tests show some impairment of the brain—a diagnosis of organic psychosis is often made, even though organic changes may not be the main cause of the observed psychological disturbance. What the members of an older person's family often notice with some alarm is generally called *disorientation:* he doesn't seem to know where he is or who his family or friends are. He can be confused about time, believing morning is evening and vice versa.

It is extremely important to understand that because there are many kinds of brain damage, totally different behavior can appear in different people. The type of personality, the cultural setting he finds himself in, and many other factors all have a bearing. A distinction must be drawn between acute, quickly developing conditions that often improve spontaneously, and those chronic, slowly developing disorders that usually do not respond with time or treatment.

Acute dysfunctions are sometimes caused by a slight stroke. When the blood is absorbed or the surrounding areas of the brain take over the functions temporarily impaired, then the disorientation and even the delusions may disappear. Infectious diseases can also produce acute, though temporary, brain disorder.

Chronic behavior changes (which are usually due to chronic brain syndrome) can be caused by a tumor or a major stroke; the changes may come on more slowly and subtly, or they can be catastrophic and involve many different functions. One group of such disorders is known as *aphasia*. The variety of aphasias is astounding: the person suffering it may either have lost all ability to speak, or he may be able to speak in one language and not another. Some can understand everything said to them but find it frustrating, and sometimes impossible, to say anything related to the subject at hand. Others can speak perfectly well but not understand the speech of their companions.

There are times when the immediate acute organic effects of a stroke have somewhat decreased but anxiety makes the brain functioning worse. In my experience, friendly reassurance or mild sedation have helped at such times.

## ACUTE AND CHRONIC BRAIN SYNDROME

The diagnostic label most frequently attached to organic brain disorders in the aged is acute and chronic brain syndrome. A syndrome is the name for a combination of symptoms of which a varying number and kind are usually present though all are hardly ever present. Such a term covers widely differing manifestations that share only some common denominators. The cause of acute brain syndrome may be one or several: vitamin defects or other nutritional deficiencies, a temporary disturbance in circulation due to problems of heart action or blood pressure, and many others, including some caused by medication. Acute brain syndrome is considered reversible—that is, patients usually recover from it.

Some chronic brain syndrome is caused by effects on the blood vessels, usually the result of a stroke (the closing off of blood vessels by small or large blood clots). If the blood clots are small, then relatively small areas of the brain are affected. Some areas of the brain are more essential to everyday functioning than others, and often other parts can take over while rehabilitation and recovery are going along. Attention to psychological problems of adjustment can help to prevent further impairment, even with chronic brain syndrome.

Fluctuations in relative functioning are frequent: the patient is sometimes better and sometimes worse. For instance, if the patient is living in an environment where life is well regulated and problems of adaptation are minor (while at the same time not being forced to live like a vegetable), the prognosis for improvement is favorable, even with chronic brain syndrome.

Among the early manifestations of brain impairment are memory defects, errors in judgment and comprehension, and disorientation (where one is, who one is, and with whom one is dealing; confusion about time of day and dates). When these problems in adaptation become very marked, it is of value to try to evaluate to what extent brain impairment is the cause. When we find we are dealing with tumors, aneurisms (blood clots) or impairment from hemorrhage (strokes), it may be possible to provide therapeutic help through surgery, medical means or rehabilitative procedures. Therefore, a brief discussion of some of the most common diagnostic procedures follows.

## PSYCHOLOGICAL TESTING

Testing can be useful for establishing both the nature of psychological conflicts and fears, and the problems leading to depression and other upsets. Testing can also identify the presence of organic brain damage. There are many tests available tailored to the determining of a variety of problems. Following is a test formulated by Dr. Alvin Goldfarb of New York City's Mount Sinai Hospital. It is a simple set of questions designed to detect the presence of organic brain syndrome.

The questions are:

1. Where are we now?
2. Where is this place located?
3. What month is it?
4. What day of the month is it?
5. What year is it?
6. How old are you?
7. When is your birthday?
8. Where were you born?
9. Who is President of the United States?
10. Who was President before him?

As can readily be seen, these questions are concerned with orientation in place and time. Questions 1 through 5 deal with present orientation; questions 6, 7 and 8 deal with memory; and 9 and 10 with general information plus memory. With zero to two errors, there is no impairment or only mild impairment. Three to eight errors indicate moderately advanced impairment; and 9 or 10 errors indicate a real brain dysfunction. This test and this scale of answers are used primarily as a rule-of-thumb investigation. More complex measures for testing abound; they should be used only by experts in psychological testing and procedures.

## OTHER DIAGNOSTIC MEASURES

Electroencephalography is probably the most widely used diagnostic technique for detecting malfunctioning of the brain. Known as an EEG, an electroencephalogram is made by placing small electrodes (similar to those used for taking an electrocardiogram, which measures heart action) on several different parts of the scalp. The procedure is neither painful nor harmful; in essence it consists of measuring the electrical waves produced by the brain. The record of the electroencephalograph shows itself in the form of waves on a strip of paper. The EEG may demonstrate some abnormalities even though the person being examined has no specific problems: for instance, the effects of certain medication, persisting for several months, can alter the wave pattern. Relatively normal aging, too, may show up as abnormalities in the EEG. To make things more complicated, disorders in the early stages, such as small tumors, may *not* show up; and a normal picture of curves does not exclude the possibility that some serious problem exists. Therefore it is not unusual for the EEG to be repeated at intervals, supplemented by other diagnostic methods.

The flow of blood through the brain is also of great importance to its function. Blood flow and hence the amount of oxygen available to the tissues of the brain can be affected by a number of conditions, chief among them (1) widespread hardening of the arteries (which not only hardens but narrows the arteries), permitting less blood and with it less oxygen to flow through; (2) tumors and other growths that block the blood flow; and (3) disorders of the functioning of the heart, which may not be pumping enough blood to the brain.

Until recently, the most popular method of estimating the amount of blood flowing through the brain consisted of injecting gases into the large blood vessel (carotid artery) at the edge of the throat, to either side of the windpipe. Depending on which side of the brain is suspected of malfunctioning, a radioactive gas is injected into the right or the left artery—or sometimes one after the other. This method is quite uncomfortable for the patient; it causes a headache and is not entirely without danger.

A new technique may render the above procedure unnecessary. Xenon 133 gas can be inhaled by the patient. Painless detecting mechanisms are placed on the scalp and a computer registers the amount of blood flowing through the white matter and other tissues of the brain. The patient has only to lie very still and breathe quietly for ten minutes. This method can measure the blood flow through both halves of the brain; it cannot give pictures for each half separately and distinctly. If either of these gas methods evidences a reduced blood flow through the brain, it is regarded as an indication of some impairment of a general nature. This can be useful information if the EEG and other techniques do not show a tumor.

Echo encephalography is so called because ultrasonic waves transmitted through the brain will be deflected in an abnormal, different way if they hit a tumor or blood clot. This deflection by echoes will show up on an oscilloscope in wavy patterns similar to those stereo enthusiasts are accustomed to seeing on their equipment. In addition to the detection of large blood clots and tumors, this method is now used for the study of the hollow space in each half of the brain called a ventricle. The size and shape of the ventricles may be affected by tumors or large blood clots pressing against them, producing changes in the outline of these chambers within the brain halves.

The ventricles can also be studied by pneumoencephalograms. Air is injected into the spinal canal in the spinal column, usually about two-thirds down the backbone, and travels directly into the ventricles. The air-containing ventricles are then X-rayed, and any changes in their shape may indicate that a tumor or large blood clot is present. Pneumoencephalography is not without its dangers, however; it usually produces a severe headache, and it is not used unless absolutely essential.

Brain scanning, on the other hand, is a harmless and painless modern detection system. Radioactive substances are administered intravenously and their distribution then mapped out. Scanning for radioactive isotopes is a familiar procedure today. The thyroid, for instance, is studied by the same technique; substances containing iodine are injected and a scanning device, something like a Geiger counter, shows just where sufficient iodine was picked up by the thyroid and where too much or too little was picked up. Similarly, the absorption pattern of radioactive isotopes in the brain may show a thickening or a lack of uptake in the brain tissue, and in that way serves diagnostic purposes.

If, by using any of the techniques mentioned above, brain impairment is discovered, surgical or medical remedies can be considered. If a severe organic situation is eliminated, then rehabilitation by psychological and social means should be started.

Definite brain impairment does not necessarily mean a poor prognosis. It need not imply drastic intervention such as surgery. Some organic brain impairment responds well to increases in intake of vitamin $B_{12}$, to hormone treatment, to improving heart functioning, and a variety of other corrections. Even in marked cases of organic deterioration, we now know that confusion, delusions and hallucinations frequently occur only when the aged person experiences little or no contact with other people and other forms of stimulation.

Beneficial effects can often be achieved quite simply. When you find an elderly relative or friend in an institution, or perhaps alone in his home, completely disoriented, you may achieve a miracle of restoration with a gentle reminder that he is apparently confused, and setting him straight on who he is, who you are, where you both are and what is currently going on. Within a half hour you may be in the company of an entirely rational person. And you will be practicing what is called reality therapy. This treatment, practiced by professionals in some old-age institutions, consists of just that kind of procedure of reminding the patient of "facts." It is often successful in preventing confusions, delusions and hallucinations, or undoing existing ones. Drugs or energizers, as discussed earlier in this chapter, can also be helpful.

# 10

# *Physical Health in Age*

*A plow that rests does rust.*
German proverb

"AGING," as we've already noted, is an imprecise term because it has so many different meanings, and there are so many separate concepts of old age. It is very hard to be definitive in discussing even the *physical* afflictions of age, but we'll try. Statistically speaking, some forms of illness are found more often in people past middle age; many people, on the other hand, live to their eighties and nineties entirely or reasonably healthy. In contrast, younger individuals may develop many, if not all, of the diseases commonly associated with advanced chronological age. As medicine continues to progress, improved diagnostic techniques and better care at the earlier stages make it highly probable that the so-called diseases of old age will become less prevalent. Thus we can anticipate that some of the physical burdens of aging will simply not occur to reduce life for much of our future older population.

## DISEASES OF THE HEART AND BLOOD VESSELS

The heart is a muscular bag or pouch that contracts and expands sixty-eight to seventy-two times a minute in the average adult. When it contracts, it forces blood into the arteries; the pulse that you can feel at your wrist or other places marks this artery expansion. When the heart relaxes, blood is sucked back through the veins. The term *blood pressure* usually refers to the pressure of the blood against the walls of the arteries as the heart contracts. A contraction of the heart muscle is called *systole,* the expansion *diastole;* hence there are systolic and diastolic blood pressures. These pressures, which are measured with a cuff around the arm, in the average adult are equal to the weight of 120 milligrams of mercury in systole and 80 milligrams in diastole. Therefore normal blood pressure is stated as 120/80, or one-twenty over eighty.

Many doctors consider the upper limits of normal pressures, even for aged people, to be 140/90. There are, however, great individual variations to this rule: some people may be better off maintaining a higher pressure rather than having it lowered by drugs. This is a matter to be left in the hands of the physician.

Exercise or emotional tension normally raises the blood pressure, particularly the systolic; the more serious forms of abnormally high blood pressure involve the diastolic. As the arteries harden with advancing age, blood pressure frequently rises. When the arterial system is young, it is supple; the blood pulses easily, distending the arterial walls with each contraction of the heart, relaxing them again as the heart relaxes, sucking the blood in. As one grows older, calcium and cholesterol are deposited in the walls of the arteries, making them more rigid and brittle. Thus when the heart contracts, the arteries are less able to dilate sufficiently to accommodate the force of blood, and the blood pressure rises. The heart has more work to do, and it becomes weaker than in its youth. Its fibers now somewhat stretched, the heart's contractions are less successful: the blood is neither pumped out nor sucked back as vigorously, causing swollen limbs and a variety of other disorders.

Besides this muscular change, the heart alters with aging in other ways. For instance, the nerves that carry the impulses sustaining the regularity of the heart rhythm may be impaired, resulting in different types of arrhythmia (irregularity of the heartbeat). The electrocardiogram can graph the electrical impulses of the heart and give excellent clues to the disturbance that exists. Electric pacemakers can often restore normal heart rhythm.

Changes in the blood vessels of the arms and legs also occur. The veins of the legs particularly become easily inflamed, sometimes from prolonged bed rest or insufficient exercise. This inflammation often results in injuries to the linings of the veins, which can produce blood clots and the interruption of the smooth flow of blood. These clots, known as emboli, may travel to such sensitive parts of the body as the brain, lungs or heart, where the damage they cause can be severe. Anticoagulants, substances that hinder the clotting mechanism of the blood, are frequently administered when the danger of clotting is great, such as after certain types of surgery or being bedridden for a long time. If patients taking anticoagulants sustain injury, as in an automobile accident, they are in special danger of bleeding to death. For this reason, it's advisable to wear an identification tag with this message (and any other pertinent medical condition), which the patient may not be in a position to transmit verbally in emergencies.

Varicose veins are another frequent affliction of old age. (They may also occur in young people, however, and are often found in women after childbirth because of the added pressure on the veins from the increased weight load of pregnancy.) Among the elderly, varicose veins develop because of diminished elasticity of the walls of the veins. They sometimes can be corrected by the wearing of some elasticized material over them.

## DISORDERS OF THE BLOOD

The most common blood disorder of the aged is anemia due to iron deficiency. If there is no abnormal loss of blood from a bleeding tumor or some other cause, the missing iron may be replaced in the form of pills or capsules. Pernicious anemia, prevalent primarily in old age, must be diagnosed by a physician. It responds successfully to a variety of drugs.

When there is an abnormal increase in the white blood cells, the disease is called leukemia. There are different types of leukemia, depending on which type of white blood cell is involved. Recent developments have made available a number of drugs that may be useful in the treatment of these disorders.

## MALFUNCTIONING OF THE BRAIN AND NERVOUS SYSTEM

If one of the large blood vessels in the neck has narrowed, it will be unable to supply an adequate flow of blood to the vessels of the brain. A disturbance of the blood flow may also be due to a spasm of the vessels. If the spasm or insufficient supply is of short duration, the symptoms of a stroke—some paralysis, the inability to speak, or other disturbing events—may last only a few minutes. If a disturbance of the blood supply to the brain lasts less than twenty-four hours, it is generally considered a spasm. If the interference lasts somewhat longer than twenty-four hours, some neurological problems usually result but tend to disappear within a few weeks. Such accidents to the nervous system, which may also be due to small leakages of blood from blood vessels in the brain itself, are called minor strokes.

These definitions are somewhat arbitrary and not entirely agreed upon. Obviously the chances of knowing precisely what went on in the living brain—spasm or small bleeding or a blocking of a tiny blood vessel—are small. By definition, a major stroke occurs when a large amount of blood leaks from a blood vessel or a large vessel is stopped up by a clot. Doctors can often tell which of these two events happened. In either case the symptoms remain for more than a few weeks, even permanently, if they do not cause death instantly.

Blood vessels in some aged people behave like a worn or overstretched garden hose. If one of those vessels is in the brain and it bulges, it is called a cerebral aneurism and it may cause paralysis by pressure on the neighboring brain tissue. Such a vessel may burst, and the leaked blood may make it impossible for the brain tissue in that area to function. If a lot of tissue is so affected, death may result; if less is involved, movement, speech, thought, feeling and other functions may be interfered with. Doctors are generally able to tell a good deal about the nature of the injury from the many details of the affliction, such as whether paralyzed limbs are stiff or flaccid and overly flexible.

Often the emotions become affected. The aged person's bewilderment may express itself in loud crying. And even though this crying is not the result of sorrow or suffering (as far as we can observe), it is nevertheless a most upsetting symptom for the patient's loved ones or those taking care of him.

The aphasia (see page 148) that attends some brain impairment is variable: in some people the ability to understand is perfect, but they are unable to form sensible sentences themselves and are very upset by the garbled speech that comes out. Other times they are unaware of the garbling and become impatient with those who can't understand them. And sometimes the patient who can speak clearly can't make sense of what is being said to him. These disturbances are due to specific interference with parts of the delicate machinery of the brain: at times they are so selective as to affect only certain musical notes and not others. More frequently a specific word or words will not be remembered or can be spoken only in a garbled fashion.

The calmer the patient and the people conversing with him can remain, the less difficulty occurs. The chances of recovery are indeed excellent when a strong wish to recover exists, accompanied by a conscious effort to remember, an ability to persevere, and an understanding of the significance of these efforts. The chances of improvement, or even complete recovery, are based on the fact that some of the blood may be reabsorbed from the brain tissue, thus permitting those particular cells to function again. But an even better chance is represented by the fact that much of the brain is customarily not used—and certainly not used to its full capacity—and therefore when one part of the brain is damaged, another part may slowly take over the function of the injured area until the patient's functioning is fully restored. Rehabilitation is possible, depending on the amount of blood leaked and the general resilience of the individual. Excellent facilities for stroke rehabilitation exist, including physical therapists, speech therapists and others.

Blood clots can also cause the brain damage discussed. The clots that "shoot" to the brain vessels and plug them up come from blood vessels in the neck. Often such blood vessels have also had their linings stretched. Once that happens, blood does not stay in its usual liquid state but may become gelatinous at the frayed parts of the blood vessel. When a piece of that gelatinous or clotted blood breaks off, it is carried by the bloodstream until it reaches a blood vessel it can't pass through. There it gets stuck and causes damage to whatever tissue is normally supplied by that vessel. If that vessel is in the brain, some of the symptoms discussed above occur.

Some blood clots from the legs to heart and lungs can be avoided: for instance, older people should not sit stationary too long with their feet down. It is better to get the feet up on a footstool, to avoid stagnation of the blood in the veins of the legs. Rocking chairs provide gentle exercise. Even lying flat out in bed for many days encourages blood clot formation in the legs, especially after operations. That is why doctors try to get people—even very old people—out of bed as soon as possible. Some drugs may prevent clotting, but they carry some other dangers with them, unfortunately.

Malnutrition may cause some disturbance of brain function and the performance of nerves throughout the body. Elderly people often have a decreased appetite, leading to an unsatisfactory diet. Malnourishment can also occur when metabolic changes in the digestive process interfere with the proper absorption of food. Neurological disturbances such as dizziness and unsteadiness arise when the cerebellum, a small portion of the back of the brain controlling movement, is "underfed." A poor or improperly digested diet also causes the thyroid to function badly, which in turn affects the brain cells. Improved diet and thyroid treatment can bring prompt relief.

Chronic alcoholism deprives the body of vitamin B. A severe deficiency of this important vitamin leads to muscle cramps and pains in the legs and arms, "pins and needles" in the hands, weakness, and general emaciation or wasting away.

Drugs, particularly those administered to lower blood pressure, and sedatives sometimes induce various side effects. If medication lowers the blood pressure too dramatically, the patient may actually suffer from an insufficient supply of blood to the brain, causing dizziness, fainting or even convulsions. Many sedatives have been known to produce loss of coordination, vertigo or drowsiness.

By far the most frequent neurologic disorder found among the aged is a tremor or involuntary quiver. Basically, two types exist. One is simply an exaggeration of a more youthful tendency toward shaking hands. Usually such a predisposition runs in families and worsens with age. The hands particularly are affected, but the head may nod and the tongue quiver as well. Because the shaking intensifies when one attempts such actions as reaching for a glass, holding a fork, shaving or writing, doctors call this an *intention tremor.* Characteristically, people who are so afflicted prefer to use two hands in certain situations, for example, holding a glass or cup. Social occasions that make greater demands on an individual increase the tendency to quake. Alcohol decreases the tremor, but there is a danger of becoming an alcoholic if an afflicted person comes to rely on drink extensively. Mild sedatives and anti-anxiety drugs help to decrease the trembling.

The second type of tremor stems from a disease of the brain that develops later in life and is called Parkinson's disease or Parkinsonism. The tremor in Parkinsonism differs from the simple intention tremor mentioned above: when the Parkinsonian reaches for something, the tremor lessens or disappears. Stiffness of the muscles is a concomitant symptom, specifically the facial muscles. (To make this manifestation graphic, recall the rigidity of Buster Keaton's poker face.) Stiffness is frequently felt throughout the body, too, particularly when it is necessary to move the hands or feet. A troublesome symptom is often slurring of speech. Other symptoms include drooling, abdominal pain, and an involuntary pill-rolling movement of index finger against the thumb.

In recent years, medical research has nearly determined that the deficiency of a substance called dopamine in the nervous system is responsible for Parkinsonism. Hence the amount of tremor can be controlled by such drugs as L-Dopa. For those whose symptoms are not relieved by L-Dopa exclusively, another drug, Amantadine, can be prescribed in conjunction with it.

In addition to these neurological difficulties, there is one that *seems* to be a skin disorder. It is, however, a bothersome and sometimes dangerous nerve affliction that occurs at any age but especially among older people with weakened resistance. Popularly called shingles, it is known to doctors as herpes zoster; it is caused by a viruslike organism that produces inflammation along the nerve fibers, primarily in the skin. (The widely occurring fever blister is also a herpes—herpes simplex.) Shingles can occur in almost any part of the body. Sometimes it follows the path of nerves along the ribs; in other cases it inflames parts of the face and is particularly dangerous if there are eruptions close to the eye. The disease is very painful, and only the strongest painkillers are effective. Antibiotic drugs and cortisone can be ameliorative, but when the disorder is acute, intense neuralgic pain may persist afterward. Herpes zoster may appear inside the cheek, on the palate, or in the ear. In some cases half the face may suffer temporary paralysis that is completely unrelated to a stroke.

## TEMPORAL ARTERITIS

Of the many complex disorders, I want to mention temporal arteritis because its early symptoms can easily be ignored and hence lead to more serious trouble. If treated early, it is usually very tractable. It can be considered either a *vascular* or a *neurological disorder*. The confusing name refers to an inflammation of an artery, specifically an artery in the temple. The chief symptoms are a severe headache at the side of the forehead and pain upon being touched there. To make the diagnosis, a doctor may have to snip a tiny part of the artery off for a biopsy. If temporal arteritis is confirmed, some variety of cortisone almost always heals it promptly. Untreated, it may progress to an inflammation of the optic nerve and even cause blindness. Since nearly all of us suffer at one time or another from headaches, it is vital to keep this one separate from all the others, which is not too difficult.

## THE DIGESTIVE APPARATUS

The digestive tract begins at the mouth, from there leading into the esophagus (food tube), then into the stomach and the intestines. Basically it is a tube that transports food and drink; it eliminates waste products through the rectum at the end of the intestines. The walls of this digestive hose, like the garden variety, are subject to weakening. First the walls stretch and bulge, then the pull of gravity forms pouches along the undermined areas, and remnants of food and bacteria are trapped in these pouches. When this occurs in the esophagus, the pockets are called esophageal diverticulae; in the intestines, intestinal diverticulae. Very often such diverticulae cause no problems, but occasionally they become inflamed. This condition is called diverticulitis, and either medical or surgical treatment is indicated.

## DIGESTIVE UPSETS

### HIATUS HERNIA

The diaphragm is a sheet of tendons running from the front to the back of the body, dividing it into the chest and the abdominal cavity. In the middle of that sheet there is an opening through which the esophagus enters the stomach from the chest. After the age of fifty, this opening often enlarges. Later in life, the stomach may tend to ride up through this enlarged opening and protrude into the diaphragm. This is called a hiatus hernia, and it interferes with the proper functioning of the stomach. Elderly patients suffering from a diaphragmatic or hiatus hernia frequently complain that they feel discomfort after eating or when lying down. Belching, regurgitation and occasional vomiting may occur, as well as heartburn and pain in the pit of the stomach. If one is overweight, reducing may be beneficial. Hiatus hernia sufferers are more comfortable when food is eaten more often in smaller portions, but definitely never before retiring. Milk and antacids may be helpful, and sleeping in a half-sitting position is of value. Surgery is rarely recommended.

## STOMACH DISORDERS

Digestive problems are fairly commonplace among the aged. The stomach secretes less acid and pepsin, both of which are necessary for appetite and digestion, as time goes on. When neither of these enzymes are in the stomach, pernicious anemia may result. A poor appetite, improper digestion and general weakness may be some of the early indications of this ailment. Drugs replacing these and other missing secretions of the stomach can remedy the situation.

Despite the absence of normal amounts of acid, ulcers are not unusual in the elderly. A poor blood supply to the stomach walls may be a cause. Also, ulcers, like various other stomach problems, may be attributable to the amount of drugs elderly people often take. Some drugs prescribed for lowering the blood pressure, such as reserpine and cortisone derivatives, may cause ulcers. In this connection, the most egregiously guilty culprit—because it is taken so often—may be aspirin. The use of buffered aspirin may avoid some side effects.

Tumors, benign and malignant, may occur in the stomach, as in other parts of the body. The differential diagnosis must be left to skilled specialists. Persistently black stools sometimes, but not necessarily, are an indication of malignancy or serious stomach trouble. (The cause may also be a relatively unimportant ulcer.) When blood passes through the stomach, it turns black from the presence there of hydrochloric acid; blood from the gastrointestinal tract below the stomach does not turn black. Before assuming the worst, however, it is important to remember that a number of foods and drugs (iron pills, for example) turn the stool black—beets turn it red—and there is not necessarily any reason for alarm.

The gall bladder is a bulblike organ enveloped by the liver which channels bile into the intestine for the proper digestion of fat. Should the duct be blocked by gallstones (which are hardened bile), the bile gets into the bloodstream, coloring the blood greenish-yellow, and lending the same hue to the skin. Even the whites of the eye get yellowish. This condition we call jaundice. The stoppage of the duct causes the expansion of the gall bladder and subsequent pain. Sometimes the stone passes through into the intestine and, temporarily, all is well again. At other times, an operation is necessary to remove the gallstone, and often the diseased gall bladder as well. Jaundice may also be caused by a tumor of the gall bladder and the liver. Whether caused by a tumor or a stone, jaundice indicates a serious problem demanding expert medical attention. Tumors, inflammation of the gall bladder and liver, and stone formations occur with surprising frequency in people over sixty-five.

## OTHER INTESTINAL DISORDERS

Among the aged one of the areas most frequently susceptible to disorder is the lower intestine, especially the colon. The formation of pockets or diverticulae (see page 165) in the large intestine develops in twenty percent of the population over sixty years of age. They may cause no problems at all, or they may lead to inflammation and infection. Usually they can be treated medically rather than surgically.

Benign tumors, such as polyps, as well as malignant tumors, grow in the intestines. The incidence of cancer of the colon and rectum among the elderly is second only to cancer of the lungs. If malignancies are discovered early, the chances for recovery are excellent. Regular examinations are advised. For diagnosis in case of suspicion, doctors who are specialists in the field use instruments resembling telescopes (a proctoscope or sigmoidoscope) for examining the colon and the rectum.

Another common difficulty among older persons is constipation, followed by very hard feces and diarrhea (see page 55). If constipation is chronic, hemorrhoids (distended veins of the rectum) may develop, a frequent affliction of middle and old age, though also occurring in the young. A form of varicose veins, hemorrhoids may result from excessive straining for a bowel movement. When these rectal veins are enlarged, dilated, stretched, they become inflamed. This inflammation and possible ensuing infection can make the bowel movement very painful. Doctors speak of hemorrhoids as internal or external, depending on whether the swollen vein is inside or outside the anal opening. When hemorrhoids are small and relatively new, keeping the stool soft (with proper diet and possibly a gelatinlike medication), and not straining for a movement, will often make them disappear. A warm "sitzbath" (just enough water to bathe the lower abdomen while sitting up) is also soothing. A variety of rectal suppositories is available at the drugstore or upon prescription. When hemorrhoids become engorged, badly infected, and bleeding, they can be removed without much difficulty—but with some postoperative discomfort. Since hemorrhoids can also be the site of malignancies, they should not be ignored, especially if they bleed.

## URINARY TRACT PROBLEMS

The inability to control urine can sometimes be treated effectively if its origin, which may be an infection, is discovered. If the muscular shutter of the bladder is unable to stop the flow of urine, bed wetting, wetting of undergarments, and even of outer clothing results. Then incontinence becomes of great importance; probably more than any other affliction, it causes families to institutionalize their aged relatives.

Incontinence of urine may be particularly serious if there is a neurogenic bladder; that is, the bladder does not function because the nerves controlling it have had some interference by a stroke or some disease of the spinal cord. The bladder is a muscular bag; in aging it loses some of its elasticity, like an old rubber bag. Its contractions are not sufficiently strong to force out all the urine at once. Thus, the bladder not being emptied, it fills up sooner again; and there is a frequent urge to urinate. Infection may follow from the bladder never being completely emptied. But even without this complication, frequency and urgency of urination are themselves most bothersome.

In older men, an enlarged prostate gland can act as a dam affecting the outflow of urine. This also is a cause of the frequent urge to urinate, infection and inflammation of the bladder, incontinence, discomfort and loss of sleep. The inability to void urine at all can be another sign of prostate enlargement. Temporary relief from this spasm of the bladder may be gained by sitting in a warm "sitzbath." Also as a temporary relief measure, the physician may insert a catheter (a thin rubber tube) to draw out the urine. Eventually surgery of the prostate may be necessary, a procedure that has been increasingly simplified in recent years.

In older women, especially those who have borne children, the muscular bottom of the abdomen, the pelvic floor, has less firmness and the bladder may protrude through it. This condition, called *cystocele,* may cause discomfort and infection.

## DISEASES OF THE JOINTS

Almost any pain of the muscles or joints is generally called *rheumatism,* although the causes and the actual disorders may differ greatly. Minor inflammations in the joints or muscles may produce pain, but so may many other complaints. One of these disorders is *rheumatoid arthritis* of the hands or feet, where the swelling leads to considerable deformity. Cortisone derivatives have been effective particularly in the acute painful phase of this disease.

Gout classically affects the big toe, turning it red, with swelling and severe pain; but gout may occur in almost any other joint as well. Those afflicted suffer from an excess of uric acid in the blood; this uric acid forms crystals in the joints and in the kidneys that cause the acute pain and inflammation. Gout does, however, respond well to a variety of drugs.

An insufficient flow of blood to the extremities, to the feet especially, is very commonplace as one ages. Often the skin of the feet has an inadequate supply, and then even a slight injury to the skin from something as ordinary as the pressure of adhesive plaster, can cause a serious skin ulcer and infection.

### HIP FRACTURE

We have already spoken some about broken hips (see page 46), a very frequent problem of the aged. What is meant most often by hip fracture is, to speak more precisely, a fracture of the neck of the femur, which is part of the hip joint. See the illustration on this page. You will notice that the neck of the long thigh bone terminates in a ball that fits into the hip socket, in which it turns like a ball joint. If an older person falls on the outside of the thigh bone, the pressure tends to snap the almost horizontal connection from the thigh to the hip.

If you study this picture, you will comprehend the most commonly employed form of treating such fractures: by nailing the joint. A "nail" made of vanadium or some other

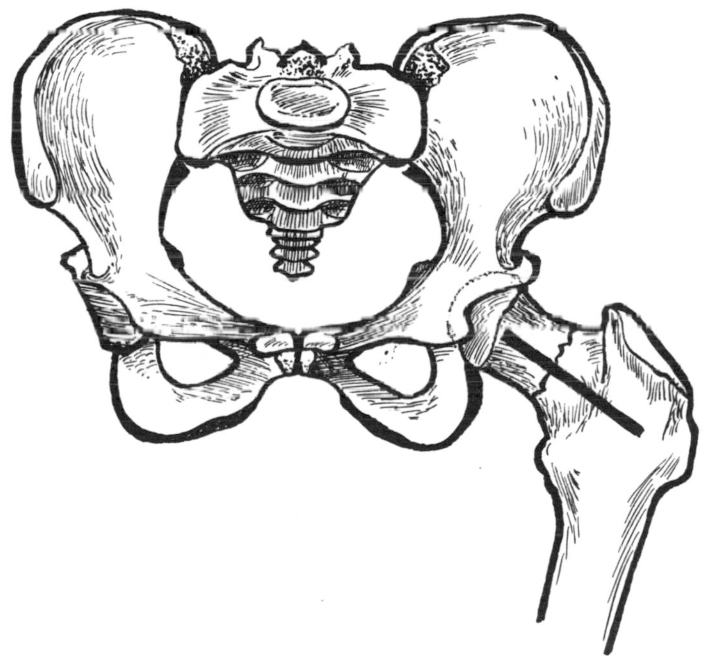

substance tolerated by the body without causing any difficulty is driven into the bone, thus providing it with an internal splint. In addition, after a while the bone starts healing, and in due course that leg is often even able to support the body's weight again. The time it takes to heal varies, of course. Appropriate exercise is part of rehabilitating the hip joint.

The hip is subject to other disorders and fractures as well, only one of which is common enough for us to go into: "absorption" of the head of the femur means that it loses some of its ball-like roundness, which then makes movement in the joint difficult, if not impossible. This loss of shape may happen with aging, but it also can occur as part of other illnesses in earlier life.

## THE SKIN—A LARGE ORGAN OF THE BODY

Often the skin is an indicator of age when other parts of the body are not. Aside from the role of heredity, exposure to sun and light probably plays the largest part in the condition of your skin. The fashionable suntan notwithstanding, excessive baring of the skin to the sun's rays tends to age it.

Skin cancer is found primarily on the parts of the body that have been exposed to sunlight over the years. People exposed to considerable sunlight in tropical climates are more prone to skin cancer than those who stay indoors or live in cooler climes. Any suspicious lesion should be examined by a skin doctor; in a number of instances innocent disorders are difficult to distinguish from potentially troublesome skin cancers. Fortunately this is usually a relatively benign condition that responds well to localized treatment. Some may be treatable by electric therapy, others can be dried out by X-ray radiation or removed surgically. Only a few types of skin cancer, such as melanoma (a darkened area of tissue), affect other parts of the body by invading it. If such dark areas enlarge, change color or become inflamed, consult a doctor.

Warts are a familiar phenomenon of the aged. Usually harmless of themselves, they need differentiating from other possibly malignant skin disorders. If warts grow or change in surface or color, consult a doctor.

A very vexing skin disorder can arise from an originally small skin infection. Elderly people can become allergic to their own skin infections and break out in a rash all over the body. The inflammation is called *autosensitization dermatitis*, meaning that it is due to an allergy in reaction to an infection of one's own skin.

Itching of the skin can be brought about by a wide variety of factors and disorders and often is bothersome enough for elderly people to consult a physician for relief. *Lichen* is the name of an itching skin condition characterized by thickening and dryness, particularly of the neck, forearms and shins. An ointment containing cortisone may be helpful.

The condition called *winter eczema* comes from changes in temperature and humidity, and especially the cool dryness of winter air. It produces fine cracks in the skin that may form a geometric pattern on the legs and cause unpleasant itching.

Dry, finely scaling skin, which may also itch, is another concomitant of aging. Alcohol rubs and certain types of bed linen may worsen the condition.

Sensitivity to some drugs is another frequent cause of itching; but often an alternative drug is available that does not induce the same sensitivity reaction. Contact with the metals in jewelry, or the use of certain soaps, detergents or cosmetics can also cause itching and skin eruptions.

Itching of the opening of the vagina and anus is usually due to oozing of secretion, urine or feces. If all special medical reasons are looked into and found irrelevant, regular bathing, the use of soothing creams, and attention to personal hygiene are most important in prevention and treatment of this annoying and embarrassing kind of itching.

Few dermatologists doubt that emotional problems can cause a variety of skin disorders. This is plausible if one bears in mind that an emotionally charged experience can cause blushing, which is a sudden expansion of the blood vessels in the skin. Fright, on the other hand, is accompanied by blanching, which is caused by the contracting of these same blood vessels. Since the supply of blood determines the resistance of the skin to the bacteria ever present on it, obviously changes in the blood supply affect its resistance to germs and viruses.

Sometimes no reason can be found for itching. The skin appears normal and even more youthful than one would expect. Such itching may come and go in response to no apparent or specific condition, and hence no successful treatment is found for it.

## THE EYE

Ophthalmologists state that only fifteen to eighteen percent of the elderly have poor vision in the absence of definite illness. The remainder have good or adequate vision to the age of ninety or more.

In the aging eye, cataracts are the most common disorder. Within the pupil of the eye lies a lens very much resembling the lens in a photographic camera; originally it is entirely transparent, but sometimes with age it becomes opaque—this is what is called a cataract. Cataracts make it increasingly difficult for a person to see with any accuracy at all. Happily, eye surgeons have developed a number of techniques for removal of cataracts: the operation is minor and usually uneventful, and eyeglasses or contact lenses take over the functions of the natural lens.

Glaucoma ranks second among disorders of the aging eye. It occurs with greatest frequency between the ages of forty and sixty-five; after that its incidence tapers off. There are different types of glaucoma, but the most typical involves an increased pressure of the fluid inside the eye. This pressure can destroy the structure within the eyeball and cause blindness. Glaucoma may be detected by blurred vision that lasts for minutes or hours, often accompanied by what resembles colored rainbows in halo forms. In some cases special eyedrops can control the condition, but at other times surgery is required. Annual eye examinations are important!

The last eye difficulty common enough in the aged for us to be concerned with is a degeneration of the macula, the center of the retina. When this occurs, there is a loss of sharp vision: peripheral vision remains intact, but vision in the center of the eye is impaired, a most annoying situation, and not one that lends itself well to correction.

## THE EAR

It is fairly well accepted as fact that most people after the age of fifty cannot hear high frequencies. But this is not of major importance since the frequencies concerned with the hearing and understanding of human speech are well below that level.

While the auditory sense may be affected by a number of relatively rare conditions, the most common malady in the elderly is *otosclerosis*. This disorder, which runs in families and usually appears in middle age, is due to a condition that immobilizes the tiny bones within the ear that transmit sound. Surgery performed on the middle ear can restore a good deal of that hearing loss, and a hearing aid can be helpful too.

Certain drugs can affect hearing. Aspirin, for example, when taken in large quantities (for arthritic pain, for instance) may induce ringing in the ears and some deafness. Such symptoms usually give way when the aspirin intake is stopped.

Sometimes deafness is caused by excessive wax in the ears: a simple reason that responds to a simple remedy—removing the wax. It should be done by a physician.

## THE SEXUAL APPARATUS

As with most other parts of the body, both male and female sexual organs undergo some changes with aging, more so of course in some individuals than in others. These changes have little or no bearing on sexual interest, or even the ability to perform or enjoy sex.

Among males, the organ most affected by the aging process is the prostate gland (often misspelled and mispronounced, it has nothing to do with being *prostrate*). The prostate is difficult for most people to visualize; this small gland sits in front of the rectum, behind and below the bladder, and surrounds the urethra. It can be felt or massaged by finger through the rectum. The normal function of the prostate is to provide secretion that combines with the semen coming up from the testicles in the normal ejaculation from the penis. When full, the spongelike prostate gland adds to the sexual urge of the male; its emptying contributes to his sexual pleasure. In young men, inadequate or incomplete ejaculations can produce discomfort, a mild inflammation or infection. Bacteria of all sorts can infect the prostate, painfully so in the case of gonorrhea, for example.

If older men sit for prolonged periods, the prostate becomes congested and unable to empty spontaneously. This causes a frequent need to urinate, a burning sensation during urination and pain that radiates into the testicles. Drugs, massage by a physician and warm sitzbaths will usually help—or the doctor may prescribe other treatment.

Sometimes in older men the tissue of the prostate enlarges. The organ actually increases in size by the addition of fibrous tissue that impinges on the bladder and its opening. The condition, called benign hypertrophy of the prostate, makes urination difficult or impossible. To sufferers it seems far from benign; and if acute, it calls for urgent measures. A warm bath will often relax a tight sphincter sufficiently to provide some comfort. If necessary, a physician can insert a catheter temporarily to drain the bladder.

If the prostate gland is enlarged, it presses against the bladder, reducing the space for containing urine. This may lead to frequent urination, infection and stretching of the bladder muscles. Enlargement of the prostate, for whatever reason, produces pressure against the rectum and a feeling of fullness there too. Passing a hard stool will, in effect, massage the prostate too roughly, causing more discomfort, even squeezing out a prostatic secretion if it is present in excess. If massage seems an advisable form of treatment, the physician can massage the gland by inserting a finger into the rectum.

Surgery may be necessary for a seriously enlarged prostate to reduce its size or remove the offending parts. Several surgical procedures are possible. In some, no abdominal incision is necessary: the prostate can be removed or decreased through the urethra by inserting instruments into the penis. In other instances, a simple incision near the bladder is preferable.

Neither sexual pleasure nor sexual functioning are significantly affected by surgery of the prostate. Men continue to enjoy sexual interest, are able to have erections and some sensation of orgasm without the external secretion (after most prostate operations, there is an internal discharge into the bladder). And for some inexplicable reason, often there is a postoperative tendency toward hiccups, which, although unpleasant, can usually be dealt with easily.

Cancerous tumors can also develop in the prostate. Surgery, the insertion of radium seeds into the prostate through the urethra, and possibly radiation by cobalt or X ray are the usual treatment procedures. The older the man is, the less active such a carcinoma is likely to be. There is relatively less danger of its spreading quickly to other parts of the body (such as to the bones as it can in younger men). In fact some specialists believe that cancerous cells can be found in the prostate glands of most men over eighty years of age, usually with no consequence whatsoever.

Except for complications with the prostate and its effect on the bladder, aging men are not likely to have sexual difficulties. Many authorities agree that an active sex life may persist into the eightieth year at least. By and large, older men are less readily aroused than younger men, have somewhat less rigid erections, ejaculate less fluid, and indulge in intercourse less often. On the other hand, once they have an erection, they are often able to maintain it longer than younger men, perhaps with some variation in firmness, but with considerable delay of ejaculation—to the increased satisfaction of their partners.

The sexual life of the aging woman, too, has been disparaged or discouraged far too much in our culture. It's true that changes in the cells of the mucous membrane of the vagina take place during menopause. The resulting dryness and possible itching may be alleviated by estrogen replacement therapy if it's indicated. If not necessary, soothing creams will provide comfort, and vaginal jellies can prevent irritation during intercourse. But the cellular change bears no relationship to sexual enjoyment: the mucous membrane is not especially the source of pleasure. Rather it is the stimulation of the clitoris and the distension and contraction of the muscular tube of the vagina in foreplay and intercourse that give pleasure, which may or may not lead to orgasm. There is no physical reason why sexual enjoyment should be affected by aging. Everyone knows about the menopause and the end of ovulation and menstruation; everyone should know also that this need not imply a negative change in either sexual functioning or the pleasure derived from it (such diminution is almost always for psychological reasons). In fact some women, free of the fear of pregnancy, enjoy full orgasm after menopause for the first time!

Both the ovaries and the uterus (womb) are possible seats for tumors, making periodic examinations a necessity. The Pap smear (named for Dr. George Nicholas Papanicolaou, inventor of this diagnostic method) consists of sampling a few vaginal cells and placing them on a glass slide for examination. The amount of estrogen (one of the female sex hormones) present is estimated, as well as a possible tendency toward some form of cancer. This test should be performed at least annually either by a gynecologist or the family doctor, for *all* adult women.

Ligaments, or tendonlike muscular bands, hold the womb in place. These muscles may stretch with age, especially after repeated childbearing. The womb may assume a position other than normal; one speaks of a prolapse if it leans forward and down, most often the disarrangement in old age. The womb is pear-shaped, and the cervix, or neck of the womb, resembles the part of the pear next to the stem. At times severely stretched ligaments permit the broader part of the pear to slip through the vaginal walls. The severely prolapsed womb may be outside of the vagina, causing discomfort and possible infection, and requiring surgical attention.

The lining of the womb is also subject to the formation of cysts—enlarged glandular sacs—or the tissue may simply thicken with growths, producing fibroids. Polyps—smooth, fingerlike growths of tissue—may also develop in the uterine area. Minor cysts, fibroids or polyps, if benign, cause few, if any, complications and are only a slight exaggeration of the norm. If these growths enlarge, however, they can cause cramps and pain. Should bleeding occur, a physician must be consulted. The cause of the bleeding may be either innocent or serious.

Removal of the ovaries and womb do not necessarily interfere with sexual pleasure or ability. If the ovaries are removed after menopause, no complications result. If the womb is removed, the vagina is left intact, and there is no reason why intercourse should not be quite normal; nor is there any physical reason for not achieving orgasm.

The breasts should be checked regularly for tumors—in all adult women. Because the breasts consist of glands, they often develop enlarged sacs or cysts, most often benign—but they must be examined and differentiated from malignant ones. Customarily the breasts lose shape and tone with aging; but exercise, proper garments and care may reduce or even prevent those changes. For cosmetic purposes, exercise of the muscles supporting the glandular and fatty tissues of the breasts may be helpful.

## METABOLIC DISORDERS

Of the many disturbances of the metabolism, gout and diabetes are probably of the most significance to the aged. Both, as well as other metabolic disorders, also occur at younger ages, but these two especially tend to have a greater prevalence in later life, from late middle age on.

Gout (already discussed; see page 170) is more often considered a disease of the joints because the uric acid crystals that form in the linings of the joints cause acute pain when their hard, sharp edges bite into the sensitive membranes. But gout can deposit too much uric acid (existing in the bloodstream) in any number of organs as well. There are now several drugs that prevent the accumulation of too much uric acid in the blood. Also a diet low in uric acid helps: avoid foods like anchovies, sardines, liver, kidneys, sweetbreads and veal. Drinking a lot of fluid helps to keep the urine relatively thin and watery, so that kidney stones are less likely to form.

Gout is much more frequent in men than in women. But

here is one cheerful thought for men suffering from gout: sexual ejaculations contain a large amount of uric acid; so one way to keep the uric acid in the body low is to have frequent orgasms.

Diabetes (by its proper name *diabetis mellitus,* by its nickname sweet or sugar diabetes) is caused by the insufficient production of insulin in the body. This substance is produced by some cells called "the islets of Langerhans" in the pancreas. The pancreas is a gland that also produces other secretions. It lies beneath the stomach in the depths of the abdomen, too difficult to chart for most people who are not medically trained. These islet cells tend to manufacture less insulin as one grows older; but there may be a familial predisposition to this malfunction as well. The intake of excessive carbohydrates (sugars and starches) generally overtaxes the insulin production. The main fact to keep in mind is that insulin not only affects the blood sugar level, but that the metabolic disturbance called diabetes can cause hardening of the arteries of the brain, the eyes and other organs. It also makes one more prone to infection, to the difficulty of healing wounds (especially of the feet and legs) and to the development of cataracts.

If diabetes is detected early, keeping the sugar and starch intake low may be sufficient treatment. If not, a more complex diet, which often has to include *some* carbohydrates for complicated chemical reasons, has to be worked out by a physician. Some drugs now exist which can be taken by mouth to lower the blood sugar level. If this is not enough, insulin injections can be administered by the patient himself or by members of his family: a simple matter easily learned. (Diabetics also easily learn to test their own urine for the amount of blood sugar present.)

Insulin is a tricky substance, of which a diabetic can get

too much. If he has not noticed the sweating, tremors or slight faintness that presage an attack—and counteracted it by a few cubes of sugar or a glass of orange juice—a patient can go into insulin shock, a very serious matter and a medical emergency of the first order. Diabetics should therefore always carry some candy or sugar lumps with them, as the blood sugar curve may dip unexpectedly some hours after insulin has been administered.

Similarly, many diabetics are required by their physicians to carry a supply of insulin and a syringe with them in case the blood sugar is suddenly increased and they suffer a diabetic coma—the opposite of insulin shock but also a medical emergency. People in diabetic coma often have a sweet smell resembling that of acetone (familiar from the odor of nail polish). Doctors can instruct you about other symptoms of insulin coma.

On the more cheerful side, it should be mentioned that relatively mild diabetes can not only be easily controlled, but may even completely disappear if a proper diet and regime are adhered to.

## TUMORS

The word tumor derives from the Latin for *swelling*. Most of us are particularly concerned with those tumors that mean an abnormal growth of cells in some part of the body. Cells normally divide; tumor cells divide *more* than normal cells. Benign tumors just grow bigger where they are and rarely cause serious trouble. (They may cause serious trouble in the brain simply because the space is limited by the bones of the skull and their pressure affects the brain tissue.)

Malignant tumors not only multiply faster than benign

ones, but they also have a tendency to spread into other tissues either directly by growing into them, or by the tumor cells traveling through the bloodstream or the lymphatic system to other parts of the body.

The body consists of different kinds of cells, and differing cells cause different kinds of tumors. The lay person tends to call every malignant tumor a cancer, or carcinoma, while doctors may call them sarcoma or by many other technical names which indicate the part of the body tissues where the tumor formed. While this is complicated, it implies different kinds of treatment and expectations to the doctor.

Some tumors are known to grow quite slowly and others very swiftly. From microscopic study after a biopsy, the physician can usually tell what kind of cells are involved, how fast-growing the tumor is and what grade (grades indicate the degree of malignancy). Some tumors are known to spread especially to some organs but not to others. Cancer of the prostate, for instance, spreads particularly readily to the tissue of the vertebrae and other large bones. Others spread specifically to the liver.

Most doctors tell their patients the facts as well as they know them. If they hedge, it is often because they don't know exactly what will happen. Some people fare much better with their malignant tumors than others. Small details such as how close to a blood vessel a tumor lies may make a great deal of difference in its spreading.

Curiously enough—and another note of cheer for the aged—the older a person is, the slower a malignant tumor progresses.

There are now several drugs available that can slow down or possibly even stop the growth of malignant tumors. Most of these drugs are still in an experimental stage. Treatment by X ray, cobalt and radium are well known; they often stop or slow down malignancies. They may also at times cause nausea and dizziness for a while, but this is increasingly avoided. The dominant fact is that the cause—or causes (it is probably complicated)—of malignant tumors is still under study and far from solved.

The American Cancer Society distributes pamphlets that discuss some early warning symptoms of different tumors. It would be a pity for you to become preoccupied with cancer symptoms; but it is helpful to be able to recognize them.

# 11

# *How and Where to Live the Later Years*

*For age is opportunity no less*
*Than youth itself, though in another dress,*
*And as the evening twilight fades away*
*The sky is filled with stars, invisible by day.*

"Morituri Salutamus" by
LONGFELLOW

THE desire to live in the best possible place is hardly new. At least as far back as the ancient Romans, people moved between summer and winter homes. The pursuit of sunlight has moved nations. Since being past middle age begins a new phase of life, it also frequently means a reexamination of the optimum conditions of residence. Sometimes for the very first time in life there is real freedom to move where one wishes: if the active earning of income does not tie you to one place any more, if you have savings or other forms of retirement income—or now that you may receive Social Security benefits in any place, including another country—

you may be free to look around as you have never been before.

Some older people don't want to move at all. Others may just move from a larger home to a smaller one that is easier to take care of and easier to reach: no steps or stairways, easy access to shopping, to recreation, to friends or grown children. Some may move seasonally: both the rich and the more modestly endowed move to Florida and other warm climates for the winter months, only to return to the temperate zone for the rest of the year.

The desire to be close to children, relatives and friends is one of the most urgent determining factors in deciding on a different abode. The state of health and finances is another. Social scientists are busily trying to find out whether living in communities for the aged only or with mixed age groups is better for the aged—and for the young. Meanwhile, elderly people are going to have their own individual ideas about this. Some welcome the comfort of being with a peer group with whom they share level of energy, outlook on life and many other characteristics. Others abhor the notion of a sort of ghetto for the aged: they want to continue to participate actively in life and community and feel that this participation includes continued exposure to people of all ages and walks of life.

Mobility, urban living and psychological changes have combined to make it much rarer that three generations live under one roof or in close proximity than used to be customary. Sociologists say that the nuclear family (father, mother, children) has replaced the extended family.

One result of this fact is that children often miss some link to their past and thus have less of a feeling of identity, of permanence, than they might otherwise. Another result is that grandparents feel more isolated and they have less of a role to play. Thus both sides lose something. (It is understood that often living under one roof created many problems for all three generations. Also, we're not necessarily speaking only of actual physical proximity in one apartment or house; even visits and psychological closeness between grandparents and grandchildren are rarer these days.)

Psychological and realistic considerations permitting, there are a number of ways in which this particular problem could be helped. If there are grandparents available, some role for them in relation to the children is most constructive for their need to be needed and to be loved. If they are not especially disturbed or excessively overindulgent or critical, it will be good for the children.

An extension of that idea, especially applicable if there is no grandparent available, lies in adopting an elderly person as grandmother or grandfather. In some communities such a plan has actually been formalized and elderly people interested in fulfilling the role of grandparents can be readily found with the help of a specific organization or a social agency. For example, in New York City the Office for the Aging interviews elderly people who have had some experience with children and directs them to institutions, hospitals and foundling homes where they work with children, often on a daily or weekly basis, providing a vitally important loving relationship which is mutually rewarding.*

An older person as babysitter may also provide a feeling of security and continuity for children and sitter alike. As with natural grandparents, foster grandparents may possibly feel "used" if the only occasion they are invited is when they are needed as babysitters.

Planned retirement communities seem to work out for the comfortable middle class if they can accept a leisure-

* See Appendix, Opportunities for Volunteer Services.

oriented role: such people seem better adjusted than those staying on in regular home communities, especially if the planned retirement community provides possibilities for an active social life. Housing that provides special amenities such as grip rails in bathrooms, doors that permit the passage of wheelchairs, and ramps in addition to stairs is desirable. Whether retirement villages of isolated units are preferred, and whether they should be high-rise apartments, scattered-site units or cottage-type dwellings are some questions which so far have not been satisfactorily answered. From a financial standpoint, a concentration of older persons and the services they need makes great sense—but many of the elderly don't like to be so segregated. The consensus seems to be that communities should provide a choice of accommodations not only as to special housing to fit special needs, but as to mixing with only your own age group or integrating with all ages.

Life within an ordinary (nonretirement) community is more desirable as long as the individual is capable of living there on his own steam, can get around and function safely, and is not unduly dependent because of his infirmities.

## RETIREMENT VILLAGES

Currently very much in fashion, and advertised to the teeth on radio, TV, by newspapers, mail and telephone, these residences are usually fairly expensive housing developed by private enterprises for a profit. Usually not too far from a metropolis, they are either garden apartments or attached townhouses that are bought outright and maintained for a monthly charge. Examples are Rossmoor in California, Sun City in Arizona, Heritage Village in Connecticut.

The cost of residence units presently ranges from about \$20,000 to \$50,000; monthly maintenance varies but is less than rent would be on a comparable apartment or house. In some of the villages within commuting distance of metropolitan areas, it is not uncommon for the residents to keep working on a part-time (or semiretired) basis. As the age level of applicants is lowered (and in some communities it is now down to fifty years of age), there will be more partially or fully employed residents. As local taxpayers, many residents become involved in the government of the larger municipality (town or county) to which their community belongs. Shopping and recreational facilities are all available on the grounds so that it is possible to have a full, active life without ever leaving the village. However, because of the security and maintenance crews, it is also possible to take a prolonged trip or vacation without the usual concerns of a homeowner.

Distinct from the retirement village, in some cities there are housing complexes arranged for the comfort and needs of the elderly. They are sponsored by insurance companies, labor unions and sometimes municipalities. These homes or apartment buildings have bathrooms with security rails, ramps next to stairs, buttons or bells for summoning aid, and usually a resident nurse, if not more extensive care facilities.

## LIFETIME CARE FACILITIES

Usually a high-rise apartment building for which each occupant pays a substantial purchase price plus a monthly maintenance charge, the lifetime care facility tends to be made up of small but adequate apartments with very minimal kitchen facilities. Meals are also available in a main dining room. There may be some club or special-interest group activities, but facilities for physical recreation are usually nonexistent. A part of the building is set aside as a nursing home. The title denotes the important strength of this type of housing—the resident is assured of lifetime care regardless of loss of income or health. If the tenant's income stops, the maintenance is assumed by the "landlord." The population tends to be older, more single occupants than couples, and people who may have had a frightening illness such as a mild stroke or heart attack. If after moving in, you decide you don't like this kind of facility, you *cannot resell it;* so it pays to investigate such a place very thoroughly before a commitment is made.

## HEALTH-RELATED FACILITIES

These residences are very similar to lifetime care facilities except that rather than an initial purchase price, there is a high monthly charge (from $800 to $1000 and up). Accommodations are usually a room rather than an apartment, with a lower price for a shared double room.

## MOBILE HOME PARKS

These residences, which used to be called "trailers," are usually occupied exclusively by former blue-collar workers. Activities are less structured in such "parks," with emphasis on entertainment rather than self-improvement.

## BOARDING HOMES

An informal arrangement whereby a family will rent out extra rooms in their house. There are no planned activities or facilities to care for a person who becomes ill. In some situations, this may become a substitute for a family; but it is just as likely to result in an aged person's being surrounded with total indifference.

## REHABILITATION CENTERS

Such centers are often available for aftercare following hospitalization for some acute problem. Many offer excellent facilities for physical rehabilitation after a hip fracture, for example, or a heart attack, a stroke or some other mishap.

## EXTENDED-CARE FACILITIES

Lying somewhere between rehabilitation centers and nursing homes, these facilities are for the patient who has progressed beyond the need for the highly prized rehabilitation bed, who is not yet in good enough shape to be able to live at home, but not impaired enough to need a nursing home.

## HOMES FOR THE AGED OR NURSING HOMES

Most of these homes are sponsored by philanthropic divisions of religious or fraternal organizations, such as Catholic

Charities, Federation of Jewish Philanthropies or Protestant Welfare Federation. There are also some homes for the aged sponsored by such special-interest groups as retired actors. These homes are always nonprofit and no one is denied admission because he lacks funds. Many such homes (particularly those with a religious orientation) have been in the vanguard in developing programs and innovative new approaches, have in fact been models for what service homes for the elderly should include. Usually they contain a full spectrum of services: separate studio apartment complexes with lunch and dinner taken in the main dining room; rooms for reasonably well, ambulatory residents who are not independent enough for their own apartments; and infirmary and nursing-home facilities as well.

The staff of these establishments includes social workers, recreational workers (including arts and crafts instructors) and psychiatric consultants. Emphasis is on keeping the resident healthy, physically active and mentally stimulated. Residents are encouraged to be involved in the larger community, doing volunteer work in such places as hospitals—especially as foster grandparents in pediatric wards—or in the school system as teacher aids. There are many musical programs and current-events lectures, as well as trips arranged to museums, concerts, the ballet, etc. Residents in such homes are urged to maintain their former interests and to develop new ones too. Continued contact with the outside community is fostered. In some such homes there are contracts with outside employers to do typing, packaging and other jobs, for which the residents are paid.

While there is usually a set monthly charge in such philanthropic homes, once an older person's financial resources are exhausted, he is helped to apply for Old Age Assistance. Children or other relatives are not expected to pay for their parents; usually the home is paid for out of the Social Security payments, with a small amount (often about $10 a month) kept as pocket money by the old-age recipient. Some of the best centers include a bank, a chapel, a beauty shop and a canteen.

Nursing homes became a large real-estate industry with the advent of Social Security legislation; only the most stringent state and local control keeps them from frank profiteering at the cost of the aged. It behooves us to see that this control is maintained and that our older population is not taken advantage of. Again, some of the least mercenary are the homes with a religious or a special-interest affiliation. In my research I was irritated, however, at finding very few homes of any kind with single-occupancy rooms. It seems to me that after giving up your own home you could at least expect your own private room.

Unfortunately, there is often a waiting period of from three months to a year for entrance into such a home. This seems grossly unfair, especially when the need for such living accommodations tends to occur suddenly.

The middle-aged adult whose parent enters a home for the aged is always left with mixed feelings compounded of relief and guilt. While the decision may appear to be an independent one, freely made on the part of your parent, there are always some unspoken questions like, "Should I have taken him into my own home?" "Am I abandoning her, after all she has done for me?" "How can I do this to him in his old age?" Also, as you are in your middle years, your own old age is not so very far off—is this what's in store for you? What will be the reaction of your children to their grandparents' going into an old-age home? Is this the right example for them? And when you visit and hear complaints about some of the personnel, you will be torn between wanting to be overprotective of your parent and being angry with her for rearousing your guilt feelings. All these reactions are to be expected; if they become too intense or too uncomfortable, counseling (for you) is usually available in some department of the parent organization. Don't feel shy about taking advantage of this important concomitant service.

## PROBLEMS OF SOCIAL RELATIONSHIPS

Officiousness is the most frequent character problem of people working in an institution, medical or otherwise, as anyone having to deal with bureaucrats well knows. Hospitalization at any age can be made a terrible blow to the dignity by nurses and doctors who treat their patients like so much merchandise, with the least amount of trouble to themselves. This kind of abuse is probably most rife in institutions for children, the mentally defective and the mentally ill; but the various institutions for the aged come next. It takes an enlightened, dedicated administration, good working conditions and appropriate pay, requirements that, tragically, are not always met in nursing or old-people's homes, to ensure the desirable attitude on the part of staff toward aged people. Just as the elderly have their own psychological problems, so do the younger people into whose care they are entrusted.

To an extent, the parent-child relationship is now reversed in an institution as well as in the family home where the elderly may have remained. The staff of an institution may tend to be patronizing, punitive or merely overcontrolling. It is not an unjust accusation to say that all the problems a younger adult has or had with his parents are likely to manifest themselves in his attitudes toward old people—they tend to repeat the posture toward these new "children" that their own parents held toward them. Man's inhumanity to man is his revenge for indignities suffered in his own childhood. Hardly anywhere does this fact manifest itself more than in the care of the aged, by their own children or by others.

Many old people, for better or for worse, tend to revert to the emotions of a child. Doctors and nurses especially are reacted to as parental figures. If the professionals can use this relationship for reassurance and guidance when the older people feel panicked, anxiously repetitious, or confused and deluded, this situation can be very constructive. If not, it may be destructive and exploitative.

Aged people who never achieved much emotional maturity are very likely to show excessive dependence and demanding behavior. This can be very trying to anyone around them. All the emotional problems they had at any age may manifest themselves, so that sibling rivalry, for example, may be a serious problem in an institutional setting.

On the other hand, institutional rules are often absurdly inappropriate to the people they serve. An example of this, briefly mentioned earlier, is the lack of privacy accorded people in many old-age homes and hospitals. In such settings, any kind of intimacy, particularly for forming sexual relationships, is impossible. This is gradually changing, with floors (and in some places even rooms) no longer segregated by sex. The provision of "courting parlors" and a more receptive attitude on the part of professionals and staff toward the possibility of affection and sexual love on the part of aged people is noticeable in some institutions now. It will, however, still take time to give all elderly people the same liberties that most college students now have in their dormitories. Higher education seems to have survived the sexual revolution, and so will old age. The problem will be more one of administrative flexibility than anything else.

The old porcupine problem stays with us to the end. We need other people, and we don't want to be too severely impinged upon by them. In organized settings, whether a home for the aged, a nursing home or hospital, or some other facility, the porcupine dilemma becomes especially acute. There are not only one's peers to live with, but also the caretakers—nurses, doctors, maintenance people, social workers. They all bring their own personalities and peculiarities along. But if they are well-trained professionals, they should learn to control their own problems and stop letting them interfere with their work.

An aged person, too, has responsibilities, "a job of work" to do on entering any new and different living situation. How well he can perform it should be carefully researched and evaluated. This chapter is concluded with a list of questions that may be helpful to you in trying to help your friend or relative arrive at a sensible decision about his "retirement" residence.

## QUESTIONS TO ASK FOR OR OF YOUR AGED PARENT

1. Do I want many planned activities such as clubs, sewing groups, etc.?
2. Do I want a facility with a trained recreational staff member who will also instruct?

3. Do I want recreational facilities such as golf courses, swimming pools?
4. Is it hard for me to make new friends?
5. Will I miss the excitement of a diverse population —will one-class, one-age-group living depress me?
6. Is it important for me to be near my friends? My relatives?
7. Is security an important factor?
8. Can I afford to buy an apartment and thereby lose the interest I'd get if the money were in the bank?
9. What are the hidden costs, such as membership fees for recreational facilities?
10. What are property taxes and are they likely to go up?
11. Will I be responsible for maintenance and landscaping?
12. How easy is it to resell this apartment?
13. Is public transportation available?
14. Are good medical facilities easily available?
15. Is medical insurance included in the cost of my apartment?
16. During short periods of illness, are there provisions for such services as homemakers, visiting nurses, etc.?

# 12

# *Senior-Citizen Economics*

> *For every thing you have missed, you have gained something else; and for every thing you gain, you lose something.*
>
> RALPH WALDO EMERSON

ECONOMIC distinctions between the well-off and the poor, unfair and hard to take at any age, are exaggerated for the aged. A person who has earned a good salary most of his years will, of course, have had more of a chance to save for his old age. His job had a greater likelihood than that of his less fortunate brother of providing fringe benefits in the form of insurance, retirement pension, health care, and so forth. He has been less likely to change jobs frequently, or be subject to layoffs; so he has had a better chance of eligibility for pensions that require a certain length of service before becoming operative. In order to qualify for the better-paying job, he may have had more education; and this fact, plus money, would give him access to knowledgeable economic advice. His higher salary will make him eligible for higher Social Security benefits than the lower-paid worker. And he was probably able to give his children "advantages" which make it possible for them to provide some of the comforts and luxuries, and surely the necessities, he may require of them when he is old.

But what of the "other half"? Statistics on the economic level of the aged in this country are very depressing: *half* the twenty million Americans over sixty-five years of age reportedly have *less than the minimum subsistence-level income* established by the Federal government. That subsistence income would buy more in some parts of the country than others, it's true, but it is still an artificial figure. When economic planners arrive at a minimal subsistence budget, they tend to pare it down until it is as low as possible, so that as few people as possible will qualify for "assistance." Therefore it is an absolutely bone-bare paper figure, usually totally unrealistic, impossible (for even the most brilliant tactician) to live by. The worst-off groups, among the aged, as in the whole economy, are blacks, ethnic minorities and women, with white women somewhat better off than "others." Inflation is particularly devastating to the elderly: their expenses continue to rise while their income remains the same. A pension that is a proportion of a salary earned ten or twenty years ago will have minimal buying power today.

The necessary expenses of the elderly include shelter, food, clothing, transportation, medical care, possibly personal care, entertainment and incidentals. Obviously, like the rest of us, they may also have need of legal and other professional services. Planners generally assume that an older person's expenses will be greatly reduced because his household is smaller. However, many people in their sixties have dependent parents or relatives, some even have young children. As life expectancy increases, this will become more common. Also, while nonworkers do not have work-incurred expenses such as transportation, lunches and work wardrobes, they may have to travel more frequently than when they were younger for medical or social services; they still have to dress and eat. Social Security benefits and pensions are not taxed as income, which is a slight help, but hardly adequate to offset the burdens.

## SHELTER

A big change in the life style of the aged is that now many more older people than previously maintain their own households even if these living quarters are nothing more than tiny, run-down rooms. There are numerous reasons for this: for instance, more of the children of the current aged established their own homes upon marriage or soon thereafter than in the past, so there is less likelihood of an adult child remaining in the parental home where the aged person has always lived. Second, modern workers are required to be far more mobile than in the past, and it is difficult for the elderly family member to continually readjust to new localities. An older parent may not want to resettle in a strange community even if the home is permanent, he feels welcome and there is plenty of room for him in his children's house. Also, modern homes and apartments, especially those built for low- and middle-income tenants, are tiny and cramped, offering no space or privacy for an extra occupant. In fact, leases usually strictly limit the number of inhabitants permitted in the "unit." There is less for an older person to contribute to a household today—fewer children to tend through fewer illnesses, to cook for, to rock to sleep. Generosity prompts many older people who don't want to be a "burden" to their offspring to live alone, even in hardship.

They know how unpleasant living with other people, and perhaps especially close relatives, can be for all concerned. Some unfortunate older people have no one, relative or friend, with whom they can share a home.

But I suspect the primary reason so many old people—even very old, single persons—maintain their own abodes is for the sheer luxury of being able to be independent, despite all the drawbacks in terms of expense, loneliness and the difficulties of handling household chores. This autonomy holds true especially for older women, who like many young women in mid-twentieth-century America, are living independently in large numbers for the first time in our history.

We all know how expensive housing is these days; and the rent or mortgage, utilities, telephone bill *must* be paid. That eats up a gigantic part of an old person's income. Some elderly people are trapped in houses or apartments that are too large for them to maintain or enjoy, or in neighborhoods whose character has drastically changed so that it is alien to them or possibly unsafe, because new housing, when available, is so exorbitantly priced and so shoddily constructed that it doesn't pay to move. Besides, to satisfy a landlord, it is necessary to show proof of income and to pay several months' rent in advance, and landlords may not want to accept an elderly tenant. Waiting lists for public housing, subsidized housing, or housing designed specifically for the elderly are long—and most of these places are priced far beyond the capacity of most old people to pay.

## FOOD

Even though aged people lead more sedentary lives and have smaller appetites than young people, and even though most aged "households" consist of only one or two individuals, the elderly still have to eat. Rising food prices are particularly hard on old people. The elderly are dependent on local markets, which may be expensive or have limited choice of products. If senior citizens have small quarters, a small income or no assistance in carrying groceries, they must buy in small quantity, which boosts the overall cost of eating. Their cooking facilities, ability, or motivation may be inadequate to make the most of inexpensive, nutritious foods. They may have poor marketing and eating habits, thus wasting their precious sustenance money. Even wealthy old people are often malnourished.

Food is one expenditure people feel they can cut, and it is typical of anxious old people to literally starve themselves. Of course this only aggravates their problems, since they become weakened, prone to accidents and illness and to the acceleration of chronic and degenerative diseases. Sometimes older people are mistakenly diagnosed as mentally ill or senile when in fact they are tragically underfed.

The habit of pilfering food, long practiced by poverty-stricken old people, can be viewed as an exciting activity to pass the time, a desperate ploy of lonely individuals to attract attention, a symbolic plea for love as represented by feeding. But above all, basically it is simply a practical response on the part of those who literally *cannot afford to eat.* The aged food lifter is likely to be furtive and ashamed of what he is doing, and to blame himself for the dishonorable state to which he has been reduced.

## CLOTHING

Perhaps you picture your grandmother in a shapeless housedress or her timeless black coat. Nowadays, however, many people dress fashionably all their lives, and as you well know, even flimsy garments cost a lot of money. Older people may be harder to fit or have need of special shoes or undergarments. They may soil themselves frequently, requiring many changes of clothing and incurring high laundry costs. In addition, they tire easily and are less mobile—they can't look in store after store until they find the perfect garment, but are limited to one or a few local shops. Thus although older people can and do economize up to a point in buying apparel, it's easy for the younger person who gives it too little thought to underestimate clothing expenses for the elderly.

## TRANSPORTATION

The availability of transportation is crucial to old people, who are largely dependent on public transit. And public transit in most communities is notoriously inadequate, expensive, and in addition difficult for physically infirm people to maneuver. New York City (and possibly others) now has a reduced rate at certain hours for people over sixty-five in its public transportation system, which is a help—but it doesn't do away with the miles of stairs that separate the elderly from most subway trains or the exceedingly high steps up to the buses.

## MEDICAL CARE

The specter of an exorbitant medical bill that wipes out one's life savings haunts all old people and their families. Even with Medicare, Medicaid and private health insurance, there are numerous "deductibles" and "exclusions" that must be paid. And recovering payments, if you are to be reimbursed, is slow and tedious.

Many people don't have a "family doctor" and don't know how to locate one. An old person may be too tired to bear the thought of a day's wait in a clinic for a brief and unsatisfactory examination. He is put off by the lack of skill in communicating with the aged exhibited by many doctors, by the superficiality and impersonality of visits with the doctor, and of course by the huge expenses of even the briefest consultation.

The inflated costs of drugs are well known these days. The elderly, who are not well-educated consumers for the most part, are unlikely to know they should specify prescriptions with generic names, which can save them *some* money. The same limitations that apply to other shopping apply here—it is particularly hard for older people to shop around for bargains.

The elderly are the least likely to have taken advantage of the preventive techniques of modern medicine, and years of neglect lead to chronic problems. In addition to what we usually think of as routine medical expenses, the aged frequently require special dental and optical care, and possibly podiatry and hearing aids.

Then there may be a need for appliances such as bedpans, catheters, walkers, wheelchairs, hospital beds, disposable diapers, safety grips, and what have you. These products are not competitively advertised. How do you know the alternate sources of supply for these items, how much they should cost, how to judge their quality? Usually you will feel rushed when the need arises and acquire them as quickly as possible—there will be too many attendant problems to go comparison shopping, even if it were possible.

## SERVICES

Older people are likely to be in need of many services—from home and automobile maintenance, to household chores, to personal care. And these services, when they are even available, are very costly.

## ENTERTAINMENT

With so much time on their hands, the aged need activities to occupy them. Spectator entertainment is increasingly expensive, and it is usually dependent on transportation. Even "public" museums often charge fees; movie tickets can cost as much as $4; parks may be unsafe to walk in. Radio and television leave much to be desired; and if your TV set breaks, forget it; on an income of $130 *a month,* who can afford a repair bill? Those lucky enough to have developed hobbies or avocations that provide them with great pleasure—and who have been looking forward to the time when they can devote much more of their energies to these entertainments—may find that hobbies are the first things they have to cut out of their budgets on retirement. This surely leaves life very drab.

## INCIDENTALS

Then there are incidentals, such as the cost of telephoning endless bureaucracies for information; trips to the Social

Security and other government offices; the cost of a cab because the bus never showed up; tips for the kid who carries the groceries up five flights of stairs; the price of a newspaper or magazine; stationery and postage; food and veterinary care for a pet; camera film and phonograph needles; batteries for a transistor radio.

Considering this dour picture of the economic needs of the aged, it is important to know every conceivable resource available to an older person and those who contribute to his happiness and his support.

## SOURCES OF INCOME—PRIVATE

### PAID EMPLOYMENT

It is only a lucky few people over age seventy, or even sixty-five, who have a choice of whether or not to continue working at the same salary and title-level they held during their earlier adult years. Current practice is to mandate retirement at an arbitrary age, usually sixty-five. Sometimes incentives are offered to encourage retirement at sixty-two. After you reach forty-five, age counts against you when applying for jobs. Here are some of the reasons usually proffered for this sad fact, some of which are pure myth.

In technological fields, skills that often require much training to acquire quickly become obsolete and experience counts for little. Younger people are more likely to be geographically mobile. Younger people are quicker to learn and adapt, less prone to accidents and illness. Older people are more expensive in terms of fringe benefits such as pension plans. "It's only fair to give young people a chance." "If everyone isn't retired arbitrarily, those who *are* 'let go' will feel bad." And so on.

Usually an older person who does land a job accepts one at lower status and pay than the job from which he "retired." Many old people say doing this is far less of a blow to the ego in the long run than not working. To further confuse a person about whether or not to work, there are all sorts of regulations limiting the amount of earned income a person may receive and still be entitled to full benefits from other sources, such as Social Security. Ironically, a wealthy, unemployed individual, receiving a hefty dividend or interest income from savings and investments (which of course are also available to him as equity) is not penalized at all in terms of Social Security benefits!

In some companies, age limits for retirement are somewhat flexible for most employees, but mandatory for executives, whose pension and retirement benefits may be contingent upon certain conditions, for instance that they may not take a job with a rival company, or that they remain available for "consultation" upon retirement. Occasionally, a particularly valuable executive is paid a high salary for years as a consultant. That fact benefits precious few of the twenty million Americans aged sixty-five and older.

## PENSIONS

One of the fringe benefits offered by some employers is a pension upon retirement. The complicated regulations governing eligibility, the financial instability of the business or the pension plan, and numerous other factors combine to disqualify a substantial number of workers from the pensions they expect to live on when they retire. (Fifty percent is considered a very conservative estimate.) And a huge proportion of the wives of covered workers, who believed they were protected, discover, upon the death of their husbands, that they are totally without means of support, particularly if they are not yet old enough to receive OASDHI survivor's benefits (see page 217).

This is a complicated topic that can only be dealt with very superficially here. For a clearer understanding of how pensions work, a critical discussion of current proposals for changing the pension system, and several proposals for a more equitable one, plus explanations of the ways we can work to change the system, I highly recommend *You and Your Pension* by Ralph Nader and Kate Blackwell (Grossman Publishers, New York, 1973). This is a short, clearly written, information-packed book.

Pensions are usually offered to workers who have reached a certain age and have been on the job for a considerable length of time. In most companies you have to work for several years before you can begin to qualify, and often you can't take your credits with you if you leave the job. If you contributed, your portion will be refunded to you when you leave the company; it will have earned little or no interest in the interim. Your employer's contribution toward your pension remains in the fund. Pensions are funded in several ways: by employer contributions, by employee contributions, by a combination of both, by profit-sharing. The money may be entrusted to a bank or trust company to hold and invest, or annuities may be purchased from an insurance company. Sometimes industry-wide multiemployer plans are formed to pool the money of small and large companies.

Regulations are varied and arbitrary, and workers are rarely provided adequate information about who qualifies, what benefits are offered and how to claim them, either at the time they enter the plan or when they leave the company. Workers usually have no information about, or control over, where the money is invested. If the company goes out of business, if the workers are laid off because there isn't enough work to go around, if workers fail to meet certain technicalities they don't even know about, if the fund runs out of money, workers may not receive the pension they were counting on. Workers usually assume their dependents will receive benefits, but there are many loopholes in this regard, and specific benefits have to be applied for. For example, *if* a wife is eligible for retirement or survivor benefits, the worker will have to accept a much lower pension himself for his wife to receive her small extra amount—and this is often impossible if the couple is to live decently.

Pensions are usually paid on the basis of a percentage of the highest salary earned under the pension plan. If your pension from a particular company is based on the salary you earned twenty years ago, it will hardly be sufficient to meet today's inflated prices. Your chances for pension benefits and their size diminish if you are laid off frequently or work intermittently. Therefore people who are unskilled, low-paid or suffer frequent job changes will be discriminated against in terms of pension income, as well as income from employment. Again, blacks, ethnic minorities and women are especially vulnerable.

## ANNUITIES

Annuities are a form of insurance purchased from insurance companies. Your money, plus interest, is paid back to you (and/or your beneficiaries, as specified) in installments after it has been left with the insurance company for a certain period of time. There are a number of different kinds of annuities. The interest, but not the principal, is taxable.

## LIFE INSURANCE

Widows, and sometimes widowers, or other relatives are usually the beneficiaries of life insurance policies, which may be counted on as a source of income in the event that the insured individual dies. There are many kinds of life insurance and most are very expensive to purchase and maintain. Benefits are often quickly used up, so life insurance cannot, as a matter of course, be relied upon as a continuing source of income in old age, although it does provide some sustenance to some people. If you are the beneficiary of a life insurance policy, you may receive a lump-sum payment or regular monthly payments. (Usually lump sums are preferable because the original policy may be cheaper to purchase, the money is available to you if you need it at a time of crisis, and if you don't need to spend it then, you can manage its investment yourself rather than being at the mercy of the life insurance company's investment policies.) One reason so many people purchase life insurance is that it is a very well-advertised business.

If you are interested in learning more about insurance, and how to formulate the right questions about the best means of insuring your family, your local library or bookstore doubtless has several current books which, taken together, will give you a basis of knowledge. *Consumer Reports* has published the second, updated version of its analysis of life insurance. See the January, February and March, 1974, issues of that periodical. Or buy *The Consumers Union Report on Life Insurance*, 1972, $2.

## INHERITANCE

In addition to being the beneficiary of life insurance, many older people also inherit estates from their spouses, relatives and friends.

## SAVINGS AND INVESTMENTS

Some older people receive income from savings banks, from savings and loan companies, from stocks and bonds and other private investments. Some of the aged benefit from real estate and royalties, as in the population at large.

## SPECIAL DISCOUNTS FOR THE ELDERLY

Your community or local organizations may offer elderly people special discounts for transportation, entertainment or services. Nongovernmental organizations for the elderly, such as the American Association of Retired Persons, may offer reduced rates for domestic or foreign travel. Vacations for the elderly may be provided by a nonprofit or church organization. You can find out about the existence of such possibilities by calling your local town hall, office of the aging, senior center, or social-service agency. While such discounts will hardly make the difference between eating and starving, they may enable the older person to brighten his life considerably. There is no stigma or shame attached to being resourceful and learning to make use of what your community offers. In fact, programs like these will not be continued unless people show a decided interest in them and make their needs and desires felt!

# 12 *Senior-Citizen Economics*

## SOURCES OF INCOME—GOVERNMENTAL*

### SOCIAL SECURITY

The Social Security Administration of the United States Department of Health, Education and Welfare administers various programs, which had their origins in the Depression of the 1930's and which, though grossly inadequate today, are the only sources of income for many of those individuals who qualify. It is important to realize that Social Security was designed as supplementary income and is still considered so today, largely contrary to fact. Political pressure is the only way to make it an effective program or to have it replaced by a more meaningful one.

There are Social Security offices throughout the United States, and sometimes, if they are some distance from your home, there is a toll-free number you can call. They will send you free of charge many brochures and a comprehensive booklet, "Social Security Programs in the United States," that describes Old-Age, Survivors, Disability, and Health Insurance (OASDHI), which is what most people mean when they refer to "Social Security." Workmen's compensation, temporary disability insurance, public assistance (familiarly known as "welfare"), and Railroad Social Insurance, Public Employee Programs and Veterans' Benefits are subsumed under OASDHI. Newer editions of this booklet will include the new supplementary security program as well. Finally, there is a brief chapter on privately organized insurance, health and pension plans. I will

* See appendix for additional information.

touch on each of these briefly, after providing something of an overview of how the system operates.

### OASDHI

Although OASDHI is called *insurance,* it operates as a tax. The amounts that beneficiaries will receive and the amounts that "contributors" (i.e., taxpayers) will pay are set by law; and during the inflationary spiral we are caught in, they change—ever upward. If you work at a job that is "covered" by Social Security, your employer must deduct the requisite amount from your salary (this appears on your W-2 form for income tax returns as "F.I.C.A.": Federal Insurance Contribution Act). Also, your employer must match this amount. He is responsible for paying both shares to the government quarterly. Every quarter of a year you earn a "credit" toward eligibility for benefits.

You cannot elect not to participate if your job is "covered." If, on the other hand, you work in a job that is *not* covered by Social Security, such as a Federal, state or local government job (which usually have their own programs), a part-time or domestic position or certain agricultural jobs, you cannot participate, even if you would like to contribute both the employee and employer amounts yourself.

Originally, only nonagricultural industries and commerce were included in the Social Security program. Only very recently domestic workers have been included, and here it is necessary that the person be paid at least $50 a quarter of a year. Self-employed individuals are taxed at a slightly higher rate than salaried individuals, but don't have to pay the employer portion.

People who work for railroads for more than ten years are

covered by Railroad Retirement programs. If they work fewer than ten years, their railroad credits are converted to Social Security. In order for employees of nonprofit organizations to be covered, the organization must formally waive tax exemption in regard to Social Security.

More people are included in Social Security now than when the program began. Nevertheless, some old person you know may *not* be eligible for these benefits. Still, Social Security is the most common source of income for older people, and that's why I'm discussing it in some detail.

When it comes time to figure out if you are eligible for benefits, you add up the number of credits you have amassed. Then an average is computed of the salaries you earned under Social Security and, on the basis of formulas that are presented in the form of tables, your benefits are figured. The higher your salary average, the higher your benefits will be. To remedy things a little for people who worked for many years for extremely low salaries—and of course the older you are, the lower your salary average for comparable jobs will be because of inflation in recent years—there is a minimum payment. Your benefits are figured according to the tables, and then compared with the minimum payment, and you get the greater amount. It is difficult, if not impossible, to figure your benefits yourself; your Social Security office will do it for you upon request.

As of 1974, benefits are tied to the cost-of-living index to take inflation into account; and the maximum base salary from which deductions are made will go up accordingly. If you earn more than a small salary (currently $2100 a year) following retirement, payments are reduced by $1 for each $2 you earn during each month you make more than $175. The amount you may earn has recently increased slightly because of inflation.

The Social Security program provides benefits for workers and their dependent spouses and children, and in some situations for their dependent parents who are aged sixty-two and over. The underlying assumption is that the worker is a male and, even if his wife is or was also employed, she is his dependent. (This is not to say that husbands cannot be considered dependents of working wives.) That is why, even if both husband and wife worked and are eligible for benefits, the wife will receive the larger of the two amounts for which she qualifies: benefits on the basis of her own earnings record *or* as her husband's dependent. If she receives dependent benefits, she will not receive any credit for the deductions withheld from her salary, and as a worker she has no choice to withhold her "contributions" even if she knows she will never benefit from participation in the program. Usually, if benefits are begun before you are sixty-five, the amounts are reduced to take into account the longer time they will be received.

The worker who is eligible for benefits receives them. His dependent spouse and children, however, receive them only under certain conditions. Usually the dependent and survivor benefits end with the termination of the dependency situation. Thus a widow or divorcee who remarries gives up the benefits she acquired as a result of being the wife of her former husband. To be eligible for dependent benefits in a new marriage, you must have been married at least a year, unless a child resulted from the marriage before that time. To be eligible for the benefits of a divorced spouse, the marriage must have lasted for twenty years prior to divorce.

A wife who is responsible for the care of minor children or disabled children is eligible for certain benefits regardless of her age. When her responsibility situation ceases, her payments also stop until she reaches the age of sixty-two.

Thus many women are suddenly left without income for a number of their late "middle" years.

There are three categories of benefits under OASDHI:

1. Retirement benefits: paid to an eligible worker at age sixty-two or age sixty-five, when he retires. Credits are granted for those who work longer (until age seventy), and their benefits are increased somewhat to take into account that they will be paid for fewer years. The worker's dependent spouse becomes eligible at age sixty-two, unless she has a child under eighteen years of age in her care, or a disabled child. An unmarried child up to age eighteen or a child who is a full-time student up to age twenty-one is entitled to dependent benefits, as is a child of any age who was disabled before age twenty-two.
2. Survivor benefits: A widow or widower aged sixty, or if disabled aged fifty, is eligible for survivor benefits of the insured spouse who has died. A widow with a dependent child under age eighteen, or twenty-one if a full-time student, and disabled children of any age are entitled to survivor benefits, as are dependent parents of the insured deceased at age sixty-two. A small lump-sum death benefit is also paid.
3. Disability benefits: These benefits are available to workers younger than age sixty-five who suffer temporary or permanent partial or total disability. You have to wait five months before receiving these benefits, and they end when you return to work. At sixty-five you become eligible for retirement benefits. Conditions for dependent benefits or disabled workers are the same as for retirement benefits.

## SUPPLEMENTARY SECURITY

Until 1974, aged people with resources below "poverty level" received assistance under welfare programs administered by the states with Federal aid. These programs were called Old Age Assistance, Aid to the Blind, and Aid to the Permanently and Totally Disabled. They have now been superseded by the Social Security Administration's new Supplementary Security Income program, which will guarantee all eligible citizens of the United States a certain income. The benefits offered by some states were extremely low, and this is an attempt to try to equalize things across the nation. However, some states have been paying more than this minimum, and people in these states who were covered under the old system will continue to receive the larger amount, with the states making up the difference. The guaranteed minimum income under this program is pathetically low. As of this writing, the amount is $130 for an individual and $195 for a couple *per month.* In addition to receiving *less than* the above monthly income in order to qualify, you must show proof of the following: an individual may not own more than $1500, a couple not more than $2500 in cash, savings, investments, cash-value life insurance, or more than a certain amount of personal property, or a house worth more than $25,000. The program is new, and the wrinkles have not yet been ironed out, causing much hardship to those eligible individuals whose checks have not arrived when expected.

If you think you are eligible, call your local Social Security office, and they will tell you what records you should bring with you when you apply.

Social Security is the total source of income for some ten percent or more of our aged citizens. When you consider how much money you spend in a day, or a week, exclusive of anything like luxuries, you can begin to realize the dreadful limitations of this support.

## HEALTH INSURANCE

Medicare is a health insurance program administered by the Social Security Administration under the aegis of the Secretary of Health, Education and Welfare. It is automatically available to all people eligible for OASDHI when they reach sixty-five, whether they are retired and collecting retirement benefits at that time or not, and to individuals who have been entitled to disability payments for at least two years.

There are two parts to Medicare: basic Hospital Insurance (HI, sometimes called "part A") and Supplementary Medical Insurance (SMI, sometimes called "part B"). There is no charge for HI, but SMI costs a small monthly premium.

When you become eligible for Medicare, you are enrolled in both parts unless you specify that you do not want SMI. The rules are somewhat confusing: Initially you have seven months in which to choose *not* to participate, starting three months before the month in which you become sixty-five and ending three months after. If you do not join then, you can enroll any year thereafter between January 1 and March 31. However, coverage will not start until the following July 1, and your premiums will be ten percent higher for each year you *could have* but *did not* participate. Also, you may cancel SMI and reenroll only once.

Medicare is available to people who are not eligible for OASDHI. They must participate in both HI and SMI and are charged monthly premiums (at present $33 for HI and $6.30 for SMI). Premiums will rise with the cost of living.

Essentially, Medicare is meant to take care of emergencies rather than routine, preventive health care. It pays for services provided by hospitals, skilled nursing facilities and home health agencies, if they meet certain standards. It is wise to find out if the agency you are dealing with is qualified under Medicare.

The amount of care covered under Hospital Insurance is limited by "benefit periods," which start when the patient is admitted to the hospital and end sixty days after he has ceased receiving hospital or skilled nursing care. In each benefit period, you are entitled to ninety days of in-patient care. During the first sixty days, you pay a total deductible of $72. For the last thirty days, you pay $18 per day toward hospital charges. Then there is a "lifetime reserve" of sixty extra hospital days that can be drawn on during any benefit period, and during these days there is a deductible of $36 per day.

Covered charges include the cost of semiprivate room and meals, regular but not private nursing, the cost of drugs, supplies, etc., that are not ordinarily furnished patients. Benefits are not available if the only reason for hospitalization is a need for general care such as assistance with feeding, walking or dressing, or help in taking medications at specified times. Furthermore, hospitalization for psychiatric reasons is limited to 190 days in a lifetime, which is often inadequate.

Supplementary Medical Insurance is designed to cover some of the emergency medical costs that are not included under basic Hospital Insurance. These include physicians' services, outpatient hospital services, an additional 100 home health visits a year, some diagnostic services, radiation therapy, costs of some medical equipment and supplies, and some chiropractors' services.

There is a deductible of $60 per year for SMI and then, for the most part, Medicare will pay eighty percent of reasonable charges, with the patient making up the difference. However, if you receive laboratory and radiology services while in the hospital, they are paid in full and the $60 deductible does not apply. And 100 percent of the costs of home health visits are covered, rather than the usual eighty percent.

On the other hand, minimal coverage is offered for some important services. Psychiatric treatment out of hospital is covered only up to $250 per year, and physical therapists' services only to $80. Routine physical checkups, prescription drugs, optical examinations, and the cost of new eyeglasses, hearing aids, routine dental care and dentures, orthopedic shoes, "personal comfort items"—the everyday necessities that are so important for the aged—are not included in Medicare coverage!

When you enroll in Medicare, you receive a Health Insurance card, which indicates the date your protection starts, a claim number which you must use whenever you have dealings with Medicare, and a Medicare handbook that will tell you the name of the "carrier" organization in your area (such as Blue Cross or an insurance company) that handles Medicare claims. Medicare will pay "reasonable" fees charged for services and the carrier determines what is reasonable for your locality.

Claims may be filed by the insured individual, on the proper form, with an itemized bill attached; in this case the patient pays the doctor and is reimbursed by Medicare. Or the doctor, if he agrees, may submit the claim and be paid directly by Medicare. Either way, the patient is responsible for any difference in cost between the total bill and the portion approved by Medicare.

The Social Security Administration suggests that, in the case of SMI, you save up the first bills until they total the $60 deductible and submit them all together. Thereafter send in each bill as it occurs so you will be paid as quickly as possible. If you have so few bills that you establish the deductible only in October, November or December of one year, those bills can count toward the deductible for the following year as well.

There is a time limit within which claims must be submitted: the time period is counted from October 1 through September 30 of a given year, and any claims incurred during that twelve-month period must be submitted by December 31 of the *following* year.

The Social Security Administration is a huge bureaucracy and claims are often misplaced. *Always* keep a record of the information in your claim, and the date the claim was submitted to Medicare.

## VETERANS' BENEFITS

The Veterans' Administration provides certain benefits, sometimes substantial, to veterans of United States wars and "conflicts." Some of these benefits are available to all people who have been in any of the armed services, some only to those who are disabled as a result of their service, or who are suffering some service-connected illness. These include loans for purchase of homes, assistance in finding employment, medical care in veterans' hospitals, education, G.I. insurance, burial benefits, pensions to veterans, their widows, children and dependent parents, use of a PX to purchase goods inexpensively. Detailed explanation of benefits can be had by calling your local Veterans' Administration office and by consulting various free publications including "Federal Benefits for Veterans and Dependents," a V.A. Fact Sheet.

### RAILROAD RETIREMENT INSURANCE

This program, administered by the Railroad Retirement Board, a three-member body appointed by the President with Senate approval, consists of representatives of the "public interest," railroad management and railroad labor. Benefits include health insurance and retirement payments for those workers employed by the railroad for at least ten years.

### PUBLIC EMPLOYEE BENEFITS

These benefits correspond to those of Social Security, but they are administered by the government under which the individual was employed, if he qualifies. Information should be requested from the appropriate government.

### WORKMEN'S COMPENSATION

This program is administered by the state governments, usually the state department of labor, but sometimes by workmen's compensation agencies or by the courts, except in a few cases that are at present administered by the Federal government, including coverage of harbor and longshore workers, and at this time miners suffering from black lung disease. People receiving workmen's compensation are paid for cases of temporary and permanent disability. If temporary, the amount paid may decrease or end when the disabling condition is stabilized and doesn't require medical care. Sometimes permanent disability payments are reduced after a period of time by law, or at the discretion of the administrator. Sometimes benefits are available to dependents of the disabled worker. Occasionally a worker may be eligible for both workmen's compensation and OASDHI, but the total amount of income received isn't supposed to exceed eighty percent of the worker's former income (even though the individual's expenses have undoubtedly increased as a result of his "disability" and the need for medical and other care!).

## INCOME TAX PROVISIONS

The special income tax provisions that are designed to take into account the unfavorable position of older Americans are spelled out in "Tax Benefits for Older Americans," publication 554, available from your local Internal Revenue Service office free of charge. You can also consult such tax preparation guides as Lasser's *Your Income Tax,* sold in bookstores and newsstands.

Among the provisions of interest to the older citizen are the following: Each person aged sixty-five and over is entitled to an extra personal deduction of $750. The deductions available to legally (that is, not necessarily totally) blind people may also apply. Furthermore, the first $2800 of gross income of people over sixty-five is not taxed, and certain sources of income, such as Social Security, are not included in this calculation because they are not subject to income tax.

Some income qualifies for deferred taxation. For example, money paid into a pension plan may not be taxed at the time it is earned, when the employee is in a high income bracket. It may instead be taxed when it is received, in the form of a pension, at which time the individual is in a lower income tax bracket because of reduced income, and therefore will pay less tax on the money.

People supporting others, in whole or in part, are entitled to certain dependency deductions, at any age.

There is a rather complicated regulation concerning gain on the sale of property used as a permanent residence for at least five of the eight years prior to sale. Depending on the size of the profit, all or part of it may be excluded from tax if the seller is over sixty-five at the time of the sale. This provision can be used only once in a lifetime. If the seller is married, his or her spouse must be a partner in the exclusion and that second individual cannot have participated in such an exclusion before—nor afterward. As of this writing, gains of up to $20,000 are entirely excluded from taxation. For larger amounts, there is a formula for determining the percentage to be taxed. You may choose this option or revoke it within the period allowed for filing claims for credit or refund of taxes—usually three years from the date the return is due, or two years from payment of taxes, whichever is later.

As you can see, tax regulations are complicated. If an accountant is not available, you can receive assistance directly from your local Internal Revenue Service office.

## GOVERNMENT ASSISTANCE AND INCENTIVES FOR PROVIDING HOUSES FOR THE ELDERLY

The Federal Housing Administration has made some attempts to remedy the deplorable situation that exists for the elderly in terms of adequate housing. For instance, the FHA may insure the mortgage of a home purchased by someone over sixty-two years of age. Construction or rehabilitation of rental housing designed in whole or in part for the aged may also qualify for FHA-insured mortgages, and so may construction of nursing homes under certain conditions.

The Public Housing Administration also assists local housing authorities in constructing or remodeling housing projects for the elderly, and the Housing and Home Financing Agency extends low-interest, long-term loans to private, nonprofit sponsors of housing for lower-middle income elderly persons as a supplement to the FHA programs.

Special regulations concerning allowable rent increases, property tax waivers and other considerations may be given to people over a certain age in your community. It is worthwhile to find out about what is available from your town offices.

## TYPICAL BUT DANGEROUS SENIOR-CITIZEN ECONOMIES

Trying to keep track of all the business that each of us is responsible for in this complex, bureaucratized society is a tremendous strain—in some cases a practical impossibility. Most of us, therefore, do the easiest thing when faced with a difficult and particularly unpleasant task, like trying to make sense out of our tangled economic situation. We ignore it in the hope that calamity will not strike and we will somehow muddle through. Muddle through we usually do, but often with results that leave us in a less advantaged situation than we are entitled to. Instead of wrestling with each separate problem in the context of a larger picture, we respond with confusion and anxiety to each pressing requirement that descends upon us as a separate entity.

Eventually someone else is going to have to deal with the aged person's finances. It may be inordinately time-consuming to try to make sense out of your aged father's economic position, but it must be done, for his welfare as well as your own. So, number one, don't just ignore it. And if it seems too tangled a thicket for you to thin out, seek help from someone who understands these things.

A common reaction to such an anxiety-producing situation as realizing suddenly that you are old and poor, or expect soon to become so, is panic. In panic people who are normally prudent, even overly cautious where small sums of money are concerned, often will invest their entire life savings in schemes that promise a high and quick return. They will do this without discussing their plans with members of the family to whom they are responsible, without consulting the family lawyer or a knowledgeable bank officer, perhaps without requiring any proof of honesty or integrity on the part of the person to whom they turn over their fortunes. And they frequently lose it all.

The "investment" may be a hot tip on the stock market, a loan or partnership in a new business, a land-development deal, or some other, less common risk-taking adventure. Sometimes an older person fails to pay proper attention to his own existing business while investing his time in frantic, unrealistic schemes to make a quick fortune to retire on.

People also are taken in because of their loneliness—or a sense of freedom and adventure that the con man promises. A notable example is the dance-class scandals, in which lonely, often aged, people sign up for interminable dancing lessons at ridiculous rates. And of course widows and widowers are often courted for their inheritance or large retirement incomes, rather than for themselves. Their money may be spent by a stranger, or go to a stranger's family when they die.

Out of panic, we often exaggerate our poverty or minimize our options. A very common response to the straitened circumstances of age is to cut down drastically on food. If the older person lives alone, has no mealtime companions, or has limited kitchen facilities, there is much less motivation to eat. And since the aged person's appetite is reduced, he does not notice hunger the way a younger person does—so it is all too easy to forget to eat. Or to eat a relatively inexpensive low-protein diet. It is crucial to insure that the old person in your care eats nourishing food regularly. It is possible to prepare varied, easily made, highly nutritious and delicious meals for surprisingly little money, even in these times, once you learn the technique and get in the habit.

Along with giving up food, a common response is to cut down so drastically on electricity and heat that one ends up living in a dangerously dark, cold environment that literally "puts one to sleep." Economizing on power expenditures and completely denying oneself minimal creature comforts are two entirely different things. Observe the difference!

A third very common practice, and one that may come before the extreme measures of starving and living virtually in the dark, is to deny oneself adequate medical care even if it is in fact available. This should be avoided at all cost. Even if you have never been to a doctor in your life before—and hate the entire medical profession on sight—after sixty-five bend a little and find out just how healthy you now are.

Finally, in an attempt to conserve their few resources, older people may well give up all entertainment, even visiting or receiving guests, and become recluses. Standards of entertainment may have to be lowered—and in fact may lower themselves in that you may take pleasure in more natural, down-to-earth and simple activities than in your "flaming youth"—but everyone needs some relief from the loneliness and routine of everyday life.

It is surprising how many people do not have wills, or have only homemade ones that may not stand up in court. A common way for money to be denied to the person who needs it, and to whom it rightfully belongs, is for an estate to be divided according to law in absence of a will. Even if your property appears paltry to you, it is worth discussing with a lawyer the advisability of a will. The ironic thing is that it often costs but $50 to $100 to prepare a standard will, which can save thousands of dollars in estate taxes or insure that the people you want to will inherit whatever you may leave behind.

Considerable economic repercussions occur because of the stereotyped division of roles in our society. Typically, older men do not possess the necessary skills to care for themselves in comfort. They may require household help, may not know how to shop wisely, may be ignorant of how to deal with bureaucracies patiently and persistently. Even though some women have had a good deal of practice in managing large sums of money and know the intricacies of managing a family business, investing money or filing income tax returns, it is typical of many families and particularly in the case of older people that the man handles all the finances and doesn't "worry the woman's pretty little head" with such details. Sometimes this is justified with the argument that the man has earned the money, thus discounting the woman's unpaid labor in caring for the family and the household, freeing her husband to concentrate on earning a living, as well as the possibility that the money was accumulated as a result of the woman's prudence and even self-sacrifice.

Since women usually outlive men, the results of this kind

of blindness and pigheadedness are often tragic. The husband may have planned his estate without consulting the wife, and his plans may be totally unsuited to the kind of life she would like to lead without him. If she is left money, she may have no idea how to handle it in her best interests. If he dies suddenly, intestate or not, there may be a business or other affairs she may be totally unprepared to manage or even dispose of in the best way.

Perhaps he was quite inept at handling money and lost much of their resources. Or, despite her entreaties, he may not have made a will; in which case the widow may be left with inadequate support, or even penniless. This can so easily be avoided by the simple measure of consulting a lawyer about a will. To neglect doing so is a needless and perilous economy—and one that may turn out to be just the opposite of saving money.

# 13

# *Some Fears to Be Allayed*

> *Oh that death were the reward of brave men only!*
> *And would refuse to free the coward from his life!*
>
> OVID

PEOPLE have quite different ideas about death and about dying—that is, the process of passing from the state that is being alive to the condition of being dead. Most people are far more concerned with and afraid of dying than of being dead. The specific fears we have about dying are often related to our preoccupations in other areas of life.

A middle-aged woman I know was virtually obsessed with the fear of one particular way of dying: if she were to fly across the ocean and the plane crashed, sharks would eat her. Not that she would drown or suffocate or die from the impact—but that she would be consumed by sharks. What really terrified her was the thought of the sharks biting chunks of flesh out of her. The fact that she would very likely already be dead when the plane crashed into the water didn't console her. Nor did it concern her especially that her plane might crash somewhere on the ground and she would be blown to smithereens. She was only afraid that the sharks might bite into her. Needless to say, such a very particular preoccupation in an otherwise quite sane woman has some special buried reasons behind it. It's easy to speculate about these fear geneses if you recall some of the more lurid fairy tales, such as many by the Brothers Grimm, or Hansel and Gretel about to be baked and eaten by the old witch, or Little Red Riding Hood who was going to be eaten by the wolf. Whether they acquired the fear from fairy tales or came by it in other ways, many people grow up with an intense fear of being devoured.

There are psychoanalysts who believe that fanatic vegetarians are people who don't want to eat meat because unconscious fantasies concerning devouring once-living flesh are troublesome to them. The unconscious mind is peculiar. Some of its notions may sound crazy to many people, but that's too easy a way of dismissing its power out of hand. Let me remind you that the Christian idea of eating the Holy Host, of partaking of the body of Jesus, is not that far away from the general ideas just mentioned. If you want something more concrete, just think back a year or so to that plane crash high in the Andes, after which the survivors found it possible to avoid starvation only by eating the flesh of their fellow passengers—who had been teammates to boot. So don't laugh off the fear of eating human flesh, or having your own consumed, as just a loony notion. Such fears have some basis in reality; moreover, we find that we all have some strange obsessions if we look closely enough.

(There are of course those people who fear dying during air travel only when the plane flies over mountains—as if one couldn't as easily die if the plane dumped onto perfectly level ground, onto a city, or anywhere else.)

For most people the fear of dying is in essence a fear of loneliness, of separation, of being left to go on entirely on one's own. As with nearly everything in our lives, the models for this particular fear—the fear of dying—can be traced to difficult and upsetting events in childhood or infancy. Many children are afraid to be left in their rooms alone when it's time to go to bed. We speak of this as early separation anxiety. Going to bed is often so hard for children that they go through a variety of processes (very familiar to most parents) to ease the pain of separation. Not only does mother have to tell a story but she has to offer reassurances that she will be there when baby falls asleep and will look in on him several times. There are many complex rituals; for instance, a child will hold onto mother's hand and as she slowly leaves the room, will say, "I'm still holding your hand, I'm still holding your hand," as a way of making the separation gradual.

A more common ritual involves what psychiatrists call "transitional objects": children become very attached to a toy animal, for instance, and that animal is really a substitute for the mother or father. As long as the child can clutch that animal in its arms or have it lying on the bed, separation from the parents and aloneness are easier. As the child matures, he is able to go to sleep without that favorite animal. That's why we call it a transitional object—it effects a transition between the real person and the child's image of the parent; it is a symbol of the parent's being nearby, and then finally not needed at all. And of course many people remain uncomfortable all their lives about sleeping alone.

Probably as popular a transitional object as the stuffed animal is the "security blanket," now a generic term in the language, but originally a literal object: unless the child has its own particular blanket, often with a corner much sucked on, he finds it very difficult to go to sleep. Those children who, for one reason or another, find it very hard to separate from their mothers cannot go away to camp even at eight or nine years of age without taking along their security blankets, however dirty or torn they may be.

Thus we see that man's beginning and his end are in many ways related, including the pains of separation and fears of being alone. The principal fear of dying is a fear of being left alone in the darkness—darkness is our usual vision of death, like the dark room that one was left alone in as a small child.

The most troublesome fear conceives of dying as a process full of pain. Of course, many people's fear of cancer is, understandably and partially realistically, fear of terrible pain. But many other people have notions of dying by choking to death, of slowly becoming breathless. This may be because they, in turn, have seen someone die a pulmonary or cardiac death—from a lung or heart disease—or perhaps as children they experienced the fairly common fear of smothering under the blankets in bed.

One woman was obsessed with the thought that when she had died, she would lie nude on the undertaker's marble slab being embalmed. The idea of lying there inert and completely exposed was unbearable to her. Obviously she had some problems with exhibitionism and a fear of her own desire to show off her body, and it took that peculiar form. It was admixed with the fear of being helpless, rather like the fantasy fears many people have of being tied up or raped.

Not unrelated to the fear of dying by being eaten by sharks is the troublesome image of being dead in a coffin and being eaten by the worms. The fantasy contents are very similar. Many people decide on cremation in order to avoid just those horrifying possibilities.

Related to the concern of what happens to one's body is another common fear of dying that is basically a claustrophobic one. As you know, we have all kinds of claustrophobias: the fear of being in a crowded elevator, the dread of accidentally being locked in a bathroom, feeling very uncomfortable in a movie theater or a department store—any place where we feel we might not be able to get out promptly. Some people feel that way about a coffin: there is the possibility of accidentally being buried alive and then finding themselves locked in the coffin, unable to get out and remove the six feet of earth on top of them. Let me remind you, these people aren't much concerned about being dead, that's not the point; they cheerfully opt for cremation, preferring to be reduced to ashes and feel nothing. So it's not the general idea of death, or of being dead, but specific fearful notions that probably have troubled them in their daily lives.

Aside from the religious ideas of a heaven (or hell) to move to when leaving the world of the living, the most frequently encountered conception of being dead is of being asleep. That's hardly surprising since death is so often spoken of as an "eternal sleep"; and household pets are euphemistically "put to sleep." Curiously enough, the idea that death is like sleep causes a great deal of trouble. Most suicides, especially by drug overdose or other methods that don't mutilate the body (as does jumping out of the window or shooting oneself) are conceived of by the victims as going to sleep. Although just as irrational as many other unconscious notions, this sleep-of-death thing is so deeply ingrained in some people that they actually don't realize that if they do put themselves to sleep supereffectively they will never wake up. One of the first tasks of a psychiatrist dealing with a potential suicide is to make it abundantly clear that if he succeeds, the situation is irreversible: it is not just some pleasant way of getting some deep sleep, then to wake up after having frightened everybody. Sometimes the impulse is expressed as "I'll show them, they'll be sorry they've been mean to me"—as if there were indeed an awakening to contrition and an undoing of the harm others have done to one. (The villains in such fantasies are usually ungrateful children, unfeeling spouses, exploitative bosses or disloyal friends.)

One of the more surprising, and yes, amusing, fears of death centers around the sense of orderliness. One middle-aged man I know is constantly preoccupied with making sure his desk is neat and clean and all his affairs "in order," well taken care of. He has really only one painful fear connected with death—that it might catch him suddenly, by accident or otherwise, and leave something unfinished, some loose papers lying around, some affairs not quite squared away and in order. Tidiness was his overriding concern. When this man had to undergo major surgery, which carried a little more than the usual danger of mortality, virtually all his time for weeks beforehand went into making sure that everything—not just his will but all business and personal affairs—was set up perfectly and understood by all his possible survivors. All bills were paid, phone calls answered, days checked off the calendar. Then he faced what would have terrified most other people—the pain and inconvenience of an operation and the subsequent convalescence, plus the real possibility of death on the operating table—with complete equanimity and calm.

Aside from giving ordinary comfort and compassion, the important thing is to try to find out the specific irrational form that the fear of death and dying take in an older person's mind. (Let me add that in order to help an older person it's important to learn the specifics of his fear of dying, rational *or* irrational.) For that matter, if the fears of an older person, rather than centering around his own death, take the form of concern about the ability of a dependent (of whatever age) to take care of himself or herself, it is reasonable that you try to provide reassurance about what can be done to protect that offspring or spouse after the person's death. This kind of concern, incidentally, is often expressed by fears about the continuity of a person's business, or anything else he is interested in.

This brings us to one of the outstanding fears about death and dying—the loss of control, over one's self or one's affairs, over the people whom one loves or hates or wishes to take care of. Some of the ways in which people deal with this fear take regrettable forms. For example, making a will and testament with provisions regulating not only (appropriately) their own funerals and the disposition of their remains—but also very complex and confounding bequests. If the estate is sizable, such stringent and irrational provisions can dictate the lives of people for years to come, unless they find ways of breaking the unreasonable wills. Indeed there are foundations that have been bequeathed millions of dollars that they are unable to spend because the terms under which the money is supposed to be dispersed are impossible to meet.

If there are no unusual phobias or peculiarities, the most helpful attitude to adopt toward people facing death, imminently or after a while, is to assure them against the most common of all human fears, that of loneliness. It *helps* to promise that a relative or a friend or a professional, or all three, will be with an aged person during his final hours until he passes from consciousness. To combat this fear of being alone, it is important to visit frequently. Holding hands as a form of comfort is of prime importance. Talking, to minimize the increasing feeling of receding from consciousness and from the world into aloneness, is an important measure.

The fear of discontinuity of existence is one for which different people have found different answers. Aristocratic families used to take comfort in the fact that there had been "Joneses" before them and there would be after them—why else the intense interest in the study of genealogy?—and that the dying person would always be remembered as part of the family tree. The idea of having one's portrait hanging among others in a dusky hall seemed to provide some relief. More ordinary people take some comfort in knowing that there is a family cemetery plot where they will be interred. Others find assurance merely in knowing where they are going to be buried. To illustrate how vital this concern is, let me remind you that millions of dollars have been spent on bringing the bodies of American soldiers home from the foreign soil on which they fell. Indeed we do not speak of "mother earth" lightly. The idea of ending one's days buried in one's motherland may complete the cycle not only of "going home," but of being reunited with that mother who tended to leave us in the evenings when we were small children, who left us more seriously on occasion to go on a trip, and whom we later left, still feeling that we were abandoned by her. Once more we feel united with mother, in death.

A novel way some people have found to deal with their fear of simply not existing any more is in deep freezing. They believe that if their bodies are deep-frozen by a special technique immediately upon dying, they can be kept in storage almost indefinitely and "reawakened" some day when science has made greater progress. (It seems that the religious idea of living on in heaven is not too widely accepted any more; this freezing business is an example of a faith in science rushing in where religious faith has faded.)

The fear of simply not existing is a powerful one and the main component of the fear of death in most people. Thus the many and varied attempts to preserve some evidence of one's having been on earth. The Egyptian Pharaohs went to great lengths (or heights) with the pyramids. The building programs of colleges and universities flourish from the donations of people who want buildings named after them; every administrator knows that it is infinitely easier to get donations for a concrete building than for a less tangible and enduring monument such as salaries for personnel.

The belief in a hereafter is probably as old as thinking humanity—that's how painful it is for anybody to conceive of simply not being there any more. The idea of transmigration of the soul and reincarnation in some other form is one way of meeting the problem. This plays a special role in religions of the Far East. The Germans had their Valhalla, at least for warriors, equipped with nectar-hefting Walküren. The Greeks had their slightly frivolous Elysium and the Romans their own variation on this theme, populated by very human(oid) gods. Judaic monotheism having nothing very colorful to offer in this line, the Christian mythology that grew out of it provided angels and other rewards, or purgatory with its miseries.

The most satisfying means of assuring oneself of some kind of immortality is to have children. In them, indeed, part of one's self lives on. For better or worse, they are likely to remember us, so that our lives don't just pass like a breath of wind with nothing to show that we have been here.

For people facing death, a simple means of comfort can be found in helping them feel perpetuated by requesting from them as a gift a treasured watch, a book of recipes, even a hair ribbon—anything that is personal and peculiarly associated with them. But the main fact to remember if you wish to help a person who will die soon is to make him feel certain that he will not be alone in the process of dying—and he will not then be forgotten in death. Whatever can promote this reassurance, whatever gives *him* comfort—is right.

# 14

# *Choices: The Right to Die and Living Wills*

*Freedom is the right to exercise a choice.*
LEOPOLD BELLAK

DISCUSSIONS about human rights include not only the choice between interment and cremation, and whether one's ashes should be kept in an urn or strewn over one's favorite patch of land or sea—but also more and more involve the question of how one chooses to die. Medical science has arrived at the point where it can often maintain us even under conditions that merely prolong a life of agony, such as in the final and often very painful stages of a malignancy. In other instances it is possible, by means of oxygen, heart stimulators and intravenous fluids, to sustain breathing and heartbeat though the dying person has no awareness of the world and is unable to move, speak or think. Society—and the medical profession—are still strongly committed to keeping people alive no matter how, and at all costs. It is still a legal offense, possibly murder, if a physician gives a lethal dose of morphine to a person in tremendous pain and only hours away from certain death.

There is of course excellent reason for hesitancy in terminating any person's life. The chances of misuse of such a power, as in all drastic uses of power, are great. Whatever can be put to good use can also be put to bad. It's quite conceivable that a physician, in judging someone fatally ill, can be wrong and the person may recover. It's also quite possible that ill-intentioned relatives, likely to profit from a person's death, can find a corrupt physician who would be willing to expedite death for a consideration. There is also the chance that some doctors could be ideological extremists who feel that anyone not actively contributing to society might as well be dead. It is well documented that physicians helped carry out mass exterminations of German citizens—not Jews or extra-nationals—who in the opinion of the Nazi authorities were not useful, some mentally ill, some chronically physically ill, some merely elderly.

The matter of if and when life should be terminated for desirable reasons is referred to as euthanasia. At one time or another, euthanasia has been advocated for various conditions—hopelessly deformed infants, severe mental illness or infants born with severe brain damage, and others. These are issues not easily decided either scientifically or morally.

It may not be necessary to enter into too much theoretical discussion when considering the matter of whether people may predetermine under which circumstances their own life should not be artificially prolonged. That is the issue which concerns us here.

In this case we are dealing with self-determination rather than determination by someone else. If someone were to use poor judgment concerning himself because of depression, and if the physical circumstances did not warrant it, it is very hard to imagine the setting in which responsible professionals or relatives would be agreeable to carrying out suicide by proxy.

Basically we are dealing then with a situation in which an aged person of sound mind, but suffering from a serious, potentially fatal disease makes it part of his will, or states in a separate document that if the time should arrive where he is near death and in agony or where he would die if not supported artificially (and if such support were extremely unlikely to lead to recovery) that either the artificial support may be withdrawn to let nature take its course or that painkillers may be used to give him comfort even if the administration of such drugs means a speeding up of his demise.

One of the drug houses, Hoffmann–La Roche, circulated a questionnaire to physicians to explore their sentiments on such matters. Their statements and the questions and responses are so instructive that we are reproducing the entire page concerning this question, with the permission of Hoffmann–La Roche:*

> Debate over the rights of an individual to determine what shall happen to his or her person, whether or not against the traditional strictures of society, now involves the question of how one chooses to die. In recognition of the development of advanced drugs and medical equipment that can sustain life beyond a useful time, a number of groups have been formed by people who wish to limit, with respect to their own persons, the traditional obligation of the physician to sustain life at all costs. Members of these groups, so-called "euthanasia clubs," prepare "living wills"

* Question #7, Report of a survey of psychiatric opinion on the social issue "The Aging Population," *Psychiatric Viewpoints Report*, Hoffmann–La Roche, Inc., 1972, p. 18.

while in good physical and mental health in which they state their desires to be allowed to die with dignity. More than 20,000 people are said to have made out such wills and a "right to die" bill has been introduced in at least one State legislature which is intended to legalize active euthanasia at the request of a terminal patient.

A number of the suggested provisions for "living wills" are listed below. Would you endorse any if they were incorporated in proposed legislation in your state? (Check those applicable as YES.)

— In the event of terminal suffering, to use the most effective analgesic irrespective of its potential for toxicity? 78%

— To accede to the patient's wish *not* to use mechanical life-support systems? 72%

— In the event of a medical emergency, to agree *not* to employ resuscitative measures after the patient is past an agreed age? 25%

— To withhold treatment that would only briefly postpone death in a terminal patient? 74%

— On a patient's request, to supply a lethal dose of medication for self-administration? 19%

— None of these. 6%

*Summary of Findings:* There was substantial agreement among approximately three-fourths of the respondents with respect to the rights of an individual to be relieved, whenever possible, of the physical suffering associated with a terminal illness. A similar proportion of respondents would help their patients avoid the indignity of prolongation of life by mechanical life-support systems or by other forms of treatment that could only delay but not alter the outcome of a terminal illness.

The physician's response is very interesting. Ninety-four percent are in favor of some "living will" provision.

Only six percent would not endorse any of these provisions.

The provision which finds little favorable response is the one which would let the physician provide a lethal dose of a drug to be administered by the patient himself. Presumably the idea of such assistance to suicide goes too much against humane and medical sentiment.

The other provision which gets little endorsement, only twenty-five percent, is the decision to use an arbitrary age limit after which no resuscitative measures would be used in a medical emergency. That is, if age seventy were agreed upon, it could mean that a man at seventy having a heart attack would be given no oxygen, cardiac stimulation or other support and would be permitted to die.

The doctors' hesitation is well taken. It is in fact surprising that as many as twenty-five percent agreed to this provision. A good deal would depend on the age chosen as a cutoff point. If it were ninety or a hundred, it would not make much sense. If it were, indeed, seventy, and adhered to generally, a lot of highly valuable and useful and happy people would be sacrificed. Aside from the general inhumanity and the common good, how would people of seventy feel if they knew that if anything serious happened to them, from pneumonia to a car accident, nothing would be done to keep them alive? It sounds like a nightmare.

On the other hand, the other provisions endorsed by seventy-two to seventy-eight percent of physicians make excellent sense. In all those provisions, we are dealing with painful, desperate or entirely useless conditions.

Thus, we have to make careful provisions for the valid judgment of when such conditions exist. For the sake of the patient and the family as well as of the physician, definite rules have to be worked out for establishing when a patient is terminal, when only an artificial support system keeps him going (and he would irrevocably die whenever the artificial support is withdrawn) or when a treatment would only briefly postpone death without obvious good.

It will probably take a certificate from three physicians to certify that such a condition exists. If a patient has signed a "living will" for any of these contingencies, it will be a matter for legal experts to examine what happens if a responsible relative should demur. Let's assume the patient is conscious, of sound mind but suffering agonies from a terminal cancer condition. The patient has expressed his wish, the physicians agree that the situation is hopeless, but a son feels terrible about letting his father die or be put to death by doses of morphine that will, on one hand, remove his pain but on the other hand, so interfere with his breathing that he is likely to be dead in twenty-four hours instead of three days. And what if the patient is unconscious, in a coma, has signed a statement, and the physicians agree that only a heart-lung machine keeps him breathing and that he will never be able to breathe on his own again and that disconnecting the machine, "pulling the plug," will end his life, but a daughter insists that the mother should be kept "alive" until another daughter can arrive? Or if an aged woman has steadily declined, wasted away and is unable to eat or drink, and one child wants her to have intravenous feedings while all the others agree that all it means is that she will have the discomfort of the needles in her arm but only live another forty-eight hours anyway, only dimly aware of anything other than discomfort?

These are questions which will arise and need discussion and regulation like so many other matters that involve life and death.

The aged are not the only ones concerned with such matters. There are middle-aged and younger people who would not want to be in the position of suffering agony after an accident or some other condition and be kept alive against all hope.

There are, indeed, people of all ages who carry some tag with them (like those issued for diabetics, hemophiliacs—people who bleed uncontrollably—and others who may need special care) which specify their desire to be permitted to die under certain circumstances.

Thus, people increasingly exercise their right to die when they feel life would be the worse alternative.

# 15

# *Reactions to Death*

*Grief pent up will burst the heart.*
RACINE

ANYONE close to the aged is bound to become familiar with losing someone through death. If a loved person hovers between life and death for days or weeks or months, the experience is indeed harrowing. One feels for the loved person. Moreover, an impending fate is generally more difficult to accept and to bear than an accomplished fact.

In addition, unconsciously you cannot help resenting the torture the dying person is inflicting on *you:* the emotional burden of suffering along with him and the weight of caring for him in one way or another are heavy. There is the feeling that you should do all you can—visit in the hospital, stay nearby—when essentially you can't help feeling useless. This futility, combined with the demand on your time and energy, makes you feel angry. And this anger, in turn, makes you feel guilty and shabby: how can I be so mean and small as to begrudge my mother, or father, or whoever, the time and effort it takes to be there when *he is dying!*

To pay the proper attention to fatally ill people is only decent. It often does give them some cheer and comfort, and it is important for *you* as well. For we all have to live within the means of our consciences, as much as within our economic means, and offending against the voice of our own conscience is usually paid for heavily. Like living high on the hog, we may get away with it for a while, but it catches up with us. Many a person who managed to be fairly callous to the death of someone close to him develops an ulcer, a skin disease or some other disorder soon afterward—which may be a way in which the previously repressed self-reproach finds expression.

On the other hand, some people mistreat themselves out of a misplaced sense of priority. The relatives who stand around a person in coma for hours and days on end are foolish if they think they are doing something for the dying person. Someone in coma does not feel or think. (In fact coma is defined by the absence of reflexes to light and sound and pain.) Therefore a brief visit to a comatose person is useful principally to the grieving relative: it is part of the leave-taking process, the dying person is still present but not really there as a needing, responding human being who can be related to. It helps begin the adjustment to the loss of a loved one.

There is increasing sentiment against all-out measures to keep dying people alive by artificial means (intravenous feeding, electrical impulses to keep the heart beating, and a forced supply of oxygen). If the patient is aged and has suffered a long, debilitating illness, and there is other medical and common-sense evidence that no miraculous change is likely, there seems little reason to maintain a life without thought, feeling, or awareness of pleasure—especially when the medical attention might be of use to someone else. In such instances, no one need have guilt feelings about permitting doctors to discontinue the artificial life-prolongation and permit a natural sequence to take its course.

## MOURNING

Mourning is a complex psychological condition that makes its progress rather predictably through different stages. In the beginning there is always some shock in hearing about a death: a life that was being lived the day before is completed, irreversibly over, finished. If for no other reason, we are shocked because we are reminded of our own mortality, and thus we react emotionally. The more closely associated we were with the deceased, the harder it is to believe at first that he is dead. It is the *discontinuity* that is hard to fathom. There he was to talk to, a part of our lives, and now he is gone. Actual interrelationship is replaced by fantasy exchanges, as one talks with the deceased loved one, thinking over past events. One is preoccupied with him or her, often temporarily forgetting that he is gone. The work of mourning has begun.

Freud called it the *work of mourning* because it consumes mental and psychic energy, often to the extent of leaving the mourner exhausted. Fatigue, in fact, is an integral part of mourning. A loss of this kind induces a feeling of disappointment, of let down, even of anger with the person who has died. Occasionally one sees a mourner fling himself over the casket and cry bitterly, "Why did you do this to me? How could you leave me?"

It is part of normal life that one "invests" love in people close to oneself. Such investment may be the reason why people generally are in love with only one person at a time: usually there is no affect left over for more than one passionate love. In fact, often when someone is in love, there seems not enough energy left over for work, or for paying attention to the ordinary things of life. Adolescents especially demonstrate that the love investment can be withdrawn from one person and then deposited with another, almost in the same way as dollars from one bank to another.

In the work of mourning, one slowly but surely withdraws the love investment from the deceased and reinvests it in other people, in one's job and daily life. The length of time it takes to do this differs, of course, with different people. For some people, death is such a grave shock that the best way they can find to deal with it is to deny that it happened. They shed no tears and they go about their business much as always. Every psychiatrist has seen people suddenly become depressed a month or a year after the shocking death, suffering from delayed mourning.

On the other hand, some people continue to mourn for months or years. Falsely romantic, they are under the mistaken impression that this constitutes evidence of a very special love and devotion. The fact is that by and large the healthier the love for a particular person was, the more promptly one will return to a full life, after appropriate mourning. Those truly capable of loving one person are able to love another.

For the psychologically healthy person in our culture, acute grief from loss of a loved one usually endures for less than two months.

Continued mourning—which then turns into morbid depression—is usually a psychiatric disorder that should receive treatment. It usually involves excessive rage, which is repressed, over having been deserted, and an overload of guilt over the rage. It may also involve excessive self-pity.

## PARTIAL GRIEF

Dr. Martin A. Berezin, a Boston psychoanalyst, points out the importance of *partial grief* in response to partial loss. The threat of loss may be precipitated by a significant anniversary of a loved one—an eightieth birthday, for instance, is likely to evoke such feelings. Even more, when a severe and possibly fatal illness is diagnosed, this affects not only the person afflicted but all those around him. In fact, as Berezin points out, retirement may start such a process of loss and grief in the person retiring as well as those around him. The presentation of the famous gold watch stirs up feelings related to those awakened at a funeral. With all the good cheer and admiration and gratitude, there is still the feeling that it is all over now—and the cold breath of death brushes over many a back.

At such an occasion, many people, on the contrary, do not recognize that they are grieving.

Erich Lindemann, Harvard Professor Emeritus and a pioneer of community psychiatry in America, has spoken of people who grieve immediately upon experiencing the loss of a person to whom they are close, others who delay their response, some in whom grief is apparently absent and others in whom it is exaggerated. When the grief response is consciously and completely absent, Lindemann (and others) feel that there may be serious repercussions. Some people begin to exhibit the symptoms of the seriously ill or deceased friend or relative. Others may become excessively active. Occasionally the nongrieving person develops psychosomatic ailments such as asthma, ulcers or skin disorders. And others may change their personal relationships, or their work habits, or show other manifestations. It is obvious that it is important not to ignore grief, be it partial, anticipatory, or in response to the final loss of a person by death.

A family conference of all those closely related to a terminally ill patient is a valuable procedure. Those not reacting can be helped to have the appropriate response, rather than repressing or exaggerating their feelings out of a sense of obligation, or some other defense. All participants can be encouraged to discuss their feelings and face the situation frankly and rationally. The distress of his family and close friends can affect a dying person adversely, so the benefits of the family conference extend crucially to the fatally ill.

## AUTOPSY

If someone dies suddenly, not from clearly evident causes, and without having been under medical care at the time of death, the law in most localities requires that there be an autopsy to determine the cause of death. This is a provision to exclude the possibility of foul play. Relatives have no choice in the matter. If someone dies in a hospital, then, under ordinary circumstances, the hospital doctor will ask the next of kin for permission to conduct the autopsy.

This is a situation that is often fraught with emotion. Many people feel reluctant to give permission for their loved ones to be "cut up." It seems a terrible indignity, if not indeed a cruelty. Actually doctors can learn a great deal about the nature of illnesses as a result of autopsies. From observing what kinds of problems caused the symptoms the deceased suffered from, the medical profession is in a much better position to make accurate diagnoses in living people with similar problems. As a doctor, naturally I am on the side of permitting autopsies. I have participated in them, have learned a great deal from them, and I know they are no more "horrible" than operations on the living. (What is more, the subject certainly doesn't mind.) The clinical-pathological conference in a hospital is often a tense, emotion-packed scene. As compared with the clinical hunches of the internist or even the surgeon, the pathologist brings out definitive facts.

In a way, the conference after the autopsy is like a court of inquiry. The reputation of a hospital, its certification by the authorities, is probably influenced more by the percentage of autopsies performed there than by any other single factor. This is how highly the medical profession values the autopsy as a means of policing the quality of medical care, as well as a source of continued study and discoveries about the human body and its functioning and malfunctioning.

It seems reasonable for me to make a plea for supporting this endeavor by permitting autopsies whenever they are requested. It should not produce uneasiness or guilt in the person who gives permission. Quite the contrary. It is one way you can make your own contribution to the advancement of science.

# 16

# *Funerals*

*All of life is a fight against gravity. . . .*
VERNA SMALL

*. . . And in the end it pulls us down.*
LEOPOLD BELLAK

As we mentioned earlier, people have very definite notions, fears and preferences about death and dying. Obviously someone preoccupied with claustrophobia and the fear of being buried alive may prefer to be cremated. Others who fear oblivion primarily will find little comfort in the idea of becoming just a small heap of ashes in a jar. The fact is, of course, that dead is dead, and fancy pyramids, marble mausoleums, or just a six-foot-deep hole in the ground makes no difference to the deceased.

It *does* make a difference to the survivor, however, and if you feel more comfortable with one method than another, that is the one to choose—if it is up to you to make the decision. Or if your feeling of pity and love is more gratified by one way of putting away the remains—then that is the best way to arrange things.

It has been said that a funeral is the third most expensive

purchase most people make in a lifetime. In our culture, the preparation and disposition of a body after death are usually done entirely by specialists. There is a considerable mystique built up about the processes employed, and few of us care to, or dare to, inquire into what goes on until it becomes necessary to arrange a funeral. Then we are under pressure, both emotionally and in time.

Funerals are sad events. They are also complicated ones that involve an entire industry. The grave diggers have a union; morticians go to school to learn the skills of embalming; a funeral parlor is a business; private cemeteries are real estate operations. These are facts to try to keep in mind when you lose someone you love.

Because most people know so little about it, and because it can be such a big expense, I am describing briefly the experience that is likely if you find yourself responsible for arranging a funeral. (For a detailed, explicit and often scathing account of the funeral industry, I highly recommend Jessica Mitford's book, *The American Way of Death.*)

The laws surrounding death vary from state to state and from locality to locality, but the basic procedures are the same throughout the United States. It is necessary for a physician to pronounce a person dead and to record this fact on a death certificate in order to procure a burial permit. Then it is up to the family, if there is one, to arrange for the disposition of the body. (In the case of unclaimed bodies, there is usually a "pauper's field" where the government inters the deceased.) There is no law in most places requiring embalming or any kind of mortician's services although health department rulings may demand the disposal of the remains within a certain number of hours after death.

A funeral establishment may be chosen by word-of-mouth

recommendation, or on the basis of discreet advertising in the telephone book or newspapers. Differences in services are not advertised; prices often are not competitive. If there is a choice between establishments, it will probably be made on the basis of a preference for the "counselor" (mortuary director or salesperson) you happen to speak with, or because one place can schedule the funeral service for a more desirable time.

Funeral procedures have been systematically worked out; they are very thorough, thus relieving the bereaved family of most responsibilities and providing a socially approved setting for getting through the initial period of mourning. The mortuary staff is usually well trained: they are calm, well organized, they speak gently and respectfully and anticipate most problems.

When someone dies, you can call a funeral home at any hour of the day or night. They will inform you that a doctor must verify the death. Then they will send attendants with a wheeled stretcher to remove the body in a vehicle. The funeral director will make an appointment to meet with you and discuss the necessary arrangements. You will be requested to provide certain information so that the funeral home can perform the services it offers: ordering copies of the death certificate, notifying organizations such as the Veterans' Administration, placing an obituary announcement in the newspapers. The basic information required is as follows: deceased's name, address, Social Security number, discharge papers or number if he was a veteran, name of physician or hospital where he was last treated, number of death certificates required, and his parents' names (if the state keeps a family tree). You will be asked to bring garments for the dead person to wear and, if you like, a photograph to help the mortician create a likeness.

Coincidentally, the information you provide may clue the

funeral director in to how much money is available in benefits earmarked for funeral expenses and thus how elaborate a service he can try to sell you. (Social Security provides a sum; so does the Veterans' Administration; so may union plans, private burial organizations and the like.) It's not necessary for you to enumerate the sources of funeral benefits if you have figured out in advance how many death certificates you will require for Social Security, Veterans' Administration, unions, pension plans, insurance companies, investment brokers, banks, and any other institutions that require official notification of death.

Although some states (New York, for instance) do require that the cost of each funeral service be separately itemized, the funeral director can gauge what price level you can afford on the basis of the information you unwittingly give him, as well as other features of your life style, to which he has learned to be sensitive.

A major decision will be the coffin. These commodities are pieces of furniture constructed, in typical modern fashion, as cheaply as possible but costing as much as the traffic will bear. It is unlikely that you will go casket shopping among several funeral establishments, or that different brands will vary very much, so you are limited to what is shown you. Nowadays one pays not only for a wooden box but for a window-dressing lining and perhaps even a posturepedic mattress. Ms. Mitford, who studied the catalogs and examined the products, concluded that the less expensive models were purposely uglified. She also reported that many of the special features, such as hermetic sealing, actually hasten certain types of decay, rather than protecting the disintegrating body. And none of the coffins will last many years. Her research indicates that you will do better if you bring along an unemotionally involved, preferably experienced companion, or a clergyman, and insist that this person accompany you when you select the coffin.

A basic expense is rental of rooms on the premises. You may choose to have an evening gathering in the presence of the body. If so, you pay the salary of a bodyguard and for the use and maintenance of the room or rooms. The day of the funeral, you will use a reception room, or rooms, and perhaps a chapel. There is usually no charge to have the body transported to a church for the service (as in Catholic funerals, for instance). But if you want pallbearers to actually carry the coffin—and they are of the mortician's staff rather than friends of the deceased—you will pay for them. Union rules and insurance regulations often mandate that employees of the funeral home, not friends, act as pallbearers. (Friends may push the casket if it is wheeled on a cart, however.)

It costs more to have the coffin transported to the cemetery by hearse than by station wagon. And there is a charge (at present about $60 in New York) for each limousine hired to pick up mourners at their homes, bring them to the funeral chapel, to the cemetery and back home. Flowers, of course, are very expensive. And often, it is rumored, florists do not provide their freshest blooms for funerals either.

Some funeral parlors (or "chapels") handle funerals of one religious group primarily or exclusively; some are multidenominational. To take care of the situation, far from infrequent, of a family that doesn't routinely practice a religion, but does desire a religious ceremony on such an occasion as death, many funeral establishments have "house" rabbis, priests or ministers on their staffs, or on call. Unless they knew the deceased well, clergy have a tendency to be perfunctory and to speak in clichés. If you want them to say something specific, it is wise to compose and present a carefully written statement, which the speaker will either read verbatim or incorporate into his address. A relative or friend may want to deliver the eulogy, or add to it. If you wish to alter tradition in some way to make it more personal, you had best discuss this in advance with all of the mourners, then make sure it is acceptable and understood with the professionals in charge.

Unless you strenuously specify otherwise, the body will automatically be embalmed. This procedure, which funeral directors like to keep secret, is discussed in considerable detail in *The American Way of Death.* The body is washed, dried, disinfected, the hair dried, dressed and coiffed, the face and hands "made up," the body clothed. Then it is lifted (by manual or hydraulic lift) and placed in the casket, where the makeup and costume are touched up in accordance with the lighting of the room where the body is to be displayed.

I repeat that embalming is *not* required by law and not necessary for health reasons. In some situations, such as a person's being buried at some distance from the place where he died, the carrier may require embalming. If you are not sure you want to agree to embalming, you can check with your local department of health. The tradition of embalming is not worldwide, and is of fairly recent origin in this country. The embalming techniques of the ancient Egyptians were designed to preserve perpetually the intact body, but it was recognized that after death the appearance of the body would change: in that hot, dry climate it would become shriveled, discolored and hard. The techniques employed by contemporary American embalmers, however, are designed for opposite results. The cosmetic aim is to recreate the semblance of a healthy, pliant, sleeping person. That image must be maintained for the brief length of time between death and burial or cremation. (This period may be legislated in terms of "a reasonable amount of time" or as a specific number of days.) In the case of autopsies the counting of hours or days begins when the funeral director receives the death certificate and can initiate the process of preparing the body.

Embalming is very costly in personnel: it reputedly takes a mortician a minimum of four hours to prepare each body. Unlike autopsy, where all organs are removed and examined, embalming does not involve the removal of any organs. With regard to the cosmetic parts of the process, it belongs to interesting trivia that the hot-air combs currently in popular vogue for the living were introduced some twenty years ago for the use of morticians!

If you do not have a family cemetery plot, the funeral home will help you to locate one. If you want to be buried outside of a cemetery, it may entail considerable legal problems, many forms to file, and probably the aid of a lawyer. In some places, such as New York City, burial outside of a cemetery is strictly prohibited except for clergy buried on church grounds.

The funeral home may not operate a crematorium, so if the body is to be cremated, and a service or reception held, you will likely be using the services of two funeral establishments. The funeral home will assume that you will want to hold a ceremony. State law or industry regulations may require that the body be transported in some kind of case, which will be assumed to be a purchased coffin, and it will be assumed that the "professionals" will bring the body to the crematorium. If you have other ideas in mind, it is up to you to make them known.

Different cultures provide different routines to get one through the period of mourning. Some hold wakes, some have a prescribed period of open house following the burial. These rituals encourage the bereaved to go through at least the ceremonies before resuming their everyday lives. Today in our pluralistic, secular culture, when so many people are agnostics, atheists or existentialists, death presents special problems and decisions. Should you go through a ceremony if it is alien to your own beliefs or practices, in deference to your relatives, or "to please" the deceased? Do you feel compelled to "put on a show" beyond your economic means? Would it comfort you to behave in an uncharacteristically traditional manner at this time? Would you yourself prefer a more elaborate ritual than the person who has died would have liked—or specified?

Here is a sampling of some of the confusing situations that can arise. The quietly pious wife of a Jewish atheist has him buried in a ritual prayer shawl. The ultramodern son of a man who wanted to be cremated arranges for the cremation to take place prior to the memorial service, but does not forewarn the mourners, who are upset by this departure from tradition. The converted eldest daughter of the deceased has him buried in the ceremonies of "her" church, rather than in the religion he observed all his life and the rest of his family expect. A great-grandmother who suffered years of illness has been metamorphosed into a beautiful young woman by an overenthusiastic mortician with the aid of facial props and cosmetics. Or someone who deteriorated rather quickly from a degenerative disease is presented without cosmetic changes and mourners are stunned by his aged and anguished appearance.

Among the many questions to consider is whether or not certain people, particularly young children, should visit the funeral establishment, the service and/or the cemetery. This decision will rest in part on the expressed wishes of the deceased or his close descendants, and on family tradition. The children's own feelings should also be considered although it is wrong to put the responsibility of the decision on their heads. Were they close to the deceased? Can they sit still during the ceremony? Will they feel abandoned by the living as well as the dead if they are "left out," or will they be upset by the event and possibly terrified by the corpse? If the adults around them have come to terms with the idea of death, they will usually be able to transmit an understanding and acceptance to the children, but if not—they cannot. It goes without saying that make-believe explanations are harmful rather than comforting, and that only as much information should be provided as is asked for by the child. He should certainly not be told that his grandparent is now "asleep": among other confusions, he may then develop a fear of going to sleep. Plain, concrete facts and unvarnished truths are best for children: they are realists. Fanciful tales about dying and death are in the service of the emotions of the adult rather than of the child.

Since most people can think of a host of reasons for leaving the children at home at the time of a death, here are some reasons for taking them along. Everything about the world is strange and new to a child and requires his acceptance. Death, which like birth happens to everyone, is not a difficult concept to absorb—although a child will not have the same conception of the event as an adult. Children are literal-minded: they like to know exactly what happens to things, and to people. It may be comforting for them to see the body put in its "final resting place."

Children live constantly with strong, passionate emotions. They can feel empathy with someone who is crying or wailing in response to great loss—that is *their* way of handling grief and they don't see why it shouldn't be the universal way. They are willing to let the adult "cry it out" and know the emotion will pass when it is relieved. It is reassuring, in fact, for a child to know that the deceased was so deeply loved and will be so intensely missed—the child can then feel that he, too, is just as warmly loved. Besides, children are capable of offering exquisitely tender and compassionate comfort to troubled people. Their questions and comments are sensible and practically never gauche. Their presence reminds everyone of the continuity of life; it demands of us a commitment to the future; it helps us to accept death and to deal with it.

To increase the usefulness of future editions, I will be happy to hear comments, suggestions and experiences from readers of this book.

EMPLOYMENT
FINANCIAL ASSISTANCE
GOVERNMENTAL AGENCIES
HEALTH—INCLUDING DAY CARE
HOME CARE
HOUSING
INFORMATION AND REFERRAL SERVICES
LEGAL AND PROTECTIVE SERVICES
NUTRITION
PSYCHIATRIC SERVICES
RECREATION
RESEARCH
SPECIAL INTEREST GROUPS
VOLUNTEER SERVICES
REFERENCES

In this appendix we attempt to provide some guide lines for getting various kinds of help. As it is impossible to provide details for each state and each community, examples of service and other help available are given.

By looking for names of the same or similar facilities in your local phone book, you should be able to find services specifically available to you.

If it is not possible to locate a specific resource, usually a call to the local branch of one of the following will direct you to the appropriate resource:

Family Service
Catholic Charities
Federation of Protestant Welfare Agencies
Jewish Family Services
Council of Social Agencies
Mental Health Association

Some of the programs listed, while not directed solely to the aged, offer services which may be of use to this group.

## EMPLOYMENT

Each state has a department of labor which operates employment services for which there is no fee. Many of them have a special division dealing only with employment opportunities for the aged. Additional information may be obtained from the nearest office of the Regional Manpower Administration, U.S. Department of Labor. Many governmental agencies sponsor programs using the elderly as paid or volunteer workers. Your union or church may also have a special employment plan for the aged.

Following is a limited sample of the types of organizations serving employment needs of the aged. (Some are volunteer and community agencies, others are profit-making corporations, but there is no fee in any.)

Baltimore Over-60 Employment Counseling Service, 309 W. Charles, Baltimore, Md.

Mature Temps, Inc., 521 Fifth Avenue, New York, N.Y. 10017 (offices in other cities also). Specializes in placing older people in temporary jobs.

Senior Aides, National Council of Senior Citizens, 1627 K Street, N.W., Washington, D.C. 20006. Employs older people in projects in various parts of the country to perform many community duties such as low-cost meal preparation.

Teacher Aides, Dade County Schools, Northeast 19th St., Miami, Fla. 33132. Employs older people to work as teacher aides in public schools.

Green Thumb–Green Light, National Director, Farmers Union, 1012 14th Street, N.W., Suite 1200, Washington, D.C. 20005. Employs older people in rural sections to beautify public areas, as aides in schools and libraries, friendly visits, etc.

Federation Employment and Guidance Service, 215 Park Avenue South, New York, N.Y. 10003.

Senior Personnel Employment Commission, 158 Westchester Avenue, White Plains, N.Y. (914-RO 1-2150).

Senior Personnel Placement Bureau, Inc., 22 Church Street, New Rochelle, N.Y. (914-BE 5-7725).

## FINANCIAL ASSISTANCE

*Social Security Benefits*

A representative in your district Social Security office is always available to you if you should wish to question the amount you are receiving, or have any questions about Medicare.

*Medicare—Part B. Hospital*

Provides hospital protection to any person over sixty-five who is entitled to Social Security or Railroad Retirement benefits. A dependent spouse sixty-five years or older is also entitled to Medicare based on the worker's record. After the patient pays the first $72, Medicare will then pay the full cost for the first sixty days and all except $18 per day for the next thirty days of any hospitalization in a benefit period (which is sixty days between the termination of one hospitalization and the beginning of another—there is no limit to the number of benefit periods a person may have). It does *not* pay for a private room (unless ordered for medical reasons), or for private duty nurses.

*Extended Care*

Also pays for "extended care facilities" or nursing homes for the first twenty days and all but $9 per day for up to eight more days. This care must be ordered by the doctor.

*Home Health Benefits*

Pays for up to 100 visits during each benefit period. Must be ordered by a doctor and patient must be confined to home. It must also follow hospitalization of at least three days for this condition.

*Part B. Supplementary Medical Insurance*

This is a voluntary medical insurance program available to those covered by Medicare Part A and costing $6.30 a month. Helps to pay doctor bills whenever the patient is seen: hospital, nursing home, office or clinic. The patient pays the first $60 of doctor bills in a calendar year. Medicare will then pay eighty percent of the charge for the rest of the year. However, the doctor's rates must be considered reasonable as determined by the Medicare carriers. It pays 100 percent of charges by doctors for radiology and pathology services if received on an in-patient basis, and ambulance service. It does *not* pay for routine physical checkups, examinations for fitting or changing eyeglasses, dental work, hearing examinations for fitting or changing hearing aids.

A Medicare Handbook which can be requested from local Social Security offices explains all of the above.

*Medicaid*

All persons who receive any public assistance are eligible for Medicaid. Others who are not receiving public assistance but whose incomes are low may also be eligible for it. A call to the Medicaid Assistance Bureau in your city or county will clarify this.

Medicaid pays for all doctors (physicians, optometrists, podiatrists, dentists), hospital, nursing home, clinic services, home nursing services (drugs, sickroom supplies, glasses and prosthetic appliances). If approved in advance, the cost of dentures may also be included.

*Tax Exemptions*

Many local governments grant some exemptions to older citizens on their real property taxes.

*Special Discounts*

Many cities have reduced fares on public transportation facilities, granted upon showing a special pass usually obtained from the bus company. This is also true of many movie houses, and in some adult education classes in both college and high school facilities. Special cards are often obtainable from local offices for the aging.

## GOVERNMENTAL AGENCIES

*Federal*

United States Department of Health, Education and Welfare, Washington, D.C. This agency is divided into nine regional offices. It also administers the Social Security Administration, which has about 700 regional offices. Listed in the telephone directory under "U.S. Government—Department of Health, Education and Welfare, Social Security Administration, District Office." In addition to Social Security benefits, this office handles Medicare.

National Council on Aging, 315 Park Avenue South, New York, N.Y. 10010 (212-777-1900). This council is divided into seven regional offices. It provides funds to state agencies (Offices of the Aging) which, in turn, make these funds available to local public and private non-profit agencies for the operation of new programs.

U.S. Office of Economic Opportunity, Washington, D.C. OEO administers funds for special projects for the aged through the Community Action Programs already in existence.

*State*

Every state has a department of the aging located in the state capital. Sometimes it is called the Office, Council, Division, or Administration of the Aging and sometimes it may be incorporated in either the state education department or the state department of welfare. In addition, state agencies such as labor and health have incorporated programs for the aged.

Medicaid is administered through state offices of welfare or social services.

*Local*

Most local programs are available through already existing public and private social agencies such as the local department of recreation and health.

## HEALTH—INCLUDING DAY CARE

As mentioned, through Medicare you are entitled to sixty days of hospital care in any benefit period. (A new benefit period starts sixty days after termination of previous hospitalization.) In addition, the first twenty days of nursing home care are completely paid for and all but $9 a day for the next eighty days in any benefit period. The transfer to the nursing home is arranged through the physician, with information about nursing homes given by the social-service department of the hospital. Additional information about nursing homes can be obtained from Information and Referral Service, Public Health Department, Mental Health Association.

Many hospitals have established day care units for older people who do not need twenty-four-hour nursing and hospital care, but who do need a medical or rehabilitation program. This is especially helpful with stroke patients. The program usually includes physical therapy, speech therapy, group psychotherapy, occupational therapy, social activities and a hot noon meal. The program lasts from five to six hours a day. Transportation is usually provided, but this assumes the residence is within a few miles of the hospital.

The following organizations offer mainly information services but in some cases additional programs:

American Cancer Association, 219 East 42nd Street, New York, N.Y. 10017 (information, medical supplies, rehabilitation and transportation to clinics, homemakers).

Cancer Care, Inc., an affiliate of National Cancer Foundation, Inc., has branches in some cities (1 Park Avenue, New York, N.Y.), provides counseling to patients and families, financial assistance in cases of advanced cancer.

American Heart Association, 44 East 23rd Street, New York, N.Y. 10010 (information service about heart disease).

Arthritis Foundation, 1212 Avenue of the Americas, New York, N.Y. 10036 (information on resources for diagnosis, treatment, and rehabilitation; also counseling).

American Foundation for the Blind, 15 West 16th Street, New York, N.Y. 10010 (information about resources for the blind and the blind-deaf; also produces talking books).

American Diabetes Association, 18 East 48th Street, New York, N.Y. 10017 (patient instruction and education).

National Parkinson Foundation, 135 East 44th Street, New York, N.Y. 10017 (information service to patients and families).

## HOME CARE

Each of the various programs described below is an attempt to help the older person remain at home as opposed to entering a hospital or home for the aged.

*Home health benefits* as described in Medicare mean skilled nursing aides and physical or speech therapists, who are ordered by the doctor within fourteen days following a hospitalization of at least two days for a medical condition. One hundred visits in a benefit period are allowed. The Visiting Nurse Association or the city or county public health department is the source for this kind of care. After Medicare benefits terminate, fees are adjusted to the patient's ability to pay. Some larger hospitals also offer this service to patients active in their outpatient clinics.

In New York and some other large cities, the municipal hospitals, as a continuation of hospital care, have doctors who make home visits and take overall responsibility for the patient (ordering and supervising such help as physical or speech therapy).

*Homemakers* are usually available through the voluntary social agencies such as Family Service, Catholic Charities, Federation of Protestant Welfare Agencies, Jewish Family Service, and American Cancer Society. Fees are usually based on ability to pay. These homemakers will do light housework, prepare simple meals, shop.

For those able to afford the prevailing rate, state employment departments, churches and some specialized commercial employment agencies also have job registries of homemakers and companions.

Mobile geriatric units, staffed by a psychiatrist, nurse and social worker, are available in some communities to make home visits to elderly people who may be depressed, anxious or confused. The patient's condition is evaluated and a treatment plan presented.

The scope of additional services aimed at making the aged person more comfortable at home is wide, but varies very much among communities. Additional in-home services such as handymen available to do minor repairs (Repairs-on-Wheels, Westmoreland County, Pa.) and a corps of teen-agers performing heavy chores and doing errands (Edmonds, Wash.) all help to make living at home more feasible.

Friendly visiting is an activity that many church groups and high school clubs have adopted. In some high schools it is known as "Adopt-a-Grandparent." Escort services for accompanying the elderly to medical appointments and personal errands are available in some local areas.

Because old people who live alone fear falling or suddenly becoming ill and being unable to call for help, "telephone reassurance" programs have been instituted in many communities. The usual arrangement is for a specific calling time, and if there is no answer after two attempts to reach the aged person, someone is sent to the home. In Nassau County, N.Y., the calling is done by residents of a home for the aged. Another variation of this is "Dial-a-Listener," where elderly professional people volunteer to be listeners for those who are lonely and want to talk with someone.

Homemakers (division of Upjohn Co.) has offices throughout the country, providing part-time and full-time employees offering a range of services—companion homemaker, home health aide and trained nurse.

Self-Help (New York City) is usually able to provide part-time companions and homemakers.

Dial-a-Listener (105 South Main Street, Davenport, Iowa).

Care-Ring (New York City), a commercial service.

Earlham Care Program (Earlham, Iowa)—homemakers and handymen.

STEP (Services to Elderly Persons), run by South Snalomish County Senior Center, 220 Railroad Avenue, Edmonds, Wash. 98020. Teen-agers perform heavy household and gardening chores.

Repair-on-Wheels (116 W. Otterman Street, Greensburg, Pa. 15601) does minor repairs.

## HOUSING

There are many retirement communities and hotels for the elderly. The real estate section of your local newspaper is a good place to begin. Some of the well-known older communities are Heritage Village, Conn., and Sun City, Ariz. Some labor unions are also building such housing. Many states have programs requiring that a specific number of apartments in middle-income and low-rental housing be reserved for elderly tenants in order to qualify for state funds.

Many sectarian social agencies operate housing facilities (apartments, homes and hospitals) for the aged. Health-related facilities are usually efficiency apartments with emergency buttons in each apartment, and special activity groups, dinner and lunch being served in a main dining room. Frequently there is a waiting period before admission can be arranged so that it is important to plan ahead for such a decision. In addition, housing is also provided for specialized groups such as "Women of the Sea" (wives of merchant mariners), people of Swiss heritage, etc.

In New York City, *as an example*, there are:

Catholic Charities, 122 East 22nd Street, New York, N.Y. 10010 (212-OR 7-5000).

Federation of Protestant Welfare Agencies, 281 Park Avenue South, New York, N.Y. 10010 (212-777-4800).

Jewish Association for Services for the Aged, 222 Park Avenue South, New York, N.Y. 10003 (212-677-2530).

National Mental Health Association, 10 Columbus Circle, New York, N.Y. 10019 (212-757-7800).

There are some health-related facilities which are a part of commercial nursing homes but are not covered by Medicare and which usually average between $700 and $1000 per month. However, they are usually an excellent compromise between living alone in an apartment or house and becoming completely dependent as in a home for the aged.

## INFORMATION AND REFERRAL SERVICES

The purpose of these services is to provide information about existing resources, follow-up to see if applicant has received service, and to determine what other services are indicated in addition to those requested. Inquiries can be made by phone.

Local Mental Health Associations almost always provide an information and referral service. United Fund and local community councils also provide telephone information service.

Many communities (state, county, local) have published free directories of the resources provided for the aged.

## LEGAL AND PROTECTIVE SERVICES

The Human Rights Act of 1968 makes it illegal to discriminate in employment practices because of age. Cases of discrimination should be reported to the local Human Rights Commission.

In New York State a law was enacted permitting the aged to obtain speedier justice. It is possible to apply for preference on the trial calendar on the basis of being a senior citizen.

The wage claim units of state departments of labor help workers having difficulty in collecting wages due them.

The Legal Aid Society, with local branches, provides legal advice and representation for those unable to pay.

A veterans' service office, usually a part of the veterans' affairs division of government (county or city), provides legal advisory service for veterans and their families with regard to veterans' rights and benefits, landlord and tenant problems, lawsuits, etc.

In larger cities, as part of the community action program, free legal service is provided for all civil cases.

New York State has a Mental Health Information Service, the purpose of which is to discuss legal rights of mental patients. Service is located in each state hospital.

Consumer aid is a specialized division of many local branches of government and will usually handle complaints.

The American Civil Liberties Union may be contacted at 22 East 40th Street, N.Y.C. (phone: 212-725-1222). At the time of writing, the ACLU takes age-discrimination cases on an individual basis. A special committee on age is under discussion. Local branches of the Civil Liberties Union may have such committees, or may form them if members express an interest. Cases of discrimination against older women may be pertinent to the Women's Rights Project of the ACLU.

## NUTRITION

Most states have taken advantage of the Federal Food Stamp Plan. This may add up to a thirty percent increase in a food buyer's power. It is not necessary to receive public assistance to qualify. Consult the county department of social service or public assistance. Nutritional education is also often available along with the food stamps.

There are many programs aimed at helping the aged receive more balanced diets. Some of them take the form of "meals-on-wheels" (a mobile unit delivering a hot noon meal and having a cold supper for a nominal fee) or "group meals," where an inexpensive nutritious hot meal is served in a neighborhood community house, center or school. There are also many commercial restaurants and cafeterias which cater to older clientele by serving meals at reduced price.

Following is a sample listing:

Senior Citizens Center of Schenectady County, 6 Lafayette Street, Schenectady, N.Y. (nutrition and counseling service).

Stanley M. Isaacs Neighborhood Center, 415 East 93rd Street, New York, N.Y. 10028 (prepared meals delivered to homebound elderly).

Serv-A-Meal, Denver, Colo., and St. Louis, Mo.

Meals-on-Wheels, Baltimore, Md.

## PSYCHIATRIC SERVICES

Psychiatric services may be obtained at the outpatient mental health clinic in your area. Medicaid will also pay for visits to a private psychiatrist. There are many psychiatrists who are particularly knowledgeable about geriatrics. A call to the local mental health agency will furnish you with some names.

In some communities a mobile geriatric unit is used where the patient cannot or will not go to the doctor's office. The psychiatrist and nurse make home visits and then recommend a plan of treatment.

Group therapy has become an important part of the program at many residences for the aged.

Individual counseling, aimed at helping to make a better adjustment to the life situation, is always available at any of the family agencies already mentioned.

Medicare will pay for a lifetime limit of 190 days in a psychiatric hospital. In New York State, Medicaid will pay $30 for an office visit, $21 for other than an office visit and $16 for a psychologist.

## RECREATION

Senior centers are the most comprehensive recreational source. In 1969 there were more than 1200. New York City has more than 100. Frequently they are incorporated with the facilities of a neighborhood house, church or "Y." The wide range of activities includes hobby groups, educational classes, meals, health education programs, physical education, paramedical services (diabetes and glaucoma screenings), planned trips and excursions, counseling and information services.

Some unions, such as the Amalgamated Laundry Workers and the Amalgamated Clothing Workers, operate day centers for retired members.

In conjunction with some of these centers, there are often vacation camps offering two-week vacation periods, with fees on a sliding scale.

## RESEARCH

There are a few governmental agencies and private centers which are doing research on problems of the aged. Some of these are:

National Institute of Mental Health, Section on Mental Health of the Aging, 5600 Fishers Lane, Rockville, Md. 20852.

*Gerontological Society* (also publishes *Journal of Gerontology*), Suite 520, 1 DuPont Circle, Washington, D.C. 20036.

Gerontology Center, University of Southern California, Los Angeles, Calif. 90007.

## SPECIAL INTEREST GROUPS

American Association for Retired Persons and National Retired Teachers Association

1225 Connecticut Avenue, N.W., Washington, D.C. 20036. Publishes a magazine, acts as a lobbying group, offers a health insurance plan, special rates on medical supplies, travel, etc. for yearly dues of $2.

Gray Panthers

3700 Chestnut Street, Philadelphia, Pennsylvania 19104. The Gray Panthers is an action-oriented national movement of young and old people dedicated to combating agism (prejudicial treatment on the basis of age). It was convened in 1970 by Maggie Kuhn and five friends who were retiring from national religious and social-service organizations. In 1973 the Gray Panthers merged with the Retired Professional Action Group sponsored by Ralph Nader's Public Citizen. Ms. Kuhn sees great potential for organizing older people because of the somewhat better health and higher educational level and aspirations of the current generation of retired people, which includes many with skills acquired in the early labor movement, the peace movement, and a few still-active members of the early feminist movement, as well as many retired social workers.

If you would like to know about Gray Panther activities in your area, the national office will be happy to provide you with names and other information. Materials available from the national office of the Gray Panthers include: a newsletter; a basic bibliography (25¢); a special bibliography on consumerism and aging (25¢); a special bibliography on advocacy and political power (25¢); *Paying Through the Ear*, a 300-page report on hearing health-care problems ($3.50 to individuals, $8.50 to organizations, businesses and libraries); a Gray Panther History (25¢); *Liberation from Agism* (25¢); an organizing manual ($1.00); a Gray Panther film (25 minutes, 16 mm., $25.00 rental fee); Gray Panther buttons and miscellaneous promotional materials. They also suggest another documentary film, *A Matter of Indifference,* which features members of the Gray Panthers (50 minutes, 16 mm., available from Hanick-Dacchile, 810 West 183 Street, N.Y., N.Y. 10033, for $50.00 rental fee).

Group for the Advancement of Psychiatry—Committee of Aging, 419 Park Avenue South, New York, N.Y. 10016

OWL (Older Women's Liberation) is an offshoot of the National Organization for Women, geared to the special needs of women in their forties and older. Local groups may be contacted through local chapters of NOW or by writing the National Chairperson of the Task Force on Older Women, National Organization for Women, 1957 East 73 Street, Chicago, Illinois 60649.

## VOLUNTEER SERVICES

The value of older people as aides and foster grandparents in child caring institutions and hospitals has been recognized as a very important therapeutic tool for these children. In some instances transportation is reimbursed and even an hourly salary paid. Day care centers are often in need of volunteer help.

In larger communities there is often a central office called "Volunteers for Service" or "Volunteer Opportunities" which will help you to locate the kind of volunteer service in which you are interested. If this is not available, a call to the volunteer department of a hospital or social agency or your church will do this.

## REFERENCES

Many references to research or professional opinion throughout our book can be found in the following three volumes. For those with a desire for technical scientific information, they are real gold mines.

*The Psychology of Adult Development,* Carl Eisdorfer, M.D., and M. Powell Lawton, editors, published by the American Psychological Association, Washington, D.C., 718 pp., 1973. This book reviews and summarizes nearly all aspects of psychological functioning. It draws heavily on research, much of it very complex and not at all easy to follow. The perspective, however, is wide, the minds of the authors most refreshingly open enough to question the soundness of anything we know so far while trying to make sense out of what data we do have.

*Mental Illness in Later Life,* edited by Ewald W. Busse, M.D., and Eric Pfeiffer, M.D., published by the American Psychiatric Association, Washington, D.C., 301 pp., 1973. It is illuminating that both the American Psychiatric Association and the American Psychological Association should have published reviews of problems of old age in the same year. It shows that aging is really getting attention.

*Clinical Geriatrics,* edited by Isadore Rossman, M.D., Ph.D., J. B. Lippincott Co., Philadelphia, 1971. This jewel of a handbook is concerned with nearly every aspect of medical phenomena in aging. It is more of a scholarly book than a manual for practicing physicians, although much of the information is clinically useful. A lay person with some understanding of biology could certainly read much of it, e.g., for specific information on one given area.

Additional technical references include:

B. Neugarten as quoted in a panel discussion on "The Experience of Separation-Individuation in Infancy and Its Reverberations Through the Course of Life-Maturity, Senescence, and Sociological Implications," reported by Irving Sternschein. *Journal of the American Psychoanalytic Association*, Volume 21, 1973, No. 3, pp. 633–645.

Martin A. Berezin, M.D., "The Psychiatrist and the Geriatric Patient: Partial Grief in Family Members and Others Who Care for the Elderly Patient," *Journal of Geriatric Psychiatry*, Volume IV, Fall 1970, No. 1, pp. 53–70.

Of general interest are:

Bellak, Leopold, M.D. *The Porcupine Dilemma*. New York: Citadel Press, 1970, C.P.S., Inc., Larchmont, New York.

Bellak, Leopold, M.D. and Bellak, Sonya Sorel. *Senior Apperception Technique* (S.A.T.). 1973. Available from C.P.S., Inc., Box 83, Larchmont, New York.

Field, Minna. *Patients Are People*. New York: Columbia University Press, 1958.

Field, Minna. *The Aged, the Family, and the Community*. New York: Columbia University Press, 1972.

The above two books illustrate the usefulness of skillful social workers in assisting families to cope with the problems of age and prolonged illness or incapacity.

Jacoby, Susan. "Waiting for the End: On Nursing Homes," *The New York Times Magazine*. March 31, 1974.

Lobsenz, Norman M. "Sex and the Senior Citizen," *The New York Times Magazine*. January 20, 1974.

Mitford, Jessica. *The American Way of Death*. New York: Simon and Schuster, 1963.

By now a classic, it describes the funeral industry in the United States.

Nader, Ralph and Blackwell, Kate. *You and Your Pension*. New York: Grossman, 1973.

How pension systems operate in the United States and what might be done to improve the situation.

Ross, Donald K. *A Public Citizen's Action Manual.* New York: Grossman, 1973.

This book provides specimen projects for individuals and groups who want to create change in such areas as health care, consumer issues, equal employment opportunities, taxation and responsive government.

Townsend, Claire. *Old Age, the Last Segregation.* New York: Grossman, 1971.

The report, by the project director, of the Nader study group on old age and nursing homes.

The National Council on the Aging, 1928 L Street, N.W., Washington, D.C. 20036, offers a catalog which itself is a guide to publications of interest in this area. This includes books, pamphlets, films, and cassettes, usually at low cost. Their current catalog lists close to a hundred items, with a summary of their content as follows:

*Older Americans—Special Handling Required*

By Marjorie Bloomberg Tiven, Program Associate, NCOA. Prepared for U.S. Department of Housing and Urban Development and the Administration on Aging, U.S. Dept. of HEW by NCOA, 1971. 118 pp. Free on request.

Basic information on the needs of older people, identifying and discussing crucial issues relevant to them in all areas of life.

*Talking Books and the Aging*

Prepared by NCOA for the Library of Congress. Free on request.

Describes the use of talking books and cassettes prepared for older, blind and disabled persons, individually or in groups.

*Community Action Programs*

Prepared by NCOA for the Community Action Program of the Office of Economic Opportunity. Free on request.

*Project SWAP* (Senior Worker Action Program)

A program designed to provide part-time employment opportunities for the elderly.

*Project: TLC* (Tender Loving Care)

Using older people as assistants in child-care institutions.

*A Nutrition Program for the Elderly*

A low-cost, nutritious meal program.

*Technical Assistance Monographs*

Prepared by NCOA for the Office of Economic Opportunity. Free on request. A series of booklets giving detailed instructions on how to set up specific programs on a variety of subjects.

*A National Directory of Housing for Older People*

Revised edition 1969. Paperback. $5.50.

Lists approximately 400 housing facilities designed or adapted to meet the needs of older people who are able to live independently. Entries include apartment houses, retirement communities, residence clubs and hotels and mobile home parks.

A significant feature is the "Guide for Selection," which discusses in detail the pros and cons of moving to a new community or into homes of relatives; what to look for and look out for in retirement housing, and the advantages, disadvantages and costs of various types of living arrangements.

Listings are arranged geographically, by state and community. Each entry includes information on sponsorship, location, size and type of facility; costs; services available on the premises and in the community; eligibility requirements; admission procedures.

*The Multipurpose Center for Older People*

32 pp., 1966. Paperback, $1.50.

Describes the Senior Center as a new focal point for social services, planning and action, in a unique position both for recruiting and remotivating older people and for channeling health and welfare services to all older persons in the neighborhood.

Papers presented by a center director, a community council director and the administrator of a home for the aged at a session of the National Conference on Social Welfare, sponsored by NCOA and three other national voluntary associations.

*Senior Centers: A Focal Point for Delivery of Services to Older People.* Published by NCOA. Summer 1972. $2.

Four papers delivered by NCOA regional meetings outlining the components of a multipurpose Senior Center and containing innovative program ideas.

"Technical Assistance Kit: How to Organize a Senior Center" Compiled by National Institute of Senior Citizens, 1972. Price on request.

Provides information and guide lines on how to organize a program for older persons. A step-by-step manual, program materials, Questions and Answers on Aging, MEMO Newsletter, catalog of publications and other related materials are included. A bibliography is also enclosed.

The U.S. Government also issues numerous pamphlets including:

*Comprehensive Care Services in Your Community*
U.S. Department of Health, Education and Welfare, Public Health Service, Washington, D.C., 1966.

*Services Available for Nursing Care of the Sick at Home,* Division of Nursing, Public Health Service, U.S. Government Printing Office, Washington, D.C., 1966.

*Homemaker Services for Older People*
U.S. Dept. of HEW, Special Staff on Aging, Washington, D.C., 1962.

*National Directory of Housing for Older People,* National Council on Aging

*Planning for Later Years,* U.S. Dept. of HEW, Social Security Administration, Washington, D.C.

*Back to Work After Retirement*
Superintendent of Documents, U.S. Government Printing Office, Washington, D.C., Stock #2900–0130, 60 cents.

*When You Grow Older*, Public Affairs Pamphlets, #131, 25 cents. 22 East 38 Street, New York, N.Y. 10016

*A Full Life After 65*, Public Affairs Pamphlets, #347, 25 cents. 22 East 38 Street, New York, N.Y. 10016

*Your Retirement Moving Guide*

*Your Retirement Job Guide*

*Your Retirement Psychological Guide*

*Your Retirement Safety Guide*

*Your Retirement Hobby Guide*

*Your Retirement Pet Guide*

*Your Retirement Home Guide* (which includes information on cooperatives, mobile homes, retirement villages)

*A Comparative Guide to State Tax Regulations* (includes federal, income, property, sales, motor vehicle, gasoline taxes)

All of the above available from:
American Association of Retired Persons and National Retired Teachers Association, 1225 Connecticut Ave., N.W., Washington, D.C. 20036

*Medicare Handbook*
U.S. Dept. of HEW, Washington, D.C. or from your local social security office.

# Index

# Index

# *Leopold Bellak*

Leopold Bellak is currently Visiting Professor of Psychiatry at Albert Einstein College of Medicine, Research Professor of Psychology, Postdoctoral Program in Psychotherapy, New York University, and Clinical Professor of Psychiatry and Behavioral Sciences, George Washington School of Medicine. He is a fellow and member of more than a dozen professional societies, the author of numerous articles and over twenty books in his field, among them *The Psychology of Physical Illness, Emergency Psychotherapy* (co-author) and the humorously human *Porcupine Dilemma.* As director of psychology at Elmurst General Hospital, he pioneered the Troubleshooting Clinic, a concept that has found acceptance on a national scale. A review of his selected papers in *Science* magazine hailed him as "a man for all seasons"; this newest book establishes him securely as physician and friend to all ages.